DEPARTMENT OF THE ENVIRONMENT
WELSH OFFICE

Review of the Development Control System

FINAL REPORT
by George Dobry QC

presented to the Secretary of State for the Environment and the Secretary of State for Wales

February 1975

LONDON
HER MAJESTY'S STATIONERY OFFICE
1975

ISBN 0 11 750896 9

To the Rt. Hon. Anthony Crosland, MP
    Secretary of State for the Environment

the Rt. Hon. John Morris, QC, MP
    Secretary of State for Wales

Sirs

I was appointed by the Secretary of State for the Environment and the Secretary of State for Wales on 3rd October 1973 to conduct a review of the development control system. My terms of reference were:

(i) to consider whether the development control system under the Town and Country Planning Acts adequately meets current needs and to advise on the lines along which it might be improved, bearing in mind the forthcoming redistribution of planning functions between local authorities and the new system of structure and local plans.

(ii) to review the arrangements for appeals to the Secretary of State under the Planning Acts, including rights of appeal and the handling of appeals in the Department of the Environment, and to make recommendations.

I submitted an interim report on 31st December 1973. On 11th March 1974, it was indicated to me that I should continue my work on the assumption that the Government would attach high priority to it, and suggested that I should provide the final report by the end of 1974. The Secretary of State for the Environment subsequently asked for my views on the control of demolition in advance of my final report and I submitted a special report on 26th July 1974.

I now have pleasure in submitting this final report.

George Dobry

J F Ballard

17th January 1975

Contents

vi

Appendices

Preface

Conduct of the Review

The Advisory Group which was appointed by the Secretary of State to assist me has brought together distinguished people from diverse backgrounds. All the professions and their Councils and Institutions, local government and its associations, the building industry, the property world and the participating public were well represented. Their experience of the present system and their advice have made this report possible. Notwithstanding their other commitments they have freely given valuable time, both as an advisory group working together and as members of study groups considering particular aspects of the present system.

The members of the Advisory Group were:

Lord Allen of Fallowfield, CBE
Professor G W Ashworth, MCD, BArch, ARIBA, PRTPI
N Borg Esq, DSC, CEng
F P Boyce Esq, LLB
D H Bretherton Esq
H J Buck Esq, FRTPI, FRICS
R B Caws Esq, FRICS
B Collins Esq, CBE, FRICS
R Graef Esq, BA
E G Hubbard Esq, LMRTPI, MBIM
Mrs J Jenkins, JP, BA
Councillor J Kotz
Alderman Sir Peter Mursell, MBE, DL
A C Phillips, Esq (until May 1974)*
F B Pooley Esq, CBE, PRIBA, FRICS, MIStructE, MRTPI
Sir Max Rayne
R E Reynolds Esq, BSC, ARICS, DipTP
D Senior Esq, BA, (Hon) MRTPI
J C Swaffield Esq, CBE
P Trench Esq, CBE, TD, BSC, FIArb
E A Vaughan-Neil Esq, MICE, MRTPI, Barrister-at-Law

There have been in all eight full meetings of the Group. These have been supplemented by many meetings of study groups on particular topics, i.e.: Special Environmental Areas; Public Involvement; Development by public bodies; Call-ins and major appeals; Inquiries; Relaxation of control; Enforcement and Demolition.

---

*Formerly Assistant Director, Countryside Commission, was a member of the Advisory Group until he was appointed to a post with the United Nations in Nairobi.

1

Evidence was taken in two stages. Early in the review a questionnaire was distributed to local authority associations, the main professional bodies, national amenity groups and others principally involved. This was designed to help potential contributors to develop their views in a way which would make them readily comparable with one another. The Interim Report (in which the questionnaire was published) proved to be a great stimulus for written evidence. I have been persuaded by the evidence I have received to amend and change in some respects the recommendations made in the Interim Report.

At a later stage I took oral evidence from a considerable variety of bodies, local authority associations, professional groups and amenity societies. The sessions provided valuable opportunities for the exploration of ideas and the testing of tentative proposals.

At a weekend seminar at Cardington on 10th-12th October 1974 I was able to test my ideas at a formative stage with the Group and other representatives of industry, local authorities, the professions and central government.

I am particularly grateful for the help given by the local authority associations, through written evidence, oral sessions and their representation at the weekend seminar. Their central position in the development control system makes their contributions of the greatest importance.

I would like to thank for their efforts everyone who took such care in contributing evidence and those who allowed me to test my ideas upon them as they evolved.*

My thanks are due to the Department of the Environment who have throughout extended very considerable help to me, not least in providing me with a secretariat who have worked with enthusiasm and continued good humour through what has been a period of very intensive work. This report could not have been written without the guidance of Mr Philip Critchley of the Department of the Environment or without the unsparing and patient help of my Secretary, Mr John Ballard. I am also deeply indebted to Mr Michael Barnes, Mr Robert Carnwath and Mr Christopher Lockhart-Mummery, Barristers, for their help at the final stage of this Review.

Finally, I must emphasise—as in my Interim Report—that the views expressed in this Final Report, and the recommendations, are entirely my own responsibility; though as I have said their formulation owes much to the help I have been given.

---

*A full list of those who submitted evidence is given in Appendix IV (i).

PART I
INTRODUCTION AND SUMMARY

CHAPTER 1

Introduction

SECTION I: THE SCOPE OF THIS REVIEW

1.1 My terms of reference were:-

(i) *to consider whether the development control system under the Town and Country Planning Acts adequately meets current needs and to advise on the lines along which it might be improved, bearing in mind the forthcoming re-distribution of planning functions between local authorities and the new system of structure and local plans.*

(ii) *to review the arrangements for appeals to the Secretary of State under the Planning Acts, including rights of appeal and the handling of appeals in the Department of the Environment, and to make recommendations.*

1.2 Because of the concern felt about delays over planning applications and appeals an Interim Report was prepared rapidly and presented just over a year ago, on the 31st December 1973. Under the critical economic pressures of the last year, the rate of development has slowed down substantially, almost drawing to a standstill in some areas; even so, the backlog of applications is such that there are still constant complaints about delays, many of them fully justified. My Interim Report concentrated on this problem of delays, but also covered many other aspects of development control. It did not, however, deal with more specialised matters such as enforcement or control of demolition.

1.3 At the request of the Secretary of State for the Environment I submitted an additional report on this last very important subject on the 26th July 1974. I advised that it was right in principle to subject the demolition of all buildings to planning control and recommended accordingly.

1.4 It may be convenient if I explain at this stage how this present, and final, report is arranged. This introductory chapter begins by outlining some of the complications which I had to deal with. It also discusses generally whether Planning Control and the arrangements for appeals meet current needs. Chapter 2 summarises my recommendations. Chapter 3 describes the new system of structure and local plans. Chapters 4 and 5 explain the way in which planning control and the arrangements for appeals operate at present, and Chapter 6 deals with current practice on enforcement. Chapter 7 is longer than the others: it is the core of this report, explaining my proposals for reforming planning control. Three important aspects of my proposed reforms are dealt with separately: Development Orders in Chapter 8, the plans and guidance that form the framework for planning control in Chapter 9 and public involvement in Chapter 10. Chapter 11 contains my suggestions for improving the procedures for appeals. The last chapter, Chapter 12, completes the picture: it covers proposed amendments to the law and to the procedures for enforcement notices and appeals.

Development by the Crown is treated separately (in Appendix I). In view of the work being currently undertaken by the Committee on Minerals Planning Control under the Chairmanship of Sir Roger Stevens, I have not considered that subject in this review.

1.5 Complicating factors. My task in writing this report has obviously been complicated, since my appointment, by several factors; by the major changes in the economic situation of the country as a whole; by the related fact that we can clearly expect no increase in resources for planning in the near future; and by uncertainty as to the effect of the proposed Government legislation to follow the White Paper on 'Land' (Cmnd. 5730).

1.6 Restricted expenditure on planning. I appreciate that the impact of current economic problems on local authorities, impose an inevitable constraint, in the short term. However, it is worth considering the scale of existing expenditure in comparative terms. I have no definite figures as to the present cost of planning, but estimates of the average cost of processing applications vary from £65 to £100 for each application, including the most trivial. The total local government expenditure on planning is estimated to have been £105 million in 1973-1974. This is small in relation to, say, the construction industry's turnover of approximately £10,000 million in 1974. In any case, this report is not intended as an interim measure; I deal both with those steps which should be taken immediately (putting present resources to better uses without increasing expenditure) and with those which should be taken as and when they become possible.

1.7 The White Paper on 'Land' (Cmnd. 5730) published in September 1974, has, in particular, made a fundamental difference to this review. It is a practical expression of the present Government's view that town and country planning is concerned not only with the physical environment but with the effect of planning on the social and economic conditions of the nation. The White Paper contains wide-ranging proposals which could alter the structure of planning control. Because of this, I was faced with a dilemma. I could either wait for the publication of the Bill on Community Land or keep to my time-table. I was encouraged, and I think rightly, to take the latter course for two reasons. Firstly, the White Paper indicates that its main proposals will be implemented gradually. I therefore do not believe that, as has been suggested, this report 'will become irrelevant almost as soon as it is published'. Secondly, I have no doubt that when the Bill comes to be considered, the assessment in this review of how the present system works and how it can be improved will be helpful even if the system is going to be changed. It will provide a background against which the development control proposals of the Community Land Bill can be measured. It may also indicate what safeguards, for owners of land and the participating public, could well be needed in the new situation.

1.8 I am very concerned not to give the impression that I underestimate the critical importance of ensuring that land is available for housing and industry. Although they are dealt with through planning control, these matters are strictly questions of policy and have occupied successive governments during the whole of my investigations — as indeed for many years before. All I can properly do is to suggest practical measures for improving the functioning of everyday arrangements for planning control and appeals, so that the machine itself does not block the way to meeting these urgent needs.

4

SECTION II: THE FINDINGS OF THE REVIEW

As an introduction to my detailed recommendations, my answers to the questions raised in the terms of reference (see para 1.1) are, very briefly, set out below.

1.9 The system is potentially very good, but its procedures do not 'adequately meet current needs'.

1.10 The planning system has achieved a great deal. The countryside, for instance, has been well defended, considering the enormous pressures upon it; the impact of suburban sprawl could easily have been catastrophic.

1.11 Regrettably, the system is slow, even at times desperately slow*, because its procedures are, as at present used, too cumbersome.

1.12 Every year a colossal planning machine deals with hundreds of thousands of applications. About 70% of them can be classified as simple, minor or uncontroversial. Over 80% of all applications are granted. The Department of the Environment struggles with thousands of appeals. Every year 75% of them fail and in many enforcement appeals a planning permission is granted. All this must involve much wasted effort. And the present position is about the same as it was, for example, 10 years ago.

1.13 Perhaps the greatest defect of planning control is its failure to identify its own failings. This report, therefore, will concentrate on offering practical solutions to the administrative defects of development control which have been ascertained in the course of this review.

1.14 Planning control 'can be improved' if the system is set free from the task of examining, at inordinate length, applications and appeals, the results of which were always predictable. It should be possible to deal with applications much more quickly and efficiently. The way to achieve this is not to relax controls but to introduce different procedures for (A) simple and (B) controversial applications. (I call them 'Class A' and 'Class B'.) Class A will comprise all applications which comply with an up-to-date development plan† and all simple or minor applications to which there are no significant objections. This arrangement will not only ensure that 'minor' developments are quickly dealt with, but would at last co-ordinate plan-making with development control. This was always the intention behind the 1947 Act.

1.15 These two classes of applications should be streamed separately, but an application should be transferred from one category to the other if it is found to have been misplaced. If it remains in Class A and is not refused within 42 days, a deemed consent would follow. This is a radical measure but not disruptive. It appears to me to follow logically from a line of thought which in fact originated many years ago, and was brought forward again recently, in evidence of great weight, in the course of this review.

1.16 The benefits of this measure should become apparent at once. In the foreseeable future planning control will have to deal with 400,000 applications annually (⅔ of the peak figure of 1973 but the same figure as, say, in 1965). I

---

*The Department was able to make a tentative assessment of the situation in the autumn of 1974, by making inquiries of a selection of local authorities. It suggests that in the three months before the presentation of this report not much more than 50% of applications in England were decided within the statutory period of 2 months.

†This may include the primary allocations of an up-to-date 'old style' development plan, but not alternative uses under a use zone chart, see para 8.23.

5

have already indicated that the very great majority of planning applications are granted anyway: in future it would not be possible to delay. As local plans are produced, the change would be even more far reaching.

1.17 These simplified procedures will also make it possible to give more attention to more complex developments of major importance to the community.

1.18 The causes of delay are not solely procedural. There is no doubt that some, though by no means all, local authorities suffer from real staff shortage. I doubt whether it will be practicable to remedy this entirely for some years. Even if there were money to pay them, which is unlikely, there are not enough qualified planners to fill the vacancies.

1.19 There are two other direct causes of delays:

(a) *Insufficient delegation.* I have evidence which suggests that where there is delegation there is much less delay; it appears also that delegation to officers saves more time than delegation to sub-committees.

(b) *Insufficiently frequent meetings.* My information shows that the interval between meetings varies in different places from between two to eight weeks. In areas where there are serious delays, meetings should obviously be held as frequently as possible, provided that the authority has sufficient staff to deal with the increased number of applications.

1.20 **The 'redistribution of planning functions between local authorities' has had an uneven effect.** It was an unfortunate coincidence that local authorities entered 1974 burdened by the weight of the largest ever flow of planning applications, just when they were suffering from the dislocation caused by the reorganisation of local government. The number of applications is now falling and in some counties the new two-tier system is beginning to settle into place. Other authorities, however, have adopted complicated 'development control schemes' encouraged by the provisions of the Local Government Act 1972. There is an overriding need for:

(a) clear division of responsibilities between county and district;

(b) a limitation of the two-way flow of paper between the two.

The practice of the best authorities should be studied and followed by those who lag behind.

1.21 **'The new system of structure and local plans' is evolving slowly.** In the preparation of structure plans authorities should 'concentrate on those issues which are of key structural importance'.* Some have done this and structure plans are already emerging, but it will be another five years before plans are available everywhere. In the meantime, steps can be taken to provide by other means (eg Handover Statements paragraph 8.7) positive guidance for immediate needs.

1.22 **'The rights of appeal' must be retained but 'the arrangements for appeals' and their 'handling within the Department of the Environment' should continue to be improved.** Here also a flexible division into (A) simple and (B) more controversial appeals is clearly needed. Increasing encouragement to appeal in writing, and in all appeals a firm timetable for everyone, including the Department†, should help to bring the long-awaited change for the better.

---

*DOE Circular 98/74 paragraph 5 (Welsh Office Circular 168/74).

†Throughout this report reference to 'the Department' stands for the Department of the Environment and the Welsh Office. Likewise, where appropriate, reference to the 'Secretary of State' stands for the Secretaries of State for the Environment and Wales.

Justified complaints about delays over appeals date back to the earliest days of planning. By now, they must and can be resolved. The Planning Inspectorate and the Appeals machinery in the Department have achieved a marked improvement during the course of this review. Estimates set out later in this Chapter, and made with the Department's approval, suggest that within a year or so a decisive further improvement can be brought about.

SECTION III: LOOKING TOWARDS THE FUTURE

1.23 **Main targets and immediate action.** The next chapter is devoted to a summary of my recommendations, with cross-references to the main text. Some will depend on finance, preparatory work and other factors for implementation. Others can and should be acted upon immediately. At the risk of duplication. therefore, I list here a number of steps (selected from the Summary in Chapter 2) which could within the limits of available resources, with benefit, be acted upon immediately.

1.24 **Improving development control:—**
(1) During the next few weeks Regional Offices should ascertain which local authorities are responsible for the worst delays. Thereafter compliance with time limits should be monitored. (As I have already mentioned, only 50% of authorities comply with the present two months time limit.)
(2) Those local authorities which are too slow should either delegate more cases or at least meet more frequently; and they should review their development control schemes.
(3) All applications should be divided into two classes.
(4) 'Class A' cases (perhaps 75%) should be processed with the minimum of formality and paper work, and with speed at all stages (including the device of 'deemed permissions' after 42 days).
(5) More difficult applications will be in Class 'B'; they will have a more generous (3 months) but an equally strict time-table.
(6) Where outline permission exists, a much shorter time-table must be accepted for detailed approval. There is firm evidence of unnecessary and costly delays in deciding reserved matters. This is possibly the area in which the most bitter complaints are made.
(7) The preparation of structure and local plans should be speeded up by concentrating on the essential.
(8) The DOE should publish an up-to-date consolidation of policy guidelines.

1.25 **Speeding up appeals:—**
Applicants and local authorities and the Department will have to accept:
(1) Enforcement of a strict time-table during preliminary procedures;
(2) Division of all appeals—like applications—into two classes ('A' and 'B');
(3) Cutting out of paper work (and formalities) in simple appeals (Class 'A'); and
(4) Written representations instead of inquiries in some cases;
(5) A time-table to be observed by the Department for the decision stage in Secretary of State cases;
(6) There should be greater use of costs as a penalty for causing delays and waste of time.

1.26 The key figures are:—
(1) About 12,000 ordinary appeals will have to be dealt with annually in the future; this is only ⅔rds of the peak in 1973.

(2) 70% of all appeals were dealt with in 1974 by written representations.

(3) Over $\frac{3}{4}$ of all appeals were transferred to Inspectors for decision, and $\frac{3}{4}$ of these were dealt with by written representation.

(4) The chances of success are now about the same whoever decides the appeal and whatever procedure is followed. (This has not always been so.)

(5) The number of appeals which the Department decides in a year now exceeds the number it receives. There is still a backlog of approximately 12 months' work.

(6) Appeals decided after a local inquiry by Inspectors take at present an average of 15 months; and those decided by the Secretary of State an average of 18 months.

(7) I am told that for *inquiry cases* there should be a gradual reduction to an average at the end of 1975 of about (a) $5\frac{1}{2}$ months* in Inspectors' cases and (b) 7 months** in Secretary of State cases.

(8) *Appeals determined after written representations* by Inspectors now take an average of 8 to 9 months; and those decided by the Secretary of State 13 months.

(9) I understand that there should be a gradual reduction during 1975 to an average of (a) $4\frac{1}{2}$ months† in Inspectors' cases and (b) 6 months†† in Secretary of State cases.

1.27 **The basic approach.** This is my final report. It gives my basic approach and many detailed recommendations. It is the former which matters most. To sum up:—

1.28 First, our modern planning system dates from 1947. Since then, a series of gradually implemented reforms have produced changes far more radical than is generally appreciated. Some of these reforms have resulted from new laws, others from changes in administrative practice. Many of these have been for the better, but overall the planning machine is too cumbersome and complex.

1.29 Second, as to whether the British planning system should be dramatically altered, I conclude that it should be retained but made more rational and efficient, especially in the field of development control which has the greatest impact on the ordinary man.

1.30 Third, an ever-increasing public interest and involvement in planning is altering the whole process. Paying lip-service to its importance only alienates the public: the proper function of public involvement should be clearly understood, encouraged but not exceeded.

1.31 Fourth, as to the individual rights, the present balance is basically correct and should be maintained but we must guard against becoming over-sensitive about this. As it is we have to cope with too many formalities.

1.32 Fifth, positive planning means not only preservation of the countryside and

---

*6 weeks for preliminary work, 12 weeks for arranging and holding the Inquiry and 6 weeks for the Inspector's decision to be issued.

**6 weeks for preliminary work, 12 weeks for arranging and holding the Inquiry and 8 weeks for the preparation of the Inspector's report and 6 weeks for the issue of a decision by the Secretary of State.

†8 weeks for preliminary work, 6 weeks to arrange and complete the Inspector's site visit, and 6 weeks for the issue of the Inspector's decision letter.

††10 weeks for preliminary work, 6 weeks to arrange and complete the Inspector's site visit and 10 weeks for the submission of the Inspector's Minutes and the issue of the Secretary of State's decision.

in towns, but also positive encouragement, and help for, development. This cliché may seem hardly worth repeating, yet there are still too many who continue to ignore it, causing serious harm to the economy and to planning.

1.33 Finally, it is not so much the system which is wrong, but the way in which it is used. The successful implementation of the proposed measures depends on a change of attitude towards a more positive and constructive approach on all sides. It may be too much to expect all attitudes to change; even if some do this Report may have served its purpose.

CHAPTER 2

Summary of Recommendations

2.1 The Report aims at:—

(i)   giving greater freedom to harmless development; but

(ii) guarding against harmful development by retaining applications for all cases, as at present;

(iii) separating from the main stream all applications which might cause harm;

(iv) disposing of applications in the main stream by rapid and routine procedures; and

(v)   applying the same approach to appeals.

SECTION I: PLANNING CONTROL

DIVISION INTO TWO CATEGORIES

2.2 To achieve these objectives a division of applications into two categories, Class A and Class B, is needed (7.4–7.8).

2.3 Class A should comprise:

(*a*) all simple cases;

(*b*) all applications conforming with an approved development plan;

(*c*) development which only just exceeds that permitted by the General Development Order, even when not allocated for that use in the development plan;

(*d*) the approval of reserved matters relating to cases classed as 'A' when outline permission was sought.

Class B should comprise all other applications (7.9–7.10).

2.4 The planning officer should have the power to transfer an application between classes provided he gives reasons for the transfer (7.11–7.17).

2.5 A repetitive application might be refused on that ground alone or, if reconsideration is warranted, transferred to Class B (7.13).

STREAMLINING PROCEDURES

2.6 There should be a uniform procedure for dealing with applications and a model code (7.22–7.23).

2.7 A single, standard application form should be used throughout England and Wales (7.24–7.27).

2.8 Time limits for consultations with authorities and the public should be enforced (7.28).

2.9 There should be a standard procedure for publicity (7.29).

MONITORING

2.10 Every planning authority should make a quarterly return to the Department stating the number of applications received, the number decided within the statutory period, and the number of applications transferred between classes (7.30).

CLASS 'A' CASES

2.11 There should be a 28 day time limit for transfer to Class B (7.11).

2.12 All Class A applications must be decided in not less than 35 and not more than 42 days (7.34–7.36).

2.13 The time limit for all consultations between and within authorities should be extended from 14 to 21 days.
It must then be understood:—
(a) that the time limit is to be strictly observed;
(b) that if no reply is received in time the decision must be taken without it (7.37–7.38).

2.14 A Class A application should be deemed to be granted unless either:
(a) the applicant has received notice of its transfer to Class B within 28 days (7.11); or
(b) the applicant has received notice of a decision within 42 days. (The date of the relevant resolution or decision of a sub-committee or an officer would be treated as the decision if made 3 days before posting and duly recorded.) (7.39–7.43).

2.15 For Class A there should be the following publicity:—

Compulsory	Discretionary
1. Site notice *or* neighbour notification	1. Notification to local societies
2. Notification of parish council.	2. Other compulsory items under Class B (see below) (7.44–7.52).

2.16 Site notices should be of uniform design and size, distinctive in colour, and written in plain, non-technical language (7.49–7.51).

2.17 Neighbour notification may be more suitable in towns. A model 'Procedure for Notification of Surrounding Residents' is shown in Appendix II C i (7.52).

CLASS 'B' CASES

2.18 There should be a three-month *time limit* for Class B applications (a six-month limit for impact study cases: see (7.59)). While there should be no deemed consent procedure, strict compliance with time limits would be demanded (7.53–7.58).

2.19 A Class B applicant should have a statutory right to consultation, if no decision is reached within the time specified (7.59).

2.20 For Class B there should be the following publicity:—

Compulsory	Discretionary
1. Site notice *or* neighbour notification	1. Notification to local societies
2. Notification of parish council	
3. Publication of lists of applications in local newspapers *or* on public notice boards *and* to registered local societies.	2. Advertisements for individual applications in local newspapers or on notice boards (perhaps allocated for that purpose) (7.29).

2.21 Some Class A applications transferred to Class B may require additional publicity (7.60).

2.22 For more important applications, a public exhibition and/or public meetings would be worthwhile (7.86).

IMPACT STUDY

2.23 An applicant will be able to submit an 'impact study' in cases of special significance and in exceptional cases will be required to do this. This would not normally apply to housebuilding (7.61–7.63).

2.24 The notice requiring an impact study should be served within 14 days of application (7.63).

2.25 An impact study would describe the proposal in detail and explain the likely effects on its surroundings. The Department should publish a Bulletin giving guidance as to the form and content of an impact study (7.64–7.65).

2.26 Proposals requiring impact studies should be prominently advertised and copies of the study should be on sale to the public (7.66–7.67).

2.27 The timetable for Class A and Class B applications should be as follows:

TIMETABLE FOR APPLICATIONS

	Class A	**Class B**
Day 1	Receipt of application.	Receipt of application.
Day 2	(a) Application registered. (b) Acknowledge application (giving class and date from which time will run and reference number). (c) State date of committee meeting or that decision to be made by officers. (d) Parish Councils and Local Amenity Societies notified within 7 days thereafter.	(a) Application registered. (b) Acknowledge application (giving class, date from which time will run and reference number of application). (c) Parish Council and Local Amenity Societies notified within 7 days thereafter.
Day 5	Site Notices sent (to be erected for 14 days). Applicant may be required to notify neighbours.*	Site Notice sent (to be erected for 14 days). Applicant may be required to notify neighbours.*
Day 7	Statutory and non-statutory consultations (21 days allowed for replies).	Statutory and non-statutory consultation (42 days allowed for replies).
Day 14		(a) Applicant informed of date when application will be considered by committee. (b) LPA must notify applicant if impact statement required.
Day 22	Applicant to certify publicity arrangements completed.	Applicant to certify publicity arrangements completed.
Day 28	(a) Any other publicity required must be completed. (b) Issue any notice of transfer to Class B.	(a) Any other publicity required must be completed.
Day 35	All consultations to be completed. First date for decision.	
Day 42	Latest date for decision. If no decision permission will be deemed to have been granted.	Receipt of any additional information for Class A application transferred to Class B.
Day 56		Latest date for decision (no impact statement).
Day 70		Submission of impact statement.
6 months		Latest date for decision (impact statement).

*There is the alternative of making local authorities responsible for all publicity. This may well be preferred: see para 7.29.

13

MEETINGS WITH APPLICANTS
A. BEFORE DECISION

2.28 Planning Committees should interview applicants if there is a marked difference of view within the Committee (7.69–7.70).

2.29 Greater use should be made of 'Section 52 agreements' to overcome particular objections (7.71).

2.30 All consultations between applicant and LPA are useful, but must be limited to cases in which they are indispensable, or are likely to be most productive (7.72–7.74).

2.31 Independently chaired meetings between applicants and local planning authorities, suggested by Circular 142/73, should at least be tried out (7.75–7.76).

2.32 The local planning authorities must always distinguish between grounds of refusal in principle and objections of detail capable of being resolved by negotiation (7.78–80).

B. AFTER REFUSAL

2.33 In Class B cases there should be a statutory duty to give reasons for a deemed refusal (7.56).

2.34 Upon a refusal of permission the applicant should perhaps be given the right to be heard by the Planning Committee or the Planning Officer. The object is to explore any possibility of compromise and to prevent hopeless appeals (7.84–7.85)

PLANNING APPLICATIONS

2.35 The borderline between 'outline' and 'detailed' applications is at present unclear and the distinction is too inflexible. There should in future be four types of application:—

(a) *Outline*. These should be accompanied only by a site plan.

(b) *Illustrative*. These should be accompanied by a site plan and illustrative plans which would determine the character of the development.

(c) *Detailed*. These should be accompanied by all building plans.

(d) *Guideline*.
   (i) These should include the general likely land use within an area. A permission would be similar in effect to an allocation in an old-style development plan.
   (ii) It will be especially useful for commerce and industry's long-term development plans.
   (iii) I suggest introduction of 'Future Development Certificate' for such cases, setting out the future use likely to be permitted.

(7.87)

2.36 Local planning authorities should have the power to grant, with the agreement of the applicant, a consent different from that originally asked for (7.113).

2.37 The applicant should be able to amend his application provided that the development proposed is of the same general nature and receives the same publicity as the original application (7.115–7.116).

2.38 There is a strong case from introducing a stamp duty or similar standard charge for planning applications; a small charge for Class A and a substantial charge for Class B (7.117–7.120).

RIGHTS OF APPEAL

2.39 Applicants should have the following rights of appeal to the Secretary of State:—

(a) in Class A cases, an appeal against a refusal or the imposition of conditions upon an express consent;

(b) in Class B cases, an appeal against a refusal, the imposition of conditions or, failure to give a decision within the stipulated time limit (7.121).

2.40 There should be no appeal against a planning officer's decision to transfer a case between classes (7.124).

2.41 Where there appears, on appeal, to have been no convincing reason for a local planning authority's delay in coming to a decision an order for costs against the authority should follow as a matter of course (7.125–7.127).

2.42 In cases which raise difficult policy issues, the local planning authority and the applicant should be able to *appeal 'by reference'* to the Secretary of State (7.128–7.131).

DESIGN CONTROL

2.43 In spite of its subjective nature, control of detailed design should be retained since:—

(a) such control is inevitable if the system of outline permission and reserved matters is to be retained;

(b) a deemed consent procedure is here inappropriate;

(c) design proposals are often extremely poor (7.132–7.133).

2.44 There is firm evidence of unnecessary and costly delays in deciding reserved matters. The process must be speeded up (7.134).

2.45 42 days should normally be the time limit for decision on reserved matters (7.137).

2.46 The local planning authority should have a limited power to stipulate an extended period for decision on reserved matters in the outline or illustrative permission, not exceeding 3 months for class B cases and 6 months for impact study cases (7.137).

2.47 Appeals to the Secretary of State on matters of detail are and should remain very much the exception. They should all go for decision to an Inspector (normally an architect), and be dealt with in writing. He will have the power to amend the plans, if the appellant agrees to it, subject to appropriate publicity. If necessary, the Inspector would hold an informal 'A' type inquiry to agree his amendments (7.137–7.138).

2.48 The use of *design guides*, for a given homogeneous area, and of *design briefs* relating to a particular site can make a major contribution to quality of design. They will be increasingly important in developing 'community land' and should be encouraged (7.139).

2.49 There are three immediate steps which should be taken to increase quality of decision on reserved matters:—

(a) Development Control Policy Note no. 10, now a decade old, should be revised (7.141).

(b) The procedure under section 50 of the 1971 Act* for appeals on matters of

---

*Throughout this report the Town and Country Planning Act 1971 is referred to as 'the 1971 Act', or 'the Act of 1971'.

external appearance and design to be heard by an independent tribunal has never been used. The Secretary of State should implement the procedure at least as an experiment (7.142).

(c) More use should be made of Conservation Area and Architectural Advisory Committees (7.143–7.145).

(d) Section 1 of the Town and Country Amenities Act 1974, should be put into effect (7.147).

2.50 Regulations should provide for specified applications by local authorities for approval of details to be made to the Secretary of State (7.148).

LOCAL PLANNING AUTHORITY PRACTICE AND PROCEDURE

2.51 Demarcation difficulties between counties and districts in the operation of Development Control Schemes are inevitable with the complex procedures of the Local Government Act 1972 (7.159).

2.52 Minimum overlapping of responsibility is essential: there is no money or manpower for duplication of effort (7.160–7.161).

2.53 Where there are delays there should be a re-appraisal of Development Control Schemes to simplify them. Monitoring of delays (see para 2.10) should indicate where this is necessary.

2.54 Since no increase in local authority staff can be expected (save in very exceptional circumstances) the only answer to staffing problems is:—

(a) greater use of unqualified staff;

(b) joint use of staff (7.165 and 7.170–7.172).

HOW COMMITTEES SHOULD OPERATE

2.55 There is surprising diversity of practice of planning authorities, in particular as to frequency of meetings and degree of delegation to sub-committees and officers, and in the ways committees work. The practice of the most efficient authorities should be followed more widely (7.173–7.174).

2.56 There must be more delegation to sub-committees and officers. Without delegation delays will never be cured (7.175–7.179).

2.57 There must be efficient sifting of applications so that committees can concentrate upon important and controversial applications without wasting time on routine cases (7.180–7.182).

2.58 The elected member of a local authority has in many ways the most unrewarding job in public life. He receives little recognition—only a barrage of criticism and complaints (7.183).

2.59 Nevertheless, if there are planning delays committees must meet more often (7.183).

2.60 There are applications which should not be decided without a site visit (7.184).

2.61 The public and the press have a right to be admitted to committees. They should normally (but not always) be admitted to meetings of sub-committees (7.185–7.189).

2.62 Experience shows that no harm is caused by publication of officers' recommendations either before or after a decision is taken at a closed meeting (7.190–7.191).

16

2.63 Pending the introduction of the proposals of the White Paper on 'Land', I recommend that generally market value should continue to be the basis of compensation for revocation orders (7.192–7.200).

SECTION II: POLICY FRAMEWORK

2.64 Individual planning decisions should not be made in a vacuum. If decisions are to be correct, fair, and, above all, consistent, they must be made within a clear and consistently applied framework comprising:—

   (i) approved structure plans and local plans which are kept up to date, or
  (ii) handover statements, that is statements which set out strategic policies and list old-style development plans and any informal non-statutory plans in force, indicating to what extent these plans are still to be applied;
 (iii) a provisional statement of its local policies by each District Council;
  (iv) Local or Particular Guidelines such as proposals affecting a particular conservation area or for a regional airport (8.1–8.35).

2.65 Speedy production of structure and local plans is crucial. There should be a national timetable for their production and they must be ready almost everywhere within the next five years (8.10–8.19).

2.66 A detailed procedure for the adoption of local plans should be settled now (8.14–8.15).

2.67 Structure planners should apply themselves to key issues. A recent Departmental circular (98/74)* advised local planning authorities to '*concentrate on those issues which are of key structural importance*'. Some counties still seem determined to prepare over-lengthy, elaborate and far too detailed structure plans. This misses the point of the whole exercise (8.20–8.22).

2.68 There should be the following general presumptions:—
 (*a*) a strong (though always rebuttable) presumption in favour of any application which conforms to an up-to-date local plan;
 (*b*) a presumption (though less strong and equally rebuttable) against an application which does not so conform (8.23).

2.69 In order to improve the quality of applications, guidelines for the public should be published:—
 (*a*) explaining how to apply for planning permission,
     and
 (*b*) explaining national and local planning policies (8.24–8.27).

2.70 Where old-style development plans are not out of date it would be helpful if local planning authorities:—
 (*a*) indicated clearly what plans or parts of plans were still being applied,
     and
 (*b*) adhered firmly to the allocations in such plans or parts of plans (8.28–8.30).

2.71 In the absence of a clear and comprehensive framework *ad hoc* decisions are an inevitable resort. This situation can mean more appeals and called-in cases, or local decisions based on wide public participation. Such policy decisions should be used in preparation of statutory plans (8.31).

2.72 In addition, policy decisions of general importance can profitably be made in advance of specific applications or appeals. For this purpose 'pilot inquiries'

---

*Welsh Office circular 168/74.

should be convened and the public examination procedure devised for structure plan inquiries used (8.36–8.41).

DEPARTMENTAL GUIDANCE

2.73 Guidance from central government is essential. Such guidance should have the following characteristics:

(a) It should be clear. Guidance contained in some circulars is hedged with so many reservations and savings as to be capable of being read as meaning anything.

(b) It should be comprehensive. The present welter of circulars, bulletins, etc., should be pruned of obsolete material and published as one comprehensive and coherent whole.

(c) It should be up to date. This means that the publication just mentioned should be kept regularly up to date and the new policy should be published promptly (8.42–8.45).

2.74 The Department should publish the following documents:

(a) a single up-to-date consolidation of policy guidance as just explained;

(b) a simple 'popular' explanation of the more important plans and policy documents;

(c) a planning control leaflet;

(d) a quarterly bulletin of topical material of interest to planners;

(e) The Department's own Desk Training Manual (8.46–8.55).

2.75 A Planning Control Consultative Committee should be established (with representation from local authorities, developers, the construction industry, some amenity societies and the professions) as a combined national forum for consultations between DOE and the public (8.56–8.60).

SECTION III: DEVELOPMENT ORDERS

2.76 A relaxation of the General Development Order (G.D.O.) would have been one way of streamlining planning control. I rejected that solution (except in special cases) (9.1 and 9.6).

2.77 The G.D.O. will, however, require considerable adjustment to attune its procedures to changes suggested in this report. Some of the permissions granted by it may well be too generous (9.10).

2.78 There is also a clear case for tightening controls in areas of special environmental importance, but this would mean some delays and additional work and expense. Putting new controls into effect must therefore wait until planning control has become more efficient (9.26–9.27).

2.79 I hope that immediate implementation of the recommendations in my Report on Demolition (September 1974) will prove possible (9.3).

2.80 Many planning applications concern development proposals exempted by the G.D.O. These should be disposed of by indicating on a standard printed form that a G.D.O. permission applies (9.12–9.13).

2.81 G.D.O. should be relaxed in order that:

Development within an existing industrial estate or premises should constitute permitted development, provided that:

    (i) it does not materially alter external appearance as viewed from outside the whole relevant premises;

    (ii) it complies with safety regulations, and

(iii) an Industrial Development Certificate has been obtained (or is available) where statute requires it.

But this extension of permitted development should not include 'bad neighbour' industry (special industry groups as defined in the Use Classes Order) (9.14–9.15).

2.82 I suggest the following amendments relating to change of use:

(1) The meaning of 'light industrial' in Article 2 should be clarified perhaps by listing processes it includes.

(2) Changes from special (bad neighbour) industrial use to general or light industrial use should constitute permitted development.

(3) Changes from light industrial use to warehousing should constitute permitted development.

(4) Changes from warehousing to light industrial use should constitute permitted development provided the buildings were completed at least five years previously. (This is to prevent evasion of I.D.C. control.) (9.16).

2.83 Agricultural buildings. No general change to the General Development Order is practical at this time but there is a clear case for some tightening of control over agricultural buildings in the future. It would not be too onerous if Class VI of the G.D.O. were amended to exclude:

(a) buildings within 100 metres of existing buildings;

(b) intensive buildings (9.29–9.31).

SPECIAL ENVIRONMENTAL AREAS

2.84 It would be helpful to divide 'special environmental areas' into those of national importance (national parks, areas of outstanding natural beauty, heritage coasts and the more important conservation areas) and those of 'local importance' (other conservation areas and other areas of town or country identified in development plans or policies) (9.33–9.37).

2.85 Special Development Orders are recommended as appropriate means for exercising control in the areas of national importance: one S.D.O. for the three landscape categories and another for the other nationally important conservation areas (9.32–9.35, 9.42–9.50 and the Annex to Chapter 9).

2.86 Article 4 directions are the most appropriate means for securing tighter control in locally important environmental areas (9.51 and Annex to Chapter 9).

2.87 Special care and stringency are needed for twilight and stress areas of cities. Here also, Article 4 directions provide the simplest and potentially most effective tool for tighter control (9.51).

2.88 Compensation under Section 165 (1) (b) of the 1971 Act should be restricted to actual damage (9.52).

SECTION IV: PUBLIC INVOLVEMENT

2.89 In this report I use:

(1) 'Public involvement' to mean both public participation and public consultation;

(2) 'Public participation' to mean taking an active part—from the outset—in the formulation of development plans and the making of major planning decisions of strategic importance;

(3) 'Public consultation' to mean giving the public an opportunity to express views on planning applications already made;

19

(4) 'Interested parties' to mean all parties other than the applicant (or appellant) and the planning authority (10.2).

2.90 The best method of involving the public must be chosen for each set of circumstances.

2.91 Public consultation must be early. In ordinary cases it should begin as soon as the local planning authority receives the application; in especially controversial or major Class B cases, pre-application publicity can help to modify development proposals before attitudes harden (10.5, 10.8 and 10.15).

2.92 The public needs to understand the nature and limits of planning control better: equally planners need a better grasp of the principles and techniques of public involvement. Public involvement must be (1) relevant, (2) more efficient, (3) constructive and selective (10.7).

2.93 Registers of planning applications should be open in lunch hours and on some evenings and should be duplicated where the planning office is difficult to reach from some parts of a district.

2.94 The existing law of copyright should be amended so that application plans can be copied (10.14).

2.95 The proper purpose of public involvement in planning is to guide, not dictate, the local planning authority's decisions (10.6).

2.96 The Department has sponsored research into public participation in plan making. This needs to be widened to include public consultation on planning control (10.46–10.47).

BETTER COMMUNICATION BETWEEN LOCAL AUTHORITIES AND PUBLIC

2.97 Local authorities should be more active in providing planning design guides, planning briefs, explanatory leaflets and information sheets (10.20–10.25).

2.98 There should be greater, and perhaps more thoughtful, coverage of planning in the local press, radio (including local radio) on television and in documentary films.

2.99 Publication of lists of applications and decisions is especially important (10.50–10.66).

2.100 Education is the key to efficient and effective public involvement. The schools, adult education institutes, universities and local societies can all make a valuable contribution (10.43–10.45).

2.101 Voluntary organisations receive insufficient help. There is a need in due course for a central national body (British Environment Council) provided with funds (10.34).

2.102 Local authorities should adopt more widely the practice of co-opting members of amenity societies and other bodies on to planning committees. This may co-ordinate consultation and help applicants (10.18 and 10.19).

2.103 Parish and community councils have a vital part to play in local planning.

2.104 In the large urban areas where they do not exist, neighbourhood councils might be considered to fill the gap (10.13).

PLANNING INFORMATION AND ADVICE

2.105 More local authority information centres and independent planning advice centres could reduce the number of abortive applications and appeals and enable objectors to present their case in proper planning terms (10.26–10.30).

2.106 There is a case for the introduction when resources permit of a Planning Aid scheme, similar to the Legal Aid scheme, for those who cannot afford professional help (10.31–10.33).

SECTION V: APPEALS

2.107 There is complaint and disquiet, not about the fairness of decisions, but about delay and over-formal procedures (11.3–5).

2.108 There is a strong case for stricter discipline at major inquiries for all parties including interested persons (11.9).

2.109 The unqualified right of appeal should not be withdrawn but the Secretaries of State should have power to exercise their discretion whether the appeal procedures should be by way of an inquiry or by way of written representations (11.13–11.16).

2.110 No case has been made out for transferring appeals to another tribunal (11.17–11.19).

2.111 Publicity. There should be the following publicity for appeals:
(a) notification to interested parties by the local authority;
(b) compulsory site notices for inquiries;
(c) discretionary publication of lists of appeals (and of the results) in local newspapers, by local authorities;
(d) in major cases, the appellants may be required to advertise.

2.112 If an advertisement had been omitted in a bad neighbour case at the application stage, the Secretary of State should have the power to accept an appeal if it is given equivalent publicity.

'A' AND 'B' APPEALS

2.113 All appeals should be divided into two classes, Class A and Class B to correspond with the class of applications (11.22).

2.114 Class A appeals should comprise:
(a) all simple cases;
(b) appeals relating to development which, within specified limits as to size, conforms to an approved up to date development plan;
(c) appeals relating to development only just exceeding the limits permitted by the General Development Order;
(d) appeals against a refusal to approve details under an 'outline' or 'illustrative' Class A application (11.22).

2.115 The decision as to which categories an appeal falls into should be that of the Department (11.24).

2.116 (1) In Class A inquiries the following simplified procedure should apply:
(a) While there should be a residual power to order Rule 6 Statements from either side such statements should not normally be required.
(b) The venue should usually be as informal as possible.
(c) The only documents to be supplied to the Secretary of State would be the application, the grounds of refusal, the grounds of appeal and a plan.

(*d*) The procedure should be as informal as possible. In particular, persons should remain seated around a table and the Inspector should play an active part in the proceedings.

(*e*) No legal representation should be allowed on either side.

(*f*) Where the decision was an Inspector's he should have the discretion to give an immediate oral decision with written reasons for the decision to follow.

(2) Class A written representations should normally require the consent of both parties but the decision could be given in about 2 months (11.26–11.32).

2.117 Priority should only be given to exceptional cases of vital importance to the national economy (11.33–11.34).

2.118 There will be a threefold and overlapping classification of appeals into:

(*a*) Class A or Class B.

(*b*) Inspectors' decisions or Secretary of State's decisions.

(*c*) Written representations or public inquiries (11.36).

2.119 The general aim should be to put as many appeals as possible into the first alternative within each of the above classifications (11.37–11.39 and 11.41–11.42).

2.120 The procedure of holding a 'hearing' closed to the public is no longer needed (11.119, see 2.139).

2.121 The status and structure of the Inspectorate should be maintained and improved (11.46–11.48).

2.122 The Inspectorate should retain the present position of a part, but an independent part, of the Department of the Environment (11.57–11.58).

2.123 One of the most important tasks of Inspectors is to write clear and comprehensive reports. The present form and content of reports is sound. There may be some scope for greater brevity in the recording of arguments (11.51–11.55).

2.124 Much would be gained from direct contact between Superintending Inspectors and Regional Directors especially on matters such as the flow and content of appeals and fluctuations of policy (11.59).

2.125 Members of the public make a valuable contribution to Inquiries but some have little idea of what is relevant and Inspectors must be given guidance on how to deal firmly with this aspect of public involvement (11.129).

2.126 There is a need for clear and well publicised central government guidance on policy. Statistical and other information should be provided not only for local authorities but also for appellants so that they may judge what chance they have of success (11.61–11.66).

2.127 Grounds of appeal should be required to be full and specific. A mere denial of the grounds of refusal should normally not be enough (11.67–11.69).

2.128 Grounds of refusal should be more selective (11.71–11.72).

2.129 A further management study is needed to speed up the work of the Administrative Division of the Inspectorate (11.75).

2.130 Much delay is caused by the parties to an appeal failing to comply with procedural requirements. A firmer line from the Department is required (11.74 and 11.76–11.78).

2.131 A standard time-table should be laid down for decisions by the Secretary of State. The Department should inform appellants how long a decision is likely to take and should provide an alternative date if the estimate is not in fact fulfilled (11.79–11.80).

2.132 The average waiting period for an inquiry has been almost halved from 15 to 8 months. The target for the end of 1975 should be an average of not more than seven months in Secretary of State cases and $5\frac{1}{2}$ months in Inspectors' cases between the date when all appellant's documents are complete and the date of the decision (11.83).

2.133 Every appeal should have a 'case officer' responsible for its progress. The officer should be available for inquiry and consultation by the parties at all stages (11.84–11.90).

2.134 The fixing and holding of inquiries at the earliest possible date is crucial for the elimination of delays. In the present circumstances it is justifiable for the Department to fix inquiries without consulting the parties. Adjournments should only be granted in the most exceptional cases (11.93–11.95).

2.135 The wider use of orders for costs is very necessary. The following points are especially important:
(a) Costs should be awarded much more readily in cases of repetitive appeals, last minute adjournments, etc.
(b) Inspectors should have power to award costs where the decision on the appeal is theirs.
(c) The Inspector should make a recommendation as to costs in Secretary of State cases.
(d) The decision letter on the appeal should generally itself deal with the question of costs.
(e) The Secretary of State should be empowered to order costs at any time even if there has been no inquiry (11.96–11.103).

WRITTEN REPRESENTATIONS

2.136 A major effort is needed to make the idea of written representations more attractive in Class B cases (as to Class A, see para. 2.116 (2)). This can only be achieved by:
(a) limiting the representations to:
   (i) the appellant's grounds of appeal;
   (ii) the local authority's (and interested parties') observations;
   (iii) the appellant's reply;
   and
(b) a set time-table, for example:
   (1) the starting time when the appellant's representations are received by the local planning authority;
   (2) the local planning authority's answer (and interested parties' representations) 6 weeks thereafter;
   (3) the appellant's reply 2 weeks later;
   (4) Inspector's visit 2 weeks after the reply;
   (5) decision letter after 5 weeks (11.104–11.111).

2.137 The total period for this procedure would be 26 weeks in Secretary of State's cases (and could be shorter – 20 weeks – in transferred cases). It would be preferable to have Statutory Rules to secure compliance with the time-table (11.112)

2.138 The Secretary of State should in appropriate cases use his power to order an Inquiry, at any time up to 28 days after the receipt of the appellant's reply (11.115).

23

INQUIRIES

2.139 Distinction between 'inquiries' and 'hearings' should be repealed. There is at present only a small distinction between 'inquiries' and 'hearings' to which the public are not admitted as of right. This serves no purpose and should be abolished. Class A appeals could be called 'informal inquiries' (11.119–11.122).

2.140 In the conduct of Class B inquiries the following changes should be achieved:

(a) The Inspector should play a more active role, particularly in bringing out relevant facts and preventing time being wasted on irrelevant and repetitive matters (11.123).

(b) Inquiries should be less formal and legalistic (11.126).

(c) Wastage of time, for example, by cross-examination on questions of opinion should be prevented by Inspectors (11.128).

2.141 The existing law of copyright should be amended so that appeal plans can be copied (11.131–11.140).

There is a need to reconcile the objectives of greater speed with the fullest participation by the public. To this end interested parties should be encouraged to give advance written notice of their case and there should be a power, to be used sparingly, to require them to provide and keep to a Rule 6 Statement (11.141–11.143).

2.142 In due course a system of 'planning aid' should be available to interested persons in carefully scrutinised cases. In the meantime it should be possible for the parties to be ordered to pay the costs of interested persons who supply helpful evidence not made available by the parties (11.143).

2.143 Costs should be awarded against interested persons who, after a full warning from the Inspector, pursue frivolous or repetitive objections (11.143).

2.144 Local planning authorities' Rule 6 (2) Statements should be served 5 weeks after the appellant's papers are complete, and the appellant's Statement of Submissions 3 weeks thereafter. The date for inquiry would be fixed at the end of the following 2 weeks (11.150).

2.145 Failure to comply with the time limits without a proper excuse should be penalised by an order for costs (11.155).

2.146 Inspectors should have power to order an exchange of proofs of evidence and to order that an attempt be made to agree a statement of facts before an inquiry starts (11.154 and 11.156).

2.147 Pre-inquiry meetings would be useful in some Class B cases (11.160–11.161).

2.148 Simple cases which raise the same question of policy and are in the same close geographical area could be dealt with at Inquiry Sessions (11.162).

2.149 The proposals in this chapter will inevitably restrict individual rights to some limited extent. The law on the review of planning decisions by the courts needs clarification. The precise grounds on which a decision may be challenged should be established. An unsuccessful party should be given an express right to apply to the High Court for an order that the decision be remitted to the Secretary of State (or an Inspector) for reconsideration on the ground that the decision was so unreasonable that no reasonable man could have come to it (11.166–11.172).

SECTION VI: ENFORCEMENT

2.150 The main problems are:

(a) the delay caused by appeals (in 65% of cases the serving of an enforcement notice leads to an appeal);

(b) the inability to serve a stop notice in respect of uses of land;

(c) reluctance to serve stop notices because of risk of liability to pay compensation;

(d) difficulties of local planning authorities (L.P.A.s) in ascertaining facts (12.2).

2.151 The large number of appeals is not really warranted. Less than 20% of successful appeals succeed on legal grounds. On the other hand about 30% succeed on planning grounds. The same result could be achieved in a less complex way (12.3).

2.152 The L.P.A. should at the outset be required to consider whether it would grant permission (and if so subject to what conditions), and if not give reasons. If it proposes to grant permission there should first be appropriate publicity (12.4).

2.153 The L.P.A. should also state in the notice any reasons (in addition to 'reasons for refusal') why it is expedient to serve it (12.5).

2.154 The model enforcement notice (issued in Circular 153/74) should always be used as a basis. (It would have to be amended if these recommendations are implemented.) (12.6).

2.155 There should be the power to add a requirement for works to be carried out as an alternative to restoring the land to its previous state (12.7).

2.156 Stop notice procedure should be extended to change of use (12.8).

2.157 Section 284 of the 1971 Act should be extended to enable L.P.A.s to require the occupier to give factual information as to use of land ('Discovery Notice') (12.9–12.14).

2.158 There should be Inquiry Procedure Rules for Enforcement Appeals (and Rule 6 Statements by both L.P.A. and the appellant) (12.15–12.17).

2.159 The power to award costs should be used freely in enforcement appeals (12.20).

2.160 There should be no power to challenge the validity of enforcement notices in Magistrates' Courts in respect of Section 88 (1) of the 1971 Act (relating to the steps required to comply with an enforcement notice and time for compliance) (12.21).

2.161 There should be power to serve an enforcement notice in respect of intermittent and temporary breaches (12.22).

PART II
THE PRESENT SYSTEM

CHAPTER 3

Development Plans

SECTION I: INTRODUCTORY

3.1 Town and Country Planning is the direct responsibility of local authorities, subject, as are all functions of local government, to central government control.

3.2. This chapter gives a description of the procedures relating to the preparation of development plans. The position both before and after local government reorganisation in 1974 is considered.

3.3 **Division of responsibilities.** The planning powers conferred on the local planning authorities by the Town and Country Planning Act of 1947, consolidated in 1971, are now exercised by the new planning authorities, i.e. county and district councils set up under the Local Government Act 1972. Before 1972 county councils and county borough councils were responsible for preparing development plans and for planning control. County councils could (and most did) delegate some of their development control work to their district councils. Now district councils have the primary responsibility for development control and it is expected that they will prepare local plans, while county councils are preparing structure plans.

SECTION II: THE HISTORY: BEFORE AND AFTER 1968

(a) The 1947 Act

3.4 **Old and new style development plans.** The original development plan system was introduced by the Town and Country Planning Act 1947 and the relevant provisions were re-enacted in the Act of 1962. A new system of structure and local plans was introduced by the Town and Country Planning Act 1968.
The relevant provisions were re-enacted in the Act of 1971 and were subsequently amended by the Town and Country Planning (Amendment) Act 1972 and the Local Government Act 1972.

3.5 **The number of planning authorities.** Local authorities (excluding those responsible for Greater London and the Isles of Scilly) which were directly responsibile for planning BEFORE the reorganisation of local government in April 1974 were:—

In England

45 county councils
79 county borough councils
the planning boards for the Peak District and
Lake District National Parks

In Wales

13 county councils
4 county borough councils

AFTER April 1974 they were replaced by:—

In England

45 county councils
332 district councils
the planning boards for the Peak District and
Lake District National Parks

In Wales

8 county councils
37 district councils

3.6 **Greater London.** The planning authorities for Greater London (since 1965) have been:—

The Greater London Council
32 London Borough Councils
The Common Council of the City of London.

As a result of the 1972 Local Government Act, the number of separate local planning authorities in England and Wales has risen from 177 to 458. It should be noted however that before April 1974 about 1,200 District Authorities exercised some development control functions under delegation arrangements.

3.7 **Old style development plans.** Development plans, prepared by the local planning authorities and approved by the Secretary of State, are in force for the whole of England and Wales. These are "plans indicating the manner in which a local planning authority propose that land in their area should be used . . .". Regulations prescribe the form and content of the plans, and procedures for their approval. (These plans will be replaced, over a period, by new plans described below.)

3.8 **County maps and town maps.** The development plan for a county consisted of a small scale county map and a written statement, supplemented by large scale town maps for urban areas. For a county borough the development plan consisted of a large scale map of the town supported by a written statement. The development plan could also include more detailed maps of areas to be comprehensively developed or redeveloped.

3.9 **The content of plans.** Development plans were based on a comprehensive land-use survey of the area in question made by the local planning authority. Any factors likely to affect development in the area were also taken into account. These might include anticipated population change, employment trends and programmed public development such as the building of motorways and trunk roads. Also, government policies affecting, for example, the distribution of industry or the conservation of agricultural land were reflected in the plans.

3.10 **The shortcomings** of the original development plan system became increasingly apparent over the years. It became clear that the approach was wrong. It dealt with land use, but it did not deal effectively with problems of transport, urban renewal or the quality of the environment. The written statement, required to concentrate upon the summarising of development proposals, was inadequate for setting out and justifying policies.

3.11 **Plans too detailed and inflexible.** The amount of specific detail tended to make a plan inflexible and the whole process of considering, modifying and

27

approving development plans, which applied equally to amending them, was slow and cumbersome. This was largely because the maps which accompanied the statements were too detailed and each one had to be closely examined by the Secretary of State. In many areas it was found impossible to keep them up to date; there was no sufficiently flexible procedure to reflect changes of policy in them.

(b) The 1968 Act

3.12 **The 1968 Act** recognised that, although important general policies should receive the Secretary of State's approval, details should be left to the discretion of the local authorities.

3.13 **Structure and Local Plans.** The revised system, therefore, brought in two kinds of plans: first, there are *structure plans* which are statements of general policy and which have to be approved by the Secretary of State; secondly, there are local plans which are intended to show in detail how these policies will be implemented. The latter will normally be adopted by the local planning authority without reference to the Secretary of State. The Secretary of State does, however, have power to call in local plans and give a decision on them himself in exceptional cases. (Responsibilities for the preparation of local plans will be shown in Development Plan Schemes (see para. 3.19 below).) In addition to dealing with development and other uses of land, the new plans concern themselves with such things as improvement of the physical environment and measures for traffic management.

The Structure Plan

3.14 A structure plan is a written statement illustrated with diagrams; it sets out the main planning policies and the most important general proposals for the area, aiming to plan as far ahead as possible. Transport and land use are also taken into account. In formulating the policy and general proposals, the local authority must also have regard to the Government's current social and economic policies for their area, also to the resources likely to be available for carrying out their proposals. The structure plan is supported by reference to surveys carried out by the local planning authority. These deal with such things as the main physical and economic characteristics of the area, the size, composition and distribution of its population.

3.15 A structure plan, therefore, has three main purposes:

(1) to outline and justify to the public and to the Secretary of State, the authority's policies and general proposals for the development and other use of land in the area concerned;

(2) to carry out national and regional policies in terms of physical and environmental planning for the area concerned; and

(3) to provide the framework for local plans.

3.16 **The Local Plan.** The preparation of local plans, including consultation with the public, can be concurrent with the preparation of the structure plan. A local plan has to be prepared for any action area (i.e. an area indicated in the structure plan as one selected for comprehensive development, redevelopment or improvement to be started within ten years). Otherwise the preparation of local plans is at the authority's discretion, subject to the Secretary of State's power to direct that plans of a particular kind should be produced.

28

3.17 **Map and written statement.** A local plan consists of a map and a written statement and its purpose is to translate the structure plan policies into suitably detailed proposals. Where appropriate it will make allocations of land. Any local plan is necessarily required to conform to the structure plan and the district council are required to obtain from the county council a certificate to this effect.

3.18 There are three main types of local plan.

(1) **District Plans** set out proposals for both public and private development or other use of land and serve as important guides for development control. They may cover the whole or a part of the local planning authority's area.

(2) **Action Area Plans** set out in detail the proposals for development, redevelopment or improvement of action areas indicated in the structure plan. They may range from closely detailed plans (especially where a local authority is the developer) to a broad brief (which will only establish guide-lines for the private developer, leaving the details to be settled by the process of development control).

(3) **Subject Plans** explain in detail the authority's policy and proposals for some particular topic, for example, conservation.

Different local plans, therefore, prepared for different purposes, may both or all be in force at the same time in the same part of a local authority's area.

SECTION III: RESPONSIBILITY FOR PREPARATION OF PLANS

3.19 **Development Plan Schemes.** County councils are responsible for the preparation of structure plans (for Greater London see para 3.21 below). District councils will prepare most local plans, but some of these may be prepared by counties. Under S.183(2) of the Local Government Act 1972, county councils are required to prepare a development plan scheme which will allocate the responsibility for making local plans and provide a programme for their preparation. This scheme is to be made in consultation with the district planning authorities and kept under review.

3.20 **National Parks.** Structure and local plans which deal with national parks are the responsibility of the appropriate county council not of the district authorities. The Peak District and Lake District National Park planning boards are responsible for development plans in their own areas.

3.21 **The Position in London.** Under the London Government Act 1963, the GLC is the strategic planning authority for Greater London. The GLC therefore prepared a general development plan for Greater London known as the Greater London Development Plan. This has been the subject of a public inquiry but has not yet been approved by the Secretary of State. Most local plans will be prepared by the 32 London Borough Councils and the Common Council of the City of London. The GLC, however, will prepare them for those action areas shown to be the responsibility of the GLC in the Greater London Development Plan.

SECTION IV: PUBLIC PARTICIPATION

3.22 The 1968 Act included new requirements for public participation in the making of plans. The authority preparing a structure or local plan must now publish a report of relevant survey material, publicise adequately the matters they propose to deal with in the plan, provide an opportunity for the making of representations about those matters and consider the representations before they finish drafting the plan. The object is to involve the public much more effectively in preparation of plans by giving them this formal opportunity to make their views known, and by ensuring that these views are considered before the local planning authority are committed to any specific solution of the planning problems of their area.

3.23 An authority submitting a structure plan to the Secretary of State for approval, or depositing a local plan before its formal adoption, must inform the Secretary of State what public participation there has been. Authorities are asked to say what issues have been raised and how they have dealt with them.

SECTION V: STRUCTURE PLANS

3.24 **The consideration of a structure plan** and the objections to it must be consistent with the nature of the plan as a broad outline of policy, illustrated only by diagrams. It is inappropriate and impracticable to deal with objections to matters of detail at this stage. The provisions for the consideration of objections to a structure plan have been designed with this in mind.

3.25 **Examination in Public.** The Town and Country Planning (Amendment) Act 1972 provides that the traditional inquiry into objections shall be replaced by an examination in public of matters selected by the Secretary of State.

3.26 **No right to be heard.** The Secretary of State is still under an obligation to consider all the objections he receives, but objectors have no statutory right to be heard. The examination, under an independent chairman, will be concerned with matters where more information is required before the Secretary of State can reach a decision or where there are matters of substantial controversy that have not been satisfactorily resolved. Participation in the discussions at an examination is by invitation. In selecting participants the basic criterion is the effectiveness of the contribution which they can be expected to make.

3.27 **Approval of Structure Plans.** The Secretary of State's powers in relation to the approval of a structure plan are more flexible than were his powers in relation to the pre-1968 plans. He may approve it in its entirety or in part, make *modifications* or '*reservations*'; or he can reject it.

3.28 **Objections to modifications; and to 'reservations'.** Under the Town and Country Planning (Structure and Local Plans) Regulations* the Secretary of State has to consider any objections made to his proposed *modifications* if they are submitted to him within six weeks from the date on which notice of the proposed modifications is first published in local newspapers. There is no right of objection, however, to the proposed '*reservations*' about those policies in the plans which the Secretary of State asks the county planning authorities to reconsider.

3.29 **Progress with structure plans.** There are now 53 counties in England and Wales. Real progress has already been made on 21 plans. Examinations in public have now been held into seven structure plans, and the modifications proposed by the Secretary of State for the first four plans to be examined were advertised in September 1974. An examination into one further structure plan was in progress on 31st December 1974. The examinations into six more plans are expected to start in March 1975. Examinations in public into the first three structure plans in Wales will be held in May 1975.

---

*Regulation No. 1486 of 1974.

30

3.30 **Target: 74 Plans.** The total number of structure plans expected in England (excluding Greater London) is seventy four. (This is in excess of the number of counties because a structure plan can be made for an area smaller than a county.) Seventeen had been submitted by 1st April 1974 and it is expected that *about half the total number will have been* submitted by the end of 1975. It is hoped that the remainder will follow by April 1978.

3.31 **The time taken to examine structure plans.** The Secretary of State's proposals for the four structure plans already examined in public have been published (on average) less than 18 months after the submission of those plans, and between five and six months after the submission of the examination panels' reports. This is to the great credit of all concerned and compares very favourably with the time taken to process development plans prepared under the 1962 Act. It indicates that the Department may well succeed in getting all structure plans submitted by April 1978 and in reaching decisions on them within one year thereafter.

3.32 **In Wales** two plans had been submitted by 1st April 1974 and a third was submitted in December 1974. The remaining seven should be submitted well before April 1978.

Informal Plans and Policy Statements

3.33 **Interim basis.** In many areas, in addition to the development plans prepared under the 1962 Act, there are informal plans and policy statements of many kinds. These can be taken into account as "other material considerations" (see S.22 of the 1971 Act) for development control purposes and, in conjunction with the development plan, serve as an interim basis for development control while formal plans are being produced.

3.34 **Advantages of informal plans.** The disadvantage of these informal plans and policy statements is that, being non-statutory, they are open to challenge in the context of planning appeals and applications for planning permission which come before the Secretary of State for decision. If they have been made subject to extensive public participation, however (as many have been) they can serve a useful purpose where statutory development plans are seriously out of date.

SECTION VI: ADOPTION OF LOCAL PLANS

3.35 **Objections and Inquiries.** Where a local planning authority intends to adopt a local plan, the same processes of public inspection, objection, inquiry and modification will be followed, as in the case of a development plan under the 1962 Act, except that responsibility rests with the local planning authority instead of with the Secretary of State. An inquiry will be held to consider objections and will, for the time being, be conducted by a Planning Inspector. The Inspector will, however, report to the local planning authority and not to the Secretary of State.

3.36 **Appointment of Inspectors.** It is expected that after an experimental period the Secretary of State will empower local planning authorities to appoint suitably qualified Inspectors of their own choice; their appointment will be governed by regulations.

3.37 **Call-in of Local Plans.** The power to call in a local plan will be exercised sparingly by the Secretary of State. It might, however, be used where the local plan raises issues of more than local significance, as in the centre of an historic town.

SECTION VII: KEEPING DEVELOPMENT PLANS UP TO DATE

3.38 **Adjustment of phasing.** All development plans are based on certain assumptions with regard to resources and so on. It is important that these should be monitored, assumptions re-examined regularly and when necessary the plan should be amended. If it is found that an incorrect assumption was made about the rate of growth, it will often be possible to adjust the plan by changing the length of time allowed for different phases. Such changes in timing would not call for proposals for alteration of the structure plan.

3.39 **Change of policy.** The policies embodied in the plan, however, may need to be changed if the assumptions on which they are based prove to be seriously wrong, or if the structure of the area is significantly affected by, for example, changes in shopping habits or methods of transport. A full review would then be required to bring about a formal alteration of the plan or the preparation of a new plan.

3.40 **Periodic revision.** A structure plan will in any case need to be brought up to date every five years or so to cover a further period. Proposals for the alteration of adopted local plans or for additional local plans may be made at any time and will be dealt with in the same way as the original proposals.

SECTION VIII: TRANSITION TO THE NEW DEVELOPMENT PLAN

3.41 **Overall development plan.** Outside Greater London, when a structure plan is approved, the overall development plan for the area it covers consists of the structure plan read together with the old-style development plan. In any case of conflict between the two the structure plan will prevail.

3.42 **Revocation of old-style development plans.** As the policy and general proposals of the structure plan are supplemented by adopted local plans, the Secretary of State, after consulting with the local planning authority, will revoke those parts of the old development plan which are out of date.

SECTION IX: ECONOMIC PLANNING COUNCILS AND ECONOMIC PLANNING BOARDS

3.43 An assessment of the system whereby plans are made would not be complete without mentioning the work of the Economic Planning Councils and Boards.

3.44 **The Economic Planning Councils.** The eight councils in England, and the one for Wales, were established in 1965. A council is made up of about 30 part-time members each of whom knows the regions and has some special experience of, for instance, industry and commerce, local government or social service. Members are not appointed as representatives of any particular interest or locality.

3.45 **Regional Development.** The councils advise Central Government on aspects of national policy which have a bearing on regional development and may themselves raise with Ministers any issue of major concern to the region's development.

3.46 Regional Strategic Plans. Of particular interest in the planning field is the councils' work in producing regional strategic plans. These are produced after analysing regional needs, taking into account the distribution of population, industry and employment.

3.47 The Economic Planning Boards are composed of representatives of Government Departments in the regions. The principal Departments involved are the DOE (which provides the Chairman), the Departments of Trade and Industry, the Ministry of Agriculture, Fisheries and Food, the Central Office of Information, the Ministry of Defence, the Department of Education and Science, the Department of Health and Social Security, the Home Office and the Department of Employment.

3.48 Co-ordination of Regional Policies. It is the task of each Board to secure co-ordination between Departments' regional policies and to assist the councils by providing information and advice and commissioning necessary research work.

CHAPTER 4

Planning Control

SECTION I: INTRODUCTORY

Local Government Act 1972

4.1 The general changes in the distribution of planning powers under the Local Government Act 1972 have already been referred to in Chapter 3 and were set out in more detail in paragraphs 3.22 to 3.27 of my Interim Report.

Development Control Schemes

4.2 I drew attention there to the possibilities of conflict in cases where the interests of county and district councils overlap and to the Department's advice (Circular 74/73*) that *"development control schemes"* should *"set out procedures for co-operation, including agreement between authorities to keep double handling to a minimum and for the rapid resolution of differences between them about the handling of planning applications in which both have an interest"*.

4.3 I understand that there were good reasons which led the Department to decide that development control schemes should not be statutory and that the Secretary of State should not have to arbitrate between county and district councils.

4.4 It is essential that there should be agreed schemes. They should also be formally adopted, kept up to date, published and explained to the public.

4.5 Above all they must be simple, sensible, and avoid duplication of paper work and of decision making. There must also be some degree of uniformity or at least a pattern, and not a mosaic of labyrinthine schemes. At present the diversity and complexity of some (but by no means all) of the schemes gives ground for deep concern; but it must be acknowledged that of 53 counties (in England and Wales) there are already over 70 schemes which are in operation.

4.6 It is essential to lay down a clear guide for determining which matters are to be dealt with at district, and which at county level.

4.7 It is intended that the county council should 'deal with applications which have an impact on its strategy' and some other applications† and the district council should process all remaining applications.

---

*Welsh Office Circular 143/73.

†ie 'county matters' are defined in paragraph 32 of Schedule 16 to the Local Government Act 1972. They include:—

(a) any application to do with the working of minerals.

(b) operations that would conflict with fundamental provisions of the structure plan or local plan prepared by the county.

(c) operations that would conflict with any statement of planning policy or proposals for development by the county, or a development plan, still in force, prepared under the 1971 Town and Country Planning Act or previous legislation.

4.8 There is no clear pattern as to *who* should determine whether an application raises a county matter:

(a) some schemes leave the *district planning officer* to decide which applications give rise to 'county matters', leaving him free to put his own interpretation on the various provisions of paragraph 32 of Schedule 16;

(b) in other cases guidance is laid down in the *Handover Statement* (see para 7.132);

(c) in one county the decision is made in practice by a *liaison branch* (employed by the county council) which meets regularly with the district planning officer to agree on whether an application raises county matters.

4.9 There is no clear pattern as to division of responsibility between county and district council.

4.10 (1) In all counties, an application which raises county matters can be *refused* by the district without reference to the county council.

(2) In one county, the county council can give *an approval in principle* to proposed development, and then leave it to the district council to process the application and to settle the details.

(3) Some county councils deal with applications within their jurisdiction after having taken *the opinion* of the district council concerned.

(4) In some counties the Development Control Scheme spells out *in detail the categories* of applications to be dealt with by the county council.

(5) In one area, *district councils are enabled to decide all applications*, including those raising 'county matters', on the advice of a joint team of county and district planning officers.

(6) In another, the district council sends *copies of all applications* to the county council each week, and county and district officers meet to discuss any case which raises county matters. The *county council* then recommend a decision to the district council.

(7) Several other county councils *insist on seeing every* application.

(8) There is an even more circuitous system whereby the *county council check every application* against approved plans and policies, and notify district councils of any potential conflicts. Major development proposals are checked by the county *plan* staff.

(9) In another case the *county council scrutinise the agenda for each district planning committee meeting*; they are thus aware of the applications coming forward for decision without having to see each one.

(10) One county council have devised an unusual way of keeping themselves informed. They pay 25% of the salary of each district planning officer, who is expected to keep the county planning officer informed, and to act for the county council on applications which raise county matters.

(11) A unique solution found provides for a *county* planning committee made up of 20 county and 10 district councillors, on the assumption that each *district* would have a planning committee of 14 district and 7 county councillors. It is, therefore, possible for the district council committee to have full delegated powers to deal with all applications. In theory this removes the need for deciding which give rise to county

---

(*d*) operations in a National Park.

(*e*) an application conflicting with any other operation 'prescribed' by the county.

This definition was deliberately drawn in very general terms, as distinct from the closely defined separate areas of responsibility in the Greater London area.

matters or for categorisation of applications, except where a proposal involves more than one district or would substantially and adversely affect county interests. In these circumstances it is referred to the county planning committee.*

SECTION II: APPLICATIONS

Workload

4.11 (1) (*a*) *The Sixties* may be described as a period of modest peaks and troughs. The annual average number of decisions made was 428,895. The two years of least activity were 1962 (397,000) and 1969 (402,000). A peak occurred in 1964 (462,000) and in 1971 463,000 decisions were made. The annual average rate of increase from 1963 to 1971 was only 1.8%.

(*b*) Against this relatively peaceful background the years of 1972 and 1973 were traumatic. After the 1971 level of 463,000 decisions there was a spectacular leap to 615,000 in 1972 (an increase of 33%) followed by a further rise (albeit of only 1.3%) to 623,000 in 1973.

(*c*) It is of course not possible at this stage to say how many applications were submitted during 1974. (The boundary changes which accompanied the re-organisation of local government will anyway make comparison with 1973 difficult.) My Secretariat have taken a random sample of some 10 county and 15 district planning authorities. This indicates that the number of applications received during the first nine months of 1974 was very roughly 25% less than in the corresponding period in 1973. On that basis some 470,000 applications will have been made in 1974.

(*d*) But the rate of fall in applications has apparently accelerated in the last quarter of this year: the Department will not receive accurate figures until about June 1975, but the present estimate is that the number of *decisions* in 1974 will in fact be of the order of at least 400,000.

(*e*) The statistical evidence over the last decade does not show a single year in which less than 400,000 decisions have been made and I conclude that this can be taken as an irreducible minimum.

(2) **Proportion of refusals:** Only 15–20% of applications on average were refused. The low was in 1969 (14–15%), also a low year for decisions. The high was in 1973 (21%), the all-time high for decisions. These are significant figures. They show that an overwhelming proportion (80–85%) of applications are approved. This immediately provokes the question of whether all applications need really go through this elaborate process.

(3) **Proportion of 'simple' applications.** It is not easy to define 'simple' or 'minor' applications. My Secretariat carried out a further sample survey asking certain authorities to give their own definition of 'minor' applications. The results of this test survey are reproduced in Appendix II A v. My guide towards a definition of 'minor' cases is given in Chapter 7 para. 7.9. On the basis of this I estimate that at least 70% of all applications would fall into what I have called 'Class A' of a two-stream system.

*Theory is not fully translated into practice because not all districts have set up joint committees: unfortunately, only 2 out of 5 districts have agreed to implement the arrangements described.

Period for determination

4.12 There is a widespread impression that planning applications are not, in general, decided within the statutory period. No statistically significant figures are available from the Department on the proportion of applications decided within this period, because the necessary monitoring system does not yet exist. Proposals are in hand to mount a comprehensive collection of statistical data, but the Department have not felt able to introduce it until the recent reorganization has been absorbed by local government. I have had therefore to rely upon a number of informal approaches to about 40 authorities. Although they do not constitute a sample survey they shed some light, however filtered, on the present position.

4.13 The proportion of applications dealt with inside the statutory two months varies considerably from authority to authority. Even the few authorities from which figures were obtained revealed a range from 0% to 100%. I am told that the particular district with a 'total failure' record takes $5\frac{1}{2}$ months on average to process an application. I understand it suffers acutely from a shortage of staff. A metropolitan district council, which achieves 95%, reports that the 'missing' 5% are largely held up either because an application is returned to the applicant for amendment, or because consultees had failed to respond. I was interested to note that one county town which decides only 48% of applications within 2 months nevertheless manages to process a further 42% if given an extra 4 weeks (i.e. a total of 90% within 3 months).

The Application Form

4.14 The Department published a model form with Circular 23/72* which they asked all local authorities to adopt, although responsibility for layout and content still rests with each individual planning authority. There is still a variety of forms in use, which is somewhat confusing.

SECTION III: DEALING WITH APPLICATIONS

4.15 In this part of this chapter I give a step by step description of the method of dealing with applications.

4.16 A new application is registered, and the papers examined to ensure that they are accurate and complete. I am told that forms are very often inadequately filled in, supporting documents are missing, and plans inaccurately drawn to an inappropriate scale.†

4.17 Some professional agents are thought to be no better in this respect than 'lay' applicants.

4.18 Consequently, the applicant often has to be asked for further information and this causes considerable delay and much additional work.

4.19 The next steps in the handling of an application vary from one authority to another, but the procedure described below is a good illustration of current

---

*Welsh Office Circular 58/72.

†Article 5(1) of the GDO provides that an application 'for planning permission . . . shall be made on a form issued by the local planning authority . . . and shall include the particulars required by such a form to be supplied and to be accompanied by a plan sufficient to identify the land to which it relates and such other plans and drawings as are necessary to describe the development which is the subject of the application'. The full text of Articles 5, 6, 7 and 16 is given in Appendix II B i.

37

practice. The example deals with a straightforward application for the erection of 1–4 houses in an area allocated for residential purposes.

4.20 I also specify the period of time which I understand is practicable at present in most cases.

4.21 In the example it is assumed that:—

(a) there is partial delegation to a planning committee and a sub-committee has the power to give advice;
(b) the council delegate some powers to officers;
(c) the district is one in which there are parish councils.

4.22 DAY 1

On receipt, the application is categorised into one of three types:

(i) suitable for decision by officers;
(ii) minor, for report to sub-committee;
(iii) major, to be advertised and subject of an individual report to planning committee.

DAY 2

It is then passed to clerical assistants, who acknowledge it and give it a reference number.

DAY 3

The application is entered in the statutory register, and the site history (if any past planning history is known) is attached to the case file.

DAY 4

Consultation is invited e.g. from the engineer's department, the highway authority, river authority, county planning department or amenity societies and adjoining owners.

DAY 5

The application goes to a technical officer for any additional consultations, advertisement, etc.

DAYS 7–9

The preparation, typing and dispatch of sub-committee agenda to members and to parish councils.

DAYS 10–28

Observations from the consulted parties are received.

DAY 29

A draft recommendation is prepared.

DAY 32

The application is considered by the sub-committee.

DAY 33

The minutes of their meeting are incorporated in a report to the planning committee.

DAY 38

The planning committee decision.

DAYS 39–44

The decision notice is then typed and documents are collated to send to the applicant.

DAY 45

The decision is issued.

DAY 47

The decision is registered and filed.

4.23 This may make the process appear simple, but it conceals a degree of overlapping between the stages, particularly where a statutory period of 21 days is required for advertisement of departures from the development plan. Hitches may occur at a number of stages apart from defects in the applications. A common cause of delay is failure on the part of other authorities to provide their comments by the prescribed date.

4.24 An early 'sticking-point' is likely to be the decision whether or not the development proposal raises 'county matters'.

SECTION IV: PUBLICITY

4.25 All local authorities publicise, notify and consult more widely than they are bound to by law.* Practice differs widely. Discretion may rest with the Chief Planning Officer, or with the full council or with the planning committee.

4.26 Public involvement means much more work for staff. For instance, the circulation each week (or month) of 100 or more lists of applications to parish councils, the county council, civic amenity and local residents' groups, local press and libraries is a considerable burden.

4.27 Under Schedule 16 to the Local Government Act 1972 a parish council have the right to ask to be notified of any proposed development and to make observations to the district council within 14 days. This right appears to have been very widely exercised. It is too early to judge whether any adjustments will need to be made, but so far no major difficulties have been reported. The question of whether or not the district planning authority should be required to send parish councils a copy of each application for which they ask is being kept under review.

4.28 Direct notification of neighbours likely to be affected by a development proposal is common. In a survey of district planning officers (undertaken by the Building Research Establishment at the request of the Department during 1974), 81% of the officers said that this was being done now.

4.29 In some districts the planning officer who makes a routine site visit informs neighbours in person or delivers postcards to adjoining properties. Elsewhere letters may be sent from the Planning Office.

4.30 The question of who constitutes a neighbour with an interest sufficient to warrant notification varies from case to case. Usually officers of the planning department decide who are the 'qualifying' neighbours. (Appendix II C i shows a possible scheme for selection of neighbours to be notified.)

4.31 Local amenity societies and residents' associations vary in their size and experience. There are many well-informed and highly responsible organisations but also some pressure groups (often originally set up in response to a single and specific situation) which are narrowly local in outlook.

4.32 Local authorities' attitudes to local amenity groups also varies. Some 'recognise' only long-established societies. Others consult a large number of local groups.

4.33 I know of one district council who do not consult any of the local societies, the societies being apparently quite content with free access to the statutory register.

---

*Advice on this is given in Circular 71/73 (Welsh Office Circular 134/73).

4.34 There may be so many local groups in a particular locality that, as happens in one district, it is felt that there can be no circulation of lists of applications to such groups because of the numbers involved. The alternative adopted is to consult not only parish councils, but also individual parish councillors.

The Press

4.35 Advertisement of applications in the local press is expensive. A single advertisement in one newspaper may cost £30. The same application may have to be advertised twice, once because it is a 'bad neighbour' case and again because it is a substantial departure from the development plan.*

4.36 Usually advertisements, even if they are not legally necessary and so in a sense voluntary, appear on the public notices page. One district council, however, advertises *all* new applications on *the entertainments page* at the cost of £600 per annum. (The sports page has also been suggested.)

4.37 More often, the local press are sent weekly, fortnightly, or monthly lists of new applications. In some areas the local press publish the whole list free of charge; in others, the editors publish notes about cases which they consider to be of general local interest.

4.38 Alternatively, the local press may be sent regularly copies of agendas of committee (or sub-committee) meetings.

4.39 A number of authorities admit the press to sub-committee as well as committee meetings.

Notice Boards

4.40 Many councils send lists of new applications to local libraries. In one London Borough this procedure is supplemented by 36 notice boards at strategic points in the borough. A list of applications for the immediate locality is posted on each board 10 days before the relevant sub-committee meeting.

Site Notices

4.41 There is increasing interest in the posting of site notices. In some areas the applicant is responsible for this. One district council have devised a bright yellow notice (with a returnable tear-off certificate of posting attached) which they send to all applicants as a matter of course (provided the proposal is for one or more new houses). A similar system is planned by other authorities.

4.42 Some councils post notices themselves; officers in the planning department decide where this is appropriate.

Officers' Surgeries

4.43 A few districts operate a system of weekly surgeries which enable anyone to attend and talk to an officer in the planning department. This can be for the whole or only part of the authority's area. Alternatively, officers may attend selected sub-centres within the district every week.

SECTION V: DECISIONS

4.44 There is great diversity as to the extent of delegation; a decision can be taken by the full planning committee, or sub-committee, or by officers. Chairmen

---

*The Department are aware of this anomaly and intend to remedy it at the first opportunity.

of committees or sub-committees commonly decide planning applications in cases of urgency, reporting the decisions for ratification.

4.45 Frequency of meetings and the degree of delegation will affect the speed with which applications can be processed. The more delegation, the greater the time which can be devoted to the most important applications. This is borne out by the informal approach to some local authorities which I mentioned in 4.12 above. It showed an apparent (and hardly surprising) link between the proportion of applications decided within two months and the proportion delegated to officers for decision. One district which achieves an overall 'success rate' of 65% say that delegated applications take 6 weeks on average; those which go before a committee take an average $8\frac{1}{2}$ weeks, apparently because the committee meet only every four weeks. In another district (in the same county) there is only limited delegation to officers but a 3-week committee cycle means that 80% of applications are determined within the statutory period.

4.46 Council resolutions delegating powers to officers are published but I think that it should always be made clear that decisions taken by officers under delegated powers have precisely the same status as decisions by the council.

4.47 'Primary delegation' (delegation by the full council to a committee) is of course very common. I know of only one authority where the planning committee have no power of decision (but in that district about 40% of applications are delegated to the planning officer).

4.48 In another district (in the same county) the planning officer has very limited powers, to deal with about 5% of applications only, while the 18-member planning committee (which meets every 3 weeks) have full delegated powers.

4.49 'Secondary delegation' (by the planning committee to a sub-committee) is also common.

4.50 The powers of committees and sub-committees may be:

(a) advisory;
(b) partial—where the sub-committee may decide on a specified range of cases;
(c) conditional—where the sub-committee's decisions are subject to consequent review;
(d) to make decision.

4.51 I know of only very few instances where committees only have an advisory function. In a former county borough (where, incidentally, there was no delegation to officers) all applications had to go first to a planning sub-committee (which met every week) and then to the public works committee (which met fortnightly). The latter, which may have had to deal at one meeting with 150 development control cases in addition to work coming forward from other sub-committees, accepted the recommendations of the planning sub-committee in 95% of cases.

4.52 Partial delegation is relatively common. For example the sub-committee may decide all applications except those which involve a major departure from the development plan. This may mean that about 10% of applications are referred to the main committee.

4.53 Conditional delegation may take the form of 'internal challenge' or 'external challenge':

(a) internal challenge: whereby members of the sub-committee/committee can require a case to be referred up to the main committee/full council.

41

(*b*) **external challenge:** whereby any member of the council may require the reference of any sub-committee or committee decision to the full council within a short period of the decision. The details by which this procedure is operated vary: in one authority any councillor is allowed to challenge any decision of the committee or sub-committee within 7 days; in another, 3 or more members may challenge a decision within 3 days.

4.54 So far as the merits of these procedures are concerned, I acknowledge that external challenge is probably acceptable, if limited to non-members of the committee, given that local government is forced to operate on a corporate basis, and in the present climate of increasing interest in planning applications on the part of councillors' constituents. I do think it is important, however, that the period allowed for challenge should not be too long. Three days seems about right; in the context of a statutory period of 2 months for determining applications, 7 days seems too long.

4.55 I am much less impressed by the system of internal challenge. This procedure seems to conflict with the principle of committee responsibility, and I would have thought it can only upset the business of the sub-committee/ committee, and encourage disunity among members.

4.56 **Delegation to Chairman.** There is no statutory power to delegate to one councillor* but it is common practice for chairmen of committees to exercise limited decision-making powers between meetings and to report for ratification any decision they have taken. Chairmen of committees or sub-committees commonly decide planning applications in cases of urgency, reporting the decisions for ratification. In one authority both the planning committee and the development control sub-committee give their chairman specific authority to act, so as to avoid holding up a case for re-submission to them. Some authorities confer powers jointly on the chairman and vice-chairman during the summer committee recess (mid-July to mid-September).

4.57 **Delegation to Officers.** In 1968 for the first time local authorities were expressly authorised to delegate some of their functions in the development control field to their officers. This innovation marked a radical departure from traditional/local government methods, and the idea was slow to gain acceptance; a number of local authorities are still firmly opposed to it.

4.58 Delegation is usually to the authority's chief planning officer; but sometimes also to one or more deputies.

4.59 The powers delegated are almost always limited. The following are typical examples:
(*a*) minor alterations and extensions to existing buildings;
(*b*) changes of use which do not conflict with the development plan or to which no objection is raised;
(*c*) the approval of details on an application already granted in outline;
(*d*) the display of advertisements;
(*e*) the felling of trees for which permission is required under a tree preservation order.

4.60 Sometimes, however—in relation to some or all of the categories delegated—officers are authorised only to refuse permission, not to grant it; and I have found one instance where officers were authorised to grant permission but not refuse it.

---

*S.101 of the Local Government Act 1972.

4.61 In one county, officers have delegated powers to act within the limits of defined policy, without delegated classes of development being specifically designated, although paragraph 7 (ii) of Circular 142/73* suggested that a list of classes to be delegated should be drawn up.

4.62 Delegation of determinations as to whether planning permission is required and of established use certificates (Sections 53 and 94 respectively of the 1971 Act) is common. In one area these decisions are delegated to the District Secretary, who is a solicitor.

4.63 In one Inner London Borough, delegation does not cover the full range of subjects described in paragraph 4.59, but it nevertheless enables officers to deal with 75% of all applications. A more typical figure is probably provided by a former county borough, in which the range was very similar to the full list given in that paragraph. This resulted in 43% of incoming applications being delegated to officers for decision.

4.64 Before 1st April 1974 some county councils delegated some powers to their officers, even where there was also extensive delegation to the district councils; county council committees then retained only cases of considerable importance for their own decision. I understand that a number of county councils are continuing these, or very similar, delegation arrangements for cases which will in future require a county council decision because they raise 'county matters'. I am not at this stage able to comment on the success or adequacy of these arrangements.

4.65 It is well worth mentioning, however, that decisions on whether applications raise county matters should as far as possible be taken by officers: the Department urged this practice in Annex 2 (para. 2 (m)) to Circular 74/73.† It stated:

". . . guide lists could be drawn up to form a working basis for officers handling applications. While there will sometimes be applications which fall outside any categorisation, arrangements which will enable officers to reach decisions of this kind will avoid delay in an area where delay must be kept to a minimum. Decisions of this kind should as far as possible be delegated to officers—with such informal consultation with members as may be appropriate." (See also para. 4.8.)

4.66 **Frequency of meetings.** Council and committee meetings take place at irregular intervals and there is no discernible pattern. Where a sub-committee has delegated planning powers, the interval between meetings is usually the same as for the main committee, but the sub-committee's meetings are staggered so that they fall half-way between, or a week before, meetings of the main committee. The infrequency of meetings is probably one of the causes of planning delays in many districts.

4.67 The interval between meetings varies considerably: a sample survey revealed intervals of 2 weeks, 3, 4, 7 and in one case 8 weeks.

4.68 The time taken for formal consultation between county and district planning authorities (see also paras 4.10, 4.24) affects the frequency of meetings.

SECTION VI: SUPPORTING STAFF
Numbers
4.69 Integration of development control work with work on forward planning is desirable. Prior to the reorganisation of local government in April 1974,

---

*Welsh Office Circular 227/73.
†Welsh Office Circular 143/73.

outside Greater London, only county and county borough councils were responsible for both preparing development plans and administering development control. Some of them integrated both functions.

4.70 Now district councils are responsible for both preparation of plans and development control. I have not been able to obtain any reliable information about deployment of staff in all new districts, some figures are given in Appendix IIA vi. I also have figures for some former county borough councils.

Former county borough	No of new planning applications per annum	No of staff employed on development control
Birmingham	7,000	19
Leicester	2,000	9
Luton	2,000	8
Norwich	3,000	10
Oxford	2,000	6
Worcester	1,800	7–8

4.71 Although it may not be realistic to present these latter figures in terms of 'cases per man', it is very tempting to do so; assuming a 5-day week, 4 weeks' leave per annum and nothing for sickness, the team at Leicester achieve an *average* of $4\frac{1}{2}$ cases per man per week. In Oxford the average is nearly 7 cases per man per week. If it is assumed that senior officers devote less time to a case than juniors, the burden of work on the juniors must be even greater. I am not able to express any view as to whether productivity of planning officers on this basis is high, particularly when compared with the effort which is put into work on development plans.* The cost to the country of the development control system seems small when contrasted with the total value of private sector construction, which I understand is running at about £5,000 m. per annum. (See also paras 7.117–7.120 on charging for an application.)

4.72 I should emphasise the difficulty of arriving at a realistic figure for staff employed on development control: even where work on local plans is entirely separate from development control, the control staff may be operating building regulations control as well. Moreover, non-professional support for the professional development controllers is organised differently within different authorities: much administrative, executive and clerical work on development control may be done in other departments, for example in those of the Chief Executive or the Solicitor. On the whole, however, each professional tends to be supported by one non-professional. (It is interesting that the same applies in the Department's Planning Inspectorate, where there are equal numbers of Inspectors and administrators.) A recent report by the University of Birmingham: Institute of Local Government Studies† gives an interesting analysis of the staffing situation and prospects and emphasises the need to make the best possible use of staff.

4.73 Another difficulty in finding out the exact number of development control staff is that many county councils have separate sections dealing with conservation areas, historic buildings, minerals, advertisements, forestry and other specialist subjects; the staff of any or all of these are likely to devote a proportion of their time to development control, and giving specialist advice to district

*The Department estimate that the cost of local authority development control staff is very roughly £40m. per annum. Decisions were issued on 623,000 planning applications in 1973.

†SSRC Inlogov Pt. 1 Manpower for Physical Planning, Manpower for the New Local Planning Authorities by T. Eddison and J. Earwicker, August 1974 price 60p.

planning officers on applications not referred formally to the county council.

Attitudes

4.74 I believe there is some feeling that development control is not rewarding: the work is often regarded as monotonous, and when committees (and indeed the Secretary of State on appeal) take decisions which run counter to professional advice, this is frustrating. The most competent development control officers are quite often older and without professional qualifications, but with much experience. Attitudes are, however, changing. Young entrants are beginning to realise that development control is important and can be interesting.

4.75 District councils are now responsible for preparation of plans as well as for control; this means that district officers can be switched from one type of work to another. In one former county borough this is thought to have benefited the staff and the quality of work. I understand that some planning officers of the new district councils enjoy their new dual role because it provides more variety for them and their staff.

Use of staff

4.76 Complaints about shortage of staff for development control are widespread; but are all authorities making the best use of their professionally qualified officers? For example, I understand that in one authority, since the number of planning applications received has declined from a peak about 9 months ago, professional staff are extensively used for public consultation experiments. Yet in one London borough most public involvement is dealt with by a non-professional group experienced in public relations.

4.77 Some authorities, faced with the problem of enforcing planning decisions, have started to recruit special enforcement officers. Their job is to try to persuade the public to comply with planning control, rather than to threaten enforcement. Apparently the most suitable type of person for this kind of work is said to be a retired policeman, rather than the professional planner. This seems a good idea, so long as one bears in mind that in most enforcement cases the overriding question is whether the contravening development should be permitted.

SECTION VII: WALES AND LONDON

4.78 Many of the differences in practice between planning authorities have already been referred to. Some points particular to London and Wales are made below.

WALES

4.79 The existing planning legislation is the same in England and Wales; the Welsh Office (formed in 1965) and the Department of the Environment work closely together in formulating and applying common policy. It is normal practice to issue joint circulars to local planning authorities. There is no *regional* planning organisation in Wales, however: all government staff are based at the headquarters in Cardiff. Day-to-day planning control work is handled by 24 (executive and clerical) staff, who have other responsibilities as well. Professional advice is provided by 25 professional and clerical staff headed by a chief planner.

Volume of work

4.80 So far as the volume of applications and appeals is concerned, Wales reflects the pattern in England. The number of applications for planning permission in 1973 was 44,000, which represented an increase of 76% over

1967 (25,000). The number of S.36 and S.53 appeals rose from 691 in 1972 to 842 in 1973, and the number outstanding at the end of 1972 and 1973 was 608 and 739 respectively.

Local authority practice

4.81 Development control is dealt with in much the same way as in England. This means that many Welsh district councils display the same caution by, for example, requiring applications to go before both a sub-committee and the planning committee. There is a certain amount of delegation to officers.

Special environmental areas/extent of control

4.82 25% (nearly 2,000 square miles) of Wales consists of national parks, areas of outstanding natural beauty and proposed *heritage coasts* compared with about 18% in England. This clearly means that development control has to be exercised with a particularly sensitive approach.

LONDON

4.83 London is a case on its own because of the powers of the GLC and its relationship with the London Boroughs. The London Government Act 1963, introduced major changes to the planning system for Greater London by setting up a two-tier structure of planning control. It made the London Borough Councils (32 in all) and the Common Council of the City of London the planning authorities for their respective areas,* and the Greater London Council the planning authority for Greater London as a whole.

4.84 The arrangements for dividing responsibility are complex. They are designed to enable the GLC to carry out strategic control:—

(a) by determining all applications for development within certain Inner London comprehensive development areas (e.g. Covent Garden); and those for certain specified developments of a strategic character (e.g. exhibition and conference centres, lecture and concert halls, sports grounds accommodating more than 2,500 people, rail, bus and air terminals, extraction of minerals) throughout London;

(b) by *directing* how certain classes of development (which a LBC wish to *allow* and have to refer to the GLC) are to be determined (e.g. new shops with an area over 250,000 sq. ft., development within 220 ft. of a Class A metropolitan road, a public car park for more than 50 cars, a substantial departure from the development plan);

(c) a LBC must *consult* the GLC about their own proposed development if the application comes within the above categories covered by (b);

(d) a LBC must *notify* the GLC about any applications which would specifically affect the character of a precinct or area defined by the Secretary of State as being of special importance. But the GLC have no power of direction in relation to such applications.

Where there is a disagreement between the GLC and a LBC over (c) or (d) above (i.e. where the GLC has no power of direction), the Secretary of State can be asked to make a decision on the proposal.

Substantial departures

4.85 If both a LBC and the GLC wish to allow proposals which constitute a substantial departure from the Initial Development Plan, the application *must be referred to the Secretary of State*, so that he can decide whether there

*Throughout the following paragraphs the abbreviation 'LBC' includes, for convenience, the Common Council of the City of London.

46

are any issues of more than local importance which would justify his making the decision on the proposal. Following the streamlining Circular 142/73,* the Department have consulted the London authorities about this procedure for dealing with substantial departures in Greater London, but there is unlikely to be any real progress in revising the procedure until the Greater London Development Plan (the future structure plan for London) is approved.

Delegation to London boroughs
4.86 The GLC may, with the consent of the Secretary of State (or if required by him) *delegate* any of its planning functions to a LBC. The GLC have made two series of delegation arrangements.

(i) In 1966, they delegated to the 7 inner LBCs concerned, powers to deal with applications for development which did not conflict with the primary use zoning. (See para 4.8 above; factories and offices, and other buildings which might substantially increase the work force of the area, were excluded from the delegation arrangement.) Certain other minor matters were delegated to these 7 councils at the same time.

(ii) In 1970, all the LBCs were given power to determine:
   (a) applications for planning permission in respect of buildings for a University or College of Advanced Technology; buildings or works for transport termini; buildings or works for a monorail or hovercraft system (and all corresponding powers in respect of revocation and discontinuance orders, enforcement notices, and appeals);
   (b) S.53 applications to determine whether a planning permission is required (and appeals).

4.87 In all the agreements the GLC reserved the right to deal with any particular application themselves. They therefore see copies of all the applications concerned, and have 10 days to decide whether they wish to recover jurisdiction. They in fact do this in difficult cases.

Duplication of controls
4.88 This is the theoretical division of responsibilities for development control between the GLC and the LBCs. Two problems arise in putting the theory into practice:

(1) the need to define the classes of development which involve the GLC's strategic functions;
(2) the need to interpret and apply this definition consistently throughout the Greater London area.

4.89 Variations occur in practice where the LBCs have some discretion in deciding whether a case should be referred to the GLC. These seem to result from the different historical backgrounds of different LBC officers. Those who have served in the former county boroughs, for example, are apparently inclined to refer fewer cases than those who used to work in the former county districts and metropolitan boroughs. A working party was set up some time ago to review the existing arrangements and the LBCs have argued for a freer use of their discretion, but are resisting any widening of the classes for decision by the GLC. I am told that the working party is still trying to agree on a solution which will reduce the number of cases dealt with at two levels, but that no firm conclusions are expected until the GLDP is approved.

Delays
4.90 The worst examples of delay probably occur when differences of opinion

*Welsh Office Circular 227/73.

47

arise between the GLC and the LBC concerned, since these can only be overcome by meetings at member level. To the extent that such differences are political in origin, as they often are, the difficulties are aggravated by the fact that changes in the political control of the GLC and of the LBCs do not happen simultaneously because the respective election dates do not coincide. Informal arrangements have been introduced to reduce the time needed for consultation at official level to a minimum.

Applications

4.91 *The GLC have to see and may give directions to the LBCs concerned on about* 8,000 *applications a year;* they actually decide about 200 more. In another 600 cases a year they have no statutory interest, but there is an agreement that the LBC will consult them before issuing a decision—see para 4.84 (*c*) & (*d*) above.

4.92 *A serious cause of delay in dealing with applications is that all GLC cases involve consultations with the LBCs. The GLC find that the latter are slow in providing comments, and the Boroughs experience the same trouble with the GLC.* An applicant sends his application to the LBC offices, from which, after some routine work, it has to be forwarded to County Hall; there, after more routine work, it is allocated to the relevant officer in the Planning Department. When allowance is made for delays in postal deliveries, routine work, weekends, the absence of officers at meetings and other unpredictable factors, it is not surprising that an application form may take a fortnight to travel from the applicant to the right desk in the GLC Planning Department.

Committee Arrangements

4.93 The GLC have a Planning Committee, who have delegated their development control powers to 4 area boards and a board of specialists in historic buildings. London Borough Councillors cannot be co-opted on to them. The Planning Committee and the 5 boards meet every three weeks. The average number of applications per meeting would break down to about 20 cases for the Historic Buildings Board (which has only recently been created), 10–12 cases for the Southern Board and about 6 cases each for the other 3 area boards.

Delegation to Chairmen and 'references up'

4.94 This has already been referred to in paragraph 4.56 & 4.53 above.

Delegation to officers

4.95 GLC elected members, including chairmen of committees and boards, visit County Hall almost daily, and certainly more often than their counterparts outside London. Perhaps in consequence delegation to the Controller of Planning and Transportation is limited. He can sanction certain minor developments by London Boroughs and by the GLC itself, and can inform LBCs in certain cases that the GLC do not wish to give any directions under the London Government Act Regulations. Even these powers can be exercised only if no LBC, and sometimes if no other GLC department, objects.

Discussion with applicants

4.96 GLC members avoid direct discussions with applicants, although quite often they will arrange a 'presentation' of an important scheme for the benefit of land owners who are concerned.

Site Inspection

4.97 GLC members undertake a good deal of site inspection. In the main, the initiative is left to them; if an area board decide that a site visit is necessary they usually send only a part of their membership. But the 'constituency councillor' is always invited, and the LBC concerned are invited to send a representative in any case where the board think this is desirable (and in every case when the GLC and the LBC disagree over the decision).

Staff

4.98 In the GLC, development control is handled by 6 sectors under the general supervision of 3 senior officers (only part of whose time is devoted to development control work). Each sector deals with 100–200 cases per month, and is commanded by a sector planner, supported by 6 or 7 professionals. Officers in other departments also spend some time on development control: most of the work on applications which affect historic buildings, for example, is done in the architect's department, and each sector probably commands 2 or 3 people who advise on civic design and highway aspects of planning applications. Moreover, although the 6 sectors process mineral applications, specialist knowledge of minerals issues is located in a different section of the Planning Department.

4.99 The full time professional staff devoted to development control therefore comes to about 60–70. Administrative support is centralised, but there are about 17 people dealing specifically with development control, and about 8 who deal exclusively with the development control aspects of development projects promoted by the GLC itself and the Inner London Education Authority.

4.100 **Conclusion.** I describe the arrangement in London in great detail, because this is the only area in which two-tier local government has existed for a number of years. It could never be used as a model, because London is a special city and its size and character are unique. Political changes, which bedevil town planning everywhere, create great complications in London. Against that, officers of both the GLC and the London Boroughs probably work as hard, and elected members perhaps even harder, than in many parts of the country. The achievements of planning in London both of GLC and of some Boroughs are considerable. There are areas in which clear division of responsibility has been achieved. But the fact must be faced that some of the strongest complaints about planning delays relate to London. They may be due partly to the complexity of the procedures laid down by the Town and Country Planning (Local Planning Authorities in Greater London) Regulations 1965.*

4.101 My initial, perhaps idealistic view, was that improvement would only come if the respective planning responsibilities of the Boroughs with the GLC could be clearly distinguished. This would mean in simplified terms that the GLC would have the *sole jurisdiction* in matters which have an impact on strategy. London Boroughs would have *sole jurisdiction* in all other matters. There would still be a third class where there are *joint interests*, to be decided by joint GLC/Borough committees or by consultation.

4.102 There is the opposing view that the local community should always have a voice through their elected representatives in as many planning matters as possible.

4.103 What is clear is that the complex political background of London Government, coupled with staff shortages and the inherent and sometimes almost insuperable planning difficulties in London, results in delays which give rise to bitter complaints. In this sense planning control in London is not an example but a warning to the rest of the country. But whatever system is adopted it will only work successfully in a spirit of co-operation. I think that in London there is now more of it than is realized. Here, as elsewhere, Local Government has come to understand the extreme public impatience with the imperfections and delays of the system.

*S.I. 1965 No 679.

E

CHAPTER 5

Appeals and called-in cases

SECTION 1: INTRODUCTORY

5.1 Central Government is directly involved in the development control process in two ways. The Secretary of State or a person appointed by him determines appeals from a refusal of planning permission by a local authority. The Secretary of State may also in certain cases 'call in' planning applications for his own decision.

Appeals

5.2 Since 1947 the Secretary of State has been the 'longstop' for the applicant who felt aggrieved by a local authority's action (or failure to take action) on his application. The Secretary of State can confirm or overrule the local authority's decision. He is able to take a detached view of the situation as a whole and the way in which regional or national, as well as local, policies should be applied.

5.3 I understand that about 70% of residential appeals which are allowed are in respect of sites which are unallocated and known as 'white land'. This tends to show that the right of appeal to the Secretary of State gives the appellant an assurance that the application will be reconsidered in the light of any relevant regional or national policies, and from a wholly objective standpoint.

Called-in cases

5.4 As planning may involve national or regional as well as local interests, the questions raised by a development proposal may be such that a local planning authority is no longer the appropriate body to determine the application. This is why the Secretary of State has the power to call in a specific planning application or all applications of a particular kind. In practice, the Department will issue a Circular if the need arises asking local authorities to notify the Secretary of State of all applications of a particular type raising special problems (e.g. out of town "stores or shopping centres of 50,000 sq.ft. or more gross floor area" (Circular 17/72)) so that the Secretary of State can call them in if he chooses. Like many of the instruments of planning control, the call-in procedure is in fact older than the 1947 Act (its origin being S.6 of the Town and Country Planning (Interim Development) Act 1943); but it was little used before the 1947 Act came into operation.

5.5 In planning, as in other fields, the Department has inherited from its predecessors a tradition of trying to interfere as little as possible with matters for which local authorities are responsible. Consequently the call-in procedure has been used sparingly. In 1973 there were 622,652 planning applications in England. The number of cases called in was 144. In Wales there were 44,000 applications; 16 cases were called in. In recent years the procedure has tended to be used only for the following kinds of applications:

(a) cases raising issues of national, regional, or otherwise more than local importance;

(b) cases which arouse more than local opposition; e.g., the redevelopment of the Monico site in Shaftesbury Avenue;

(c) cases which, for any reason, it might be unreasonable to ask the local planning authority to decide: e.g., involving development proposed by foreign governments (the decision on which could be diplomatically sensitive), or development raising unfamiliar problems on which adequate technical advice was not available to the local planning authority; e.g., the first application for a processing plant for North Sea Gas;

(d) cases associated with a different issue which can be decided only by the Secretary of State; e.g., applications for town centre redevelopment associated with a compulsory purchase order.

5.6 Planning applications are not necessarily called in simply because they involve a substantial departure from the development plan; indeed paragraphs 8–12 of circular 142/73, 'Streamlining the Planning Machine' (soon to be incorporated in a new Development Plan Direction), indicate that the Secretary of State wishes to limit his interventions even more strictly. Nor are applications called in simply because they cause a good deal of local opposition. There are, however, cases in which a local planning authority refuses permission for controversial development simply to force the Secretary of State to take the responsibility on appeal for making an unpopular decision with which the local planning authority may, in fact, agree. This point illustrates the fine distinction between called-in cases and major appeals.

5.7 It may be very difficult to decide whether or not an application should be called in. A quarter of a century's experience of administering planning law has probably helped to evolve a consistent attitude to this problem, but the reluctance to call cases in is justified at present on grounds of expediency, as calling in does cause delay.

SECTION II: LEGISLATIVE POSITION

5.8 The law as to called-in cases and appeals is as follows:—

(1) **Called-in cases.** Under S.35 of the Town and Country Planning Act 1971 the Secretary of State can give directions requiring planning applications to be referred to him instead of being dealt with by local planning authorities. Such a direction may relate either to a particular application or to all applications within a specified class. The Secretary of State's decision on an application 'called in' in this way is final. He must, however, give an opportunity to the applicant and the local planning authority (if either of them so wish) to appear before, and be heard, by a person appointed by him for the purpose. In practice the hearing always takes the form of a local inquiry.

(2) **Appeals.** Under S.36 of the 1971 Act, an applicant may appeal to the Secretary of State if he is aggrieved by a local authority decision to refuse his application for planning permission, or to grant it subject to conditions.

51

There is also a right to appeal against a local authority's failure to give a decision within the prescribed period of two months. The applicant has to give notice of his appeal within six months. As in (1) above, the Secretary of State's decision is final, a local inquiry having been held if either party desires one. The Secretary of State may not only allow or dismiss the appeal, he may reverse or vary any part of the decision of the local authority; he may deal with the application as if it had been made to him in the first instance. This is an important and useful power, which is not always understood.

(3) **Transferred appeals.** Schedule 9 to the 1971 Act provides that a person appointed by the Secretary of State can, subject to certain exceptions, determine appeals in prescribed classes*.

(4) **Recovery of jurisdiction.** The Schedule also provides machinery by which the Secretary of State can recover jurisdiction to decide any such appeal himself. This can only be done by means of direction, which has to be served on the person appointed, the appellant, the local planning authority and any person who has made representations under the provisions of Section 29 (statutory third parties). It must also state the reasons why the Secretary of State has decided to determine the appeal.

5.9 (1) **Secretary of State's** appeals are those which are reserved for his own decision (whether made personally by him or made, in fact, on his behalf by another Minister or an official of the Department).

(2) Secretary of State's appeals can proceed either by way of written representation or a local public inquiry, but there must be an inquiry if either party so insist.

(3) There is also a considerable increase in the number of appeals dealt with by written representations. Whether the cases are transferred or to be determined by the Secretary of State, about 70% of all appeals are now dealt with in this way. This does mean, however, that an increased burden of work is falling on decision branches. Where an appeal is not transferred, the decision branch has to read the representations on the file, and the Inspector's site visit report, and then draft the decision letter *ab initio*. This is a serious consequence of written representation procedure and my conclusions take this into account. In contrast, where an Inquiry has taken place, the decision letter can often be confined to a summary of the Inspector's recommendation and a simple statement that this is accepted. All other relevant material is obtainable from the Inspector's report, a copy of which always accompanies the decision.

SECTION III: PROCEDURE

5.10 The procedure adopted in the Department for dealing with appeals and called-in cases is substantially the same in each case. In both cases if there is to be an inquiry the local planning authority is required to produce a Rule 6 statement setting out the submissions it proposes to make. For called-in cases

---

*The Town and Country Planning Act 1968 gave a power to transfer certain kinds of cases to Inspectors for decision. These 'transferred cases', like other appeals, may be dealt with either by written representations or by arranging an inquiry. Transfers started in 1969 and have since then increased progressively to the point where they now comprise about 75% to 80% of all appeals in England (65% in Wales). The kinds of appeal which Inspectors can decide are set out in the Town and Country Planning (Determination of appeals by appointed persons) (Prescribed Classes) Regulations 1972 (S.I. 1972 No. 1652). Most of these appeals relate to residential development for areas of up to 2 hectares or the building of up to 60 houses.

the Department produces a statement of the issues which it considers relevant and wishes to see brought out at the Inquiry. This information is, of course, also given to the Inspector. The individual steps are set out in diagrammatic form in Appendix III i.

5.11 The administrative processes in the Department, the procedure at the Inquiry, the form and content of the Inspector's report and the way in which the case is considered subsequently, are much the same for appeals and for called-in cases. Accordingly, for the remainder of this chapter I shall, for the sake of convenience, confine my attention to appeals.

SECTION IV: WORKLOAD

5.12 (1) Between 1963 and 1971 the number of appeals received in the Department annually was within the range of 8,500 to 14,500, giving an average of 11,250 a year. The figure rose to over 15,000 in 1972 and escalated to over 19,000 in 1973. The approximate figure for 1974 is 14,000. In statistical terms there appears to be a return to the conditions of the 1960's.

(2) **Backlog.** In the 1960's the number of appeals outstanding at the end of each year varied between 6,000 and 9,000, and the annual average for 1963-1971 was 7,157. Averages can be misleading, but these figures suggest that on the whole the average time for a decision was not much more than a year. (The average number of decisions each year during this period was 7,643.)

(3) **1972/3.** The number of appeals submitted rose to 15,099 in 1972 and 19,213 in 1973. In January 1973 there was a backlog of 13,500 cases. Notwithstanding a record number of decisions (11,400) in 1973, 17,400 appeals were pending at the end of that year. The total of new appeals received in 1974 is likely to be about 14,000, a drop of 27% compared with 1973. As recent figures emphasise a continuing downward trend, we may well get back next year to a figure closer to 11,000, about the yearly average for the country in the 1960's.

(4) **Improvement.** The total number of appeals decided in 1974 was about 12,500–13,000; more than double the number in 1972 and over 10% more than in 1973. Allowing for appeals withdrawn, the backlog had gone down to 15,000 at the end of November.

(5) **Written representations.** The proportion of appeals decided by the use of the written representations method in 1963 was 36%. The proportion was fairly constant between 1965 (45%) and 1971 (47%) – apart from a 'peak' of 54% in 1968 – but there was a steep rise to 65% in 1972. In 1973 the figure was 76% and in 1974 it was 70%.

(6) **Transferred Appeals.** In 1969 760 cases were transferred to Inspectors for decision (i.e. $11\frac{1}{2}$%). In 1973 Inspectors made about 8,800 decisions and in 1974 about 10,000 (well over three-quarters of all decisions issued).

(7) **Success Rate.** Between 1969 and 1973 the appellants were successful in about 25% of cases ranging from 29% in 1969 to 22% in 1973. In non-transferred cases the Secretary of State disagreed with the Inspector's recommendation in only 5% of cases.

SECTION V: THE ADMINISTRATIVE PROCESS FROM RECEIPT OF AN APPEAL TO ISSUE OF DECISION

5.13 When completed appeal forms are received in the Planning Inspectorate Administration Division, they are registered and a file is opened. Details of the case are entered on an index card which is used as a location record for the file and to record the progress of the appeal. The appeal is checked to make sure it is in time and that all the necessary documents have been enclosed and are in accordance with the General Development Order.

5.14 Receipt of the appeal is then acknowledged and any missing documents are requested. A copy of the appeal form containing the appellant's grounds of appeal* and his wishes as to procedure is sent to the local planning authority together with a questionnaire (which should be returned within 14 days) which asks for basic information about various matters relevant to the proposed development. It also asks whether the local planning authority would agree to the appeal being dealt with by the written representations procedure. (The time taken to return the completed questionnaire is often the first major source of delay.)

5.15 At this point details of the appeal are recorded on an ordnance survey map in the Land Use Records Section, and a brief is provided indicating, for example, whether the site is in a green belt or conservation area. The brief will also state what other planning matters are being dealt with by the Department in the vicinity of the appeal site or have been dealt with within the last 5 years.

5.16 The file then goes to a Procedure Branch where, when the questionnaire arrives back from the local authority, the appeal is checked again to ensure that the Secretary of State has jurisdiction. At this point it will be decided whether the appeal:
  (i) falls within one of the classes transferred to an Inspector for decision (see para 5.8 (2) above); *or*
  (ii) falls within the prescribed classes but, because of particular circumstances (e.g. political sensitivity), jurisdiction has to be recovered; *or*
  (iii) is for decision by the Secretary of State.
If necessary, consultations are carried out with other branches of the Department and other Government Departments (e.g. if the site is in a safeguarded area of an airfield, the Ministry of Defence or the Civil Aviation Authority are consulted).

5.17 At this stage the decision is made whether to proceed by means of written representations (if the parties have agreed to it) or to hold a local inquiry. There are no hard and fast rules. An inquiry is held, for example, where facts are in dispute, because at an inquiry they can be tested in cross-examination. Where the issues are simple and straightforward, written representations are generally more suitable.

SECTION VI: PUBLIC INQUIRY METHOD

5.18 Once it has been decided whether to hold a local inquiry or to follow the written method, procedures diverge. Where there is to be an inquiry, the parties are notified and are told whether or not the appeal is to be transferred to an Inspector for decision. A Senior Inspector indicates which Inspectors would be able to take that particular appeal. A date is then arranged; this may take some time if either party claims that the date offered is not acceptable. Formal notice of the inquiry is given to the parties at least 6 weeks before it is to take place.

---

*The appellant's grounds of appeal are expected to be comprehensive and should, taken with the local planning authority's reasons for refusal of the application, indicate the main issues upon which the case will turn.

5.19 The local planning authority is, if necessary, reminded to submit a Rule 6 Statement to the appellant to the Department and to any third parties who have made representations and who may, under Section 29 of the 1971 Act, be entitled to receive one. Failure to submit the statement soon enough may lead the appellant to ask for the inquiry to be postponed on the grounds that not enough time is left to prepare an answer to the authority's case. Late Rule 6 Statements are therefore another source of delay.

Three weeks before the inquiry the parties are told which Inspector has been instructed to hold the inquiry (and where it is a transferred case, appointed to determine the appeal). Briefing material is provided for the Inspector in the form of a general regional brief, a report on the development plan situation in the relevant county, etc.

5.20 The inquiry follows. If the appeal is to be decided by the Secretary of State the Inspector then writes a report on the proceedings and recommends a decision. The report, together with all the other papers relating to the case, goes to an administrative division which, after any necessary consultations, issues a decision letter. If the decision is to be taken by the Inspector, he prepares a decision letter which, after processing, i.e., typing, checking and correction, is issued.

SECTION VII: WRITTEN REPRESENTATION METHOD

5.21 If it has been decided to proceed by means of written representations, the parties are notified that this procedure is to be followed. The local planning authority is asked to supply a written statement within one month of the date of the request, and to notify local residents of the appeal and invite their representations.

5.22 When the statement is received it is checked to see whether any further consultation is necessary with other branches of the Department and whether, in the case of transferred appeals, any issues are raised which make it desirable to recover jurisdiction for the Secretary of State to determine the appeal. A copy of the statement is sent to the appellant (or his agent) with a request that any comments on it should be submitted within 14 days. Both parties are informed whether the appeal is to be determined by an Inspector or by the Secretary of State.

5.23 An Inspector is allocated and arrangements are made for the site inspection. In transferred cases the name of the Inspector to determine the appeal is also notified. The site visit, which may be accompanied*, is normally arranged to take place after an interval of not less than 4 weeks from the date on which the local authority's statement is sent to the appellant for observations. The reason for this is to have the representations completed before the site visit takes place. It quite frequently happens, however, that the applicants do not send their comments within 14 days, but nevertheless do warn the Department that they intend to make a further submission.

5.24 For transferred appeals, 7 days before the site visit the Inspector's regional briefing material is attached to the file which is then sent to the Inspector. After he has made the visit he prepares his decision letter and this is issued after

*A site visit is invariably accompanied if one of the parties so requests, or if the Inspectorate Administration decide that it is necessary for the Inspector to go to the relevant land, as opposed to viewing it from adjacent land.

the necessary processing. If the appeal is for determination by the Secretary of State, the Inspector writes a report assessing the impact of the proposed development on the surrounding area. The file is then sent to the appropriate administrative division where, after consideration of the Inspector's site visit report and the representations on the file, a decision letter is issued.

SECTION VIII: TIMING

5.25 We have now seen possible causes of delay:—

(i)   the local authority may fail to complete and return the questionnaire within 14 days (para 5.13 above);

(ii) inquiries. It may take time to arrange a date for the inquiry (para 5.18 above);

(iii) the local authority may fail to supply their Rule 6 Statement 28 days before the Inquiry date (para 5.19 above);

(iv) written representations. The local authority may fail to supply within one month the written statement for which they are asked when notified that this procedure is to be followed (para 5.21 above);

(v)   the appellant may subsequently fail to send his statement within 14 days (para 5.22 above).

5.26 The delay in fixing dates for Inquiries has been due primarily to the problems of the Department and local authorities in coping with the backlog of appeals. Some effective progress has recently been made towards reducing this in that the Department has now introduced a programme system for appeals. *The number of appeals awaiting the arranging of a local inquiry has been reduced from over 4,000 at the start of last year to a few hundred by the end of 1974.* One consequence has been that Inspectors are deployed more efficiently; another is that local authorities now find themselves committed systematically to a series of inquiries. While the backlog is being cleared, however, there is still a delay before dates can be fixed for new inquiries. This delay is at present six or seven months. A contributory factor has been the upheaval caused by local government reorganisation. The Department has in the past taken a fairly sympathetic attitude in arranging dates to suit the wishes of the appellant and the local authority but there is now some evidence of a hardening of attitudes. It also happens quite frequently that an appellant may ask for a postponement without giving any really adequate reason. The same difficulty can arise even over the apparently straightforward exercise of arranging a site visit, although I understand that this is fairly unusual.

Decision Stage

5.27 I suggested in my Interim Report (Appendix 3) that under the best conditions it is possible to determine an appeal within:—

13 weeks (transferred/by written representations);
15 weeks (Secretary of State/by written representations);
16 weeks (transferred/Inquiry appeals);
21 weeks (Secretary of State/Inquiry appeals).

In practice these time limits are not achieved. The average times taken on those appeals which were decided during 1974 were (for the four types of appeals) 8-9 months, 13 months, 15 months and 18 months respectively.

5.28 The length of the period between receipt of the appeal and the holding of the local inquiry or the site visit in written representation appeals (see para 5.23) accounts for most of the wide disparity between the average times and the optimum periods. However the outlook for the future appears somewhat brighter if we consider the figures for appeals received since 1 January 1974 and the reducing size of the backlog.

SECTION IX: DECISION STAGE: ORGANISATION

5.29 The decision branch of the Department is located in the area to which the application relates. The office for East Anglia and the South East is at the Department's Headquarters in London, but there are now a further six regional offices for planning purposes at Birmingham, Leeds, Manchester, Newcastle, Bristol and Nottingham. Since 1972 they have been responsible for the main part of the Department's statutory functions as regards planning in their respective areas. Besides making recommendations to the Secretary of State on particular called-in applications or appeals, their tasks include the assembly of a regional brief for Inspectors. Other duties include work connected with structure and local plans and with historic buildings, footpaths and open spaces.

SECTION X: WALES

5.30 In Wales there is some variation from the English practice. In order to provide the flexibility needed to deal with a fluctuating flow of work, the Welsh Office uses the Planning Inspectorate of the Department of the Environment. There are at present 7 Welsh-based Inspectors seconded from the DOE and in addition English-based Inspectors regularly deal with Welsh cases. The Welsh-based Inspectors occasionally take cases in the western parts of England. The allocation of cases to the Inspectorate is handled by the Inspectorate Administration in London.

5.31 The average time taken to decide Welsh appeals is much the same as that taken to decide English appeals (from 27 to 66 weeks), but whereas in England about 70% of appeals are dealt with by written representations, before my Interim Report only 35% were dealt with by this method in Wales. This was because the Welsh Office had accepted without question the right of either party to opt for a local inquiry. I am glad to report that the Welsh Office has now adopted the DOE practice of urging the benefits of the written representations method wherever it seems appropriate. This has already resulted in such an increase that 65% of appeals were dealt with by written representations in the first 6 months of 1974 with consequent benefits apparent in the average time taken to reach decisions.

5.32 A small difference in the arrangements for determining Welsh appeals has come to my notice. In England, when the written representations procedure is adopted for an appeal which is to be decided by the Secretary of State, the site visit is undertaken by an Inspector. In Wales, however, it is carried out by one of the Welsh Office's professional planners. Although no part of the Inspectorate is exclusively assigned to Welsh appeals, this practice makes a marginal difference to the amount of work required of Inspectors handling Welsh business. It derives, apparently, from a time (before the Welsh Office was set up) when the regional offices of the Ministry of Housing and Local Government, including its office in Cardiff, operated a similar system in order to relieve an exceptionally heavy burden on the Inspectorate; the practice was discontinued in England but has continued in Wales.

CHAPTER 6

Enforcement Practice

SECTION I: INTRODUCTORY

6.1   It is hardly necessary to remind anyone that effective enforcement is indispensable in order to make planning control effective. Over the years, enforcement, because of legal technicalities involved, has probably been the weakest link in the planning control system. This is not surprising. The draftsmen of the 1947 Act, without prophetic powers, could not have foreseen what experience has taught us since. The radical changes introduced in 1960 and 1968* have been for the better but now a further leap forward is needed and is possible. My suggestions as to what should be done are set out in Chapter 12. This chapter describes briefly how the system now works.

6.2   **Existing Powers and Practice.** Since the 1947 Act local planning authorities have been able to serve enforcement notices requiring that unauthorised buildings should be removed, or that unauthorised uses should cease, or to secure compliance with planning conditions. In 1960 the enforcement appeals were removed from magistrates' courts and taken over by the Ministry of Housing and Local Government. The 1968 Act abolished immunity from enforcement for breaches consisting of a material change in the use (except change of use to a single dwelling house) or failure to comply with a condition (other than a condition relating to carrying out of operations), if the breach occurred after the end of 1963. Under the 1968 Act a new concept, a stop notice, was also introduced. Such notices can be served *only in respect of operational development* (*not uses of land*), and only when an enforcement notice has been served and has not become effective.

6.3   But local planning authorities have seemed very reluctant to serve stop notices. There is evidence which indicates that many authorities do not realise that it is only in very limited circumstances that the service of a stop notice can render them liable to a claim for compensation.

SECTION II: OPERATIONS

6.4   Although it is a breach of planning control to erect or extend buildings without having first obtained planning permission, or where there has been failure to comply with a planning permission which has been granted, this is not an offence. Where such a breach is brought to the attention of a local planning authority, they may serve an enforcement notice. The serving of such a notice is not a statutory requirement but a step which may be taken at the discretion of the local authority, if they think it expedient, having regard to the

---

*ss. 33 to 40 of Caravan Sites and Control of Development Act 1960; ss.15, 16, 19 and 20 of Town and Country Planning Act 1968.

provisions of the statutory development plans or other material considerations. The notice must be served on the owner and occupier of the land to which it relates and on any other person who has an interest in that land, being an interest which, in the opinion of the local authority, is materially affected by the notice. The enforcement notice specifies to those involved the steps which the local planning authority requires them to take in order to remedy the breach by restoring the land to its condition before the development took place (which may in some cases mean demolition), or to secure compliance with the conditions or limitations subject to which the planning permission was granted. The notice becomes effective at the end of a specified period. Such period must not be less than 28 days after the serving of the notice, and an appeal can be made to the Secretary of State within that period, in which case the notice does not come into effect until the appeal is finally decided or is withdrawn.

6.5 Where the local authority considers it desirable that the development should cease within a shorter period they may at any time, before the enforcement notice takes effect, serve a further notice, known as a stop notice. This notice must be served upon the same persons as the enforcement notice and comes into effect on a date specified which shall be not less than three and not more than fourteen days after its service. Its purpose is to call a halt until such time as the enforcement notice comes into effect. One of the purposes of the stop notice is to prevent work proceeding to the point at which the local authority would be faced with a 'fait accompli', in which situation the authority or the Secretary of State on appeal may well deem it unreasonable to demand the demolition of the whole building. In effect the local planning authority may be forced into granting a permission which would otherwise have been refused. Rare cases have been reported in which, after service of a stop notice, a contractor has brought a large labour force onto a site so as to complete the work before the notice becomes effective, but in general stop notices have been effective.

6.6 A developer who ignores an enforcement notice relating to the carrying out of operations is liable to a fine in accordance with section 89 of the 1971 Act, which provides that a person not complying with an enforcement notice "shall be liable on summary conviction to a fine not exceeding £400 or on conviction on indictment to a fine", and if the failure to comply with the notice is continued after conviction he is liable to a fine (of an amount not exceeding £50 for each day of the continuing offence on summary conviction or of an unlimited amount on conviction on indictment). The same penalties are imposed, by section 90(5) of the Act, in respect of failure to comply with a stop notice.

SECTION III: CHANGE IN THE USE OF LAND

6.7 It is in general* a breach of planning control to make a material change in the use of land without having first obtained the permission of the local planning authority.

6.8 Changes of use raise very complicated questions for local planning authorities. When it comes to their attention that an unauthorised change of use has been made, the authority may, if it deems it expedient, serve an enforcement notice which comes into effect after not less than 28 days (if there is no

---

*Certain material changes of use can be made without permission by virtue of the provisions of section 23 of the Act.

appeal). However, if the use in question has been established since before 1964 such a notice cannot be served, even if no planning permission for the use has ever been obtained.

6.9 It is at this point that the local authority's enforcement powers differ according to whether they are dealing with operational development or with changes of use. If an appeal is made they cannot bring the use under control by serving a stop notice during the period before an enforcement notice comes into effect. The reason given for this restriction when stop notices were introduced was that only in the case of operations was continuance of the activity, pending the coming into effect of the enforcement notice, likely to affect the outcome of any appeal. In addition there were thought to be problems due to the degree of uncertainty when a material change of use takes place. If the local planning authority could serve stop notices in respect of material changes of use they would run a considerable risk of interfering with lawful activities, even to the extent of serious and permanent damage to a business. In this case substantial claims for compensation against the local authority might be made.

6.10 Once an enforcement notice served in respect of unauthorised change of use has come into effect, anyone who does not comply with the notice is guilty under section 89(5) of the 1971 Act of an offence and is liable on summary conviction to a fine not exceeding £400 or on indictment to an unlimited fine. If the use is continued after conviction, a further offence is committed and there is liability to a fine not exceeding £50 on summary conviction for each day on which the use is continued, or an unlimited fine on conviction on indictment.

SECTION IV: APPEALS

6.11 An appeal may be made under section 88 of the 1971 Act on the following grounds:—

"(a) that planning permission ought to be granted for the development to which the notice relates or, as the case may be, that a condition or limitation alleged in the enforcement notice not to have been complied with ought to be discharged;

(b) that the matters alleged in the notice do not constitute a breach of planning control;

(c) in the case of a notice which, by virtue of section 87(3) of this Act, may be served only within the period of four years from the date of the breach of planning control to which the notice relates, that that period has elapsed at the date of service; this applies where the breach relates to operations or to a change of use to a single dwelling house;

(d) in the case of a notice not falling within paragraph (c) of this sub-section, that the breach of planning control alleged by the notice occurred before the beginning of 1964;

(e) that the enforcement notice was not served as required by section 87(4) of this Act;

(f) that the steps required by the notice to be taken exceed what is necessary to remedy any breach of planning control;

(g) that the specified period for compliance with the notice falls short of what should reasonably be allowed".

6.12 Where an appeal is brought under this section the enforcement notice is of no effect pending the final determination or withdrawal of the appeal.

Furthermore an appeal against an enforcement notice acts as a deemed application for planning permission for the development to which the notice relates even if ground (a) is not pleaded (section 88(7)). This is why in many appeals it is necessary to consider both the planning merits of the development and any legal grounds pleaded.

6.13 An average of about 45% of enforcement appeals are withdrawn each year and of the remainder between 65% and 70% of the notices are upheld and 30%-35% quashed.

6.14 **Statistics.** Approximately 4,000 enforcement notices were served in 1973. During the last decade the number of appeals made has gone up from 1,620 in 1964 to 3,095 in 1973 before falling back to 2,678 in 1974. This represents an overall increase of 65%, the rate of increase varying from year to year from 26% in 1964 to 4% in 1967 (with an actual drop in 1969 and 1974).

6.15 **Proportion of enforcement appeals.** On average in the last few years in 75% of cases the serving of an enforcement notice has led to an appeal. This is a substantial proportion. In recent years about 35% of enforcement appeals were successful as compared with 24% in planning appeals.

6.16 **Transferred enforcement appeals.** Ordinary appeals are far more often transferred to inspectors than enforcement cases: 75-80% of ordinary planning appeals as compared with approximately 25% *of all enforcement appeals.*

6.17 **Success rate in Secretary of State's cases.** The latest statistics indicate that in Secretary of State's enforcement appeals last year about 36% succeeded. Of these 20% succeeded on planning grounds, 10% on legal grounds and 6% succeeded on technicalities, eg the notice is a nullity because its form is defective.

6.18 **Success rate in transferred cases.** 35% of transferred appeals were successful, virtually all of which succeeded on planning grounds.

6.19 From the above figures it can be seen that less than 10% of all appeals succeed on the grounds that the service of the notice was not legally justified. Two thirds of all successful appeals raise planning merits as the sole issue. Accordingly they should in so far as is practicable be streamed into a separate class.

6.20 It is clear that the great edifice of enforcement appeals imposes an unfair burden on the authorities, as, subject to planning merits, the vast majority of enforcement notices served are sound and therefore the work involved and the complexity of the system is out of proportion to the need to protect individual rights. There does seem to be a case here for doing some streamlining and trying to take a few short cuts.

6.21 The task of keeping appeals moving at a "satisfactory rate" has been made more difficult following the judgement of the Court of Appeal in the case of *Howard v The Secretary of State.** The Court held that the time limit set by section 88(1) and the requirements of section 88(2) of the 1971 Act were mandatory to the extent that an appeal had to be made in writing within the period specified in the notice as the period at the end of which it would take effect. On the other hand, it held that a notice of appeal was valid even if it was not accompanied by any indication of the grounds of appeal, or any statement of the facts on which it was based. This means in practice that there is no longer a statutory time limit within which an appellant must provide grounds of appeal. I deal with the problem in paragraphs 11.15-11.18.

Howard v Secretary of State for the Environment (1972) 23 P & C.R. 324.

PART III

THE FUTURE

CHAPTER 7

Planning Control: Towards a Better System

7.1 **A quicker and more rational procedure.** This chapter sets out a procedure for members of the public making planning applications and for local authorities dealing with them. It is designed to make planning control quicker, simpler (or at least more rational) and more efficient to the advantage of all parties.

7.2 **Streamlining not replacement.** The changes proposed amount to a streamlining of the present system rather than its replacement by totally new and unfamiliar procedures. They are aimed at drawing a realistic balance between what is desirable and what is workable. With goodwill and determination, those responsible should find it possible to implement them—even in present conditions—and so enjoy the savings and bonuses they offer.

7.3 Among the more important features of the proposed system are:

(i)   a single standard application form;
(ii) a leaflet explaining how to fill it in;
(iii) information centres and (later) advice centres to help applicants and interested parties;
(iv) full publicity, to nationally laid down standards, for all planning applications;
(v)   the division of planning applications into two classes:
    (A) minor and uncontroversial and
    (B) major and/or controversial;
(vi) a simpler and speedier treatment for Class A applications, and a realistic but strict time-table for Class B applications;
(vii) a firm time-table for the principal steps for processing applications is set out in para 2.27;
(viii) separate public consultation codes for each of these classes;
(ix) the device of deed permissions for Class A applications, so that in default of a decision they are automatically approved;
(x)   a clearer, stricter definition of responsibility for handling planning applications as between district and county councils;
(xi) complete revision of the General Development Order to make it clearer and more comprehensible to the public (see para 9.10).

SECTION I: TWO KINDS OF APPLICATIONS

The case for making a distinction

7.4 It is tempting to assume that minor developments are automatically simple, and that planning authorities, therefore, always need less information and less time to reach sound decisions on them. That is clearly not so. As amenity societies and professional bodies were quick to point out, in commenting on the tentative distinction made in my Interim Report between house-holder applications and others, some quite 'small' proposals raise major questions of principle.

7.5 It should not be necessary for a small and relatively simple proposal, unlikely to arouse much objection, to run the gamut of the same stringent procedures as a major or controversial proposal. Nor ought it to wait as long for a decision.

7.6 Some cases, however, including otherwise minor ones which give rise to issues of principle or could arouse controversy, will always demand a lengthier, more stringent appraisal. And so long as we have only one procedure applying to all applications, there is little hope of achieving simplicity and speed for the majority of applications. They will tend to move at the pace of the complex or controversial few.

Suggested categories 'A' and 'B'

7.7 **Development proposals should be divided into two categories.** It is, therefore, suggested that applications should be divided into two categories: those that are minor and uncontroversial (called 'Class A' in the rest of this report); and those that are major or controversial or both (*including proposals requiring an impact statement* (see para 7.63) ('Class B')). Applications would be streamed accordingly.

7.8 **Initially, an applicant could choose** in which category to place his application. An explanatory leaflet would help him to decide whether A or B better fitted his needs. He would make his application on a standard form. A wrongly categorised application would be re-streamed as a matter of course by the local authority and the applicant notified.

7.9 **Defining Class A.** An attempt to lay down rigid rules for defining Class A applications is doomed to failure. I hope that local authorities will want to stream as many as possible into the faster, simpler procedure. Some guidance should, however, be given in the form of a *national code of practice*. This would ensure that at least the following are treated as Class A (Appendix II A iv sets out a list of developments which could fall into Class A):

(i)   all simple cases;
(ii) all applications conforming with an approved development plan; (this may have to be subject to specified limits for an experimental period);
(iii) development which only just exceeds that permitted by the General Development Order, including Class I (development within the curtilage of a dwellinghouse), Class VI (agricultural) and VIII (industrial) developments;
(iv) the approval of reserved matters relating to cases classed as 'A' when outline permission was sought.

7.10 **Guidelines.** To supplement the national code of practice, district councils should be encouraged to produce guidelines indicating what types of application would be treated as Class A and B, either throughout the district or in particular parts of it. In addition to applications complying with old-style development plans or approved local plans, Class A might include applications in accord with an informal plan widely canvassed and tested by public participation.

Switching categories

7.11 Discretion to transfer. The planning officer will examine each 'A' application and at his discretion may transfer it to the Class B stream (and should it arise, vice versa). There should be a time limit for transfer of 28 days. Cases where he does so will include those where proposals:—

(a) conflict with the scale and character of a site's surroundings, especially if they comprise an area of homogeneous character;

(b) provoke public concern or controversy on true planning grounds (see para 7.18-7.20) submitted within 28 days of receipt of the application (see para 7.29).

7.12 A planning officer should not need to switch many applications from Class A to Class B. If an application conforms to a council's published policy for the area, and if that policy was adequately publicised at the appropriate time, he should be able to gauge the strength of probable public reaction. Small extensions to houses, factories and other existing buildings sometimes arouse opposition. In the great majority of cases, however, the objections are 'private' ones.

7.13 Repetitive applications. Where an applicant in the face of refusal of permission makes the same Class A application again with material changes, and reconsideration is warranted, it could be transferred to Class B. This may be convenient because:

(i) a file on the case would exist, allowing officers to use collated material;

(ii) repetitive applications require the wider publicity given to Class B applications; and

(iii) an earlier refused application may have brought firm comments from interested parties.

Serious consideration should be given as to whether a recent refusal of a similar planning application should by itself be a sufficient reason for refusal.

7.14 Reasons for transfer. Whenever a planning officer transfers an application from Class A to Class B, he should state his reasons for doing so in writing. One standard reason would be that the application had provoked substantial opposition on relevant planning (not private) grounds (see 7.19). Another would be that it presented substantial planning difficulties. But neither reason by itself would be precise enough.

7.15 Precise reasons. In giving reasons, the planning officer must also specify the nature of the difficulties or the reasons for the opposition, e.g. allegedly inadequate traffic capacity or main drainage capacity, or possible visual intrusion on the neighbourhood.

7.16 The fact that the local planning authority (LPA) had consulted another authority and not received its reply in time would not be an acceptable reason for transfer, any more than for failure to keep within time limits (7.38).

7.17 Transfer is not a refusal. Every notification of transfer should make it clear that 'transfer' means 'further investigation' and is not a refusal. *A clear distinction also needs to be drawn between 'reasons for transfer' and 'grounds of refusal'.* When a planning officer gives reasons for transfer, they do not imply that he or his authority believe the difficulties or opposition need be fatal to the application. He is simply saying that they amount, so to speak, to a *prima facie* case meriting more careful consideration.

7.18 **Distinction between 'Public' and 'Private' objections.** The planning officer will have to ensure that objections on purely *private* grounds are not entertained. But equally he will be responsible for seeing that objections on genuinely *public* planning grounds (even if made by a single individual) carry due weight.

7.19 Many attempts have been made to define this distinction between public and private interests in planning. For example, in Development Control Policy Note No 1 (para 14) it was said that 'the effect of a proposed development on its neighbours, including its effect on the value of neighbouring property, is a consideration which can properly be taken into account in deciding a planning application. But the material question is not whether owners and occupiers of neighbouring properties would suffer financial or other loss, but whether the proposal would affect the locality generally and lead to a change in its character which would be contrary to the public interest'.

7.20 I do not myself think a precise definition possible, but I do consider that where a proposal will lead to a neighbourhood intrusion it may constitute a planning objection (see para 10.2(*e*)). It is rather a 'matter of fact and degree'. This is the formula which lawyers often use to describe what is in effect a discretionary power, but which they hope will be used with common sense.

7.21 I have no doubt that the best authorities will be able to use this discretion sensibly. It must, however, be left to local authority associations and to the public to persuade less enlightened councils into adopting the best practice.

SECTION II: STREAMLINING OF PROCEDURES AND MONITORING

(a) Model Procedure

7.22 **Importance of a model procedure.** A uniform practice in acknowledging and processing applications offers great advantages. Certain steps should therefore follow the receipt of *every* application, and these should be set out in a circular which should also describe detailed steps for dealing with Class A and Class B applications.

7.23 **Simplicity of procedure.** I have selected and put as Appendix II A iii two development control schemes adopted in Leicestershire and West Sussex. They offer two contrasting solutions both of which work well. There will be others that are just as good. The essential point is that the codes adopted by LPAs need to be simple to operate and easy for the applicant to understand.

(b) Standard form

7.24 **Present diversity confusing.** At present the General Development Order (Article 5(1)) provides for applications to be made on a form supplied by the LPA. Circular 23/72 suggests a good model, but in practice forms still vary. Some are clearer and better in presentation than others (see Appendix II A i for an example).

7.25 The variations are confusing. It is only commonsense to have one standard form throughout the country. In the past local authorities have been anxious to retain their right to produce their own forms. This opposition to a national form may now be reduced—the County Councils' Association sees merit in a standard form to ensure consistency between districts in a particular county.

7.26 **A standard form.** The model form in Circular 23/72 would in any case need to be re-designed to accommodate the Class A/Class B division. Some improvement of the form too should be possible to achieve greater clarity and simplicity.

65

The Department should now get together with the authorities and representatives of potential users and produce a model form quickly.

7.27 Information storage. The new form must be so designed that it can be used in computer systems. Some district councils have already arranged to use the existing 'model' form to store and classify applications.

(c) Standard consultation procedure

7.28 Limits to consultation. If the model procedure is to work satisfactorily, it must not be bogged down by delays. Strict compliance with time limits for consultation (21 *days for Class A and* 42 *days for Class B*) is the key to its success —and that includes compliance by those *authorities* whom the local planning authority is bound to consult (see para 7.38).

(d) Publicity

7.29 It also includes *consultations with the public.* Class B cases require more extensive publicity than Class A and will need to be publicised more widely. More time must also be allowed in some cases for comment and objections. There should be a standard period for comment by all consulted and for public comment. For convenience I itemize below the different forms of compulsory and discretionary publicity which I consider appropriate for Class A and Class B applications. If the applicant is made responsible for publicity he will be required to certify that it has been completed.

Compulsory and discretionary publicity

	COMPULSORY	DISCRETIONARY
Class A	1. Site notices *or* neighbour notification	1. Notification to local societies
	2. Notification of parish council	2. Other compulsory items under Class B
Class B	1. Site notice *or* neighbour notification	1. Notification to local societies
	2. Notification of parish council	2. Advertisements for individual applications in local newspapers or on notice boards (perhaps specially allocated for that purpose)
	3. Publication of lists of applications in local newspapers *or* on public notice boards (perhaps specially allocated for that purpose) and to registered local societies	

The timetable for A and B applications is set out in para 2.27 and in a diagrammatic form as an Annex to this chapter.

(e) Monitoring—statutory duty to make a quarterly return

7.30 To enable all concerned to judge the effectiveness with which the new procedures are operated, every local planning authority should have a statutory duty to make a quarterly return to the Department giving the following information *in respect of both A and B cases:*

(1) the number of planning applications received in each class;

(2) the number decided within the relevant statutory time limits;

66

(3) the number not so decided;
(4) the number transferred from Class A to Class B.
LPAs should also have a statutory duty to publish this information in local newspapers.

SECTION III: CLASS 'A' APPLICATIONS

(a) Advantages of directing applications into Class A

7.31 **Class A procedures: its advantages.** The aim of the new system will be to direct at least $\frac{1}{2}$, and I hope up to $\frac{2}{3}$, of all planning applications into the faster, simpler, Class A procedure. Statistics are admittedly unreliable; it is difficult to tell from past figures how many applications were 'minor' and how many 'major'. But there appears to be general agreement that at least 40%-50% of present applications are 'minor' ones—and some estimates would put it as high as 70% or 80%. (Appendix II A v summarises the information on this point collected by my Secretariat.)

7.32 There is a counter-argument: that even this high proportion of minor applications takes comparatively little time to process and does not clog the system. Present rules, it is said, are simple enough. I find it impossible to believe this. My own assessment to the contrary draws support from some very experienced local authority officers whom I have consulted.

7.33 What will be achieved by siphoning off the simpler, non-controversial development proposals? (I have already indicated the method of transfer in paragraph 7.11.) The object is to enable local authorities to concentrate time and skilled manpower on those applications that matter most: Class B. It should also serve to free resources for positive planning, so that authorities are not always on the defensive. Public participation, too, is plainly most effective when interest and attention are concentrated on major or potentially controversial cases.

(b) Quicker decisions

7.34 **Realistic time-table.** At present a local authority has two months, under Article 7(3) of the GDO, to inform an applicant of its decision. Compliance with that time limit has been patchy. Some councils meet the deadline in most cases. Others clearly fail to meet it in a substantial proportion of cases. I can produce no precise figures. During local government reorganisation monitoring of performance did not take place in many areas. Nonetheless I have the firm impression, based on extensive enquiries, *that no more than 50% of applications are currently decided within the two month time limit.*

7.35 I therefore consider that it would be quite wrong to retain that time limit generally. A realistic time limit would be shorter for Class A cases, longer for Class B.

7.36 Class A applications are, by definition, unlikely to be controversial. They can therefore be taken by an officer or a sub-committee acting under delegated powers. *Given a simpler standard publicity procedure, not less than 35 and not more than 42 days should be long enough to reach a decision.* (For Class B applications I suggest three months, except where an 'impact study' is required, see paragraph 7.63.)

(c) Quicker consultations

7.37 In many instances the present consultation procedure does not appear to work as intended. There are two basic reasons for this. LPAs consult too many

67

authorities and bodies on too wide a range of applications; and the consultations themselves are too protracted. My proposals for more extensive publicity should in many cases serve to alert other bodies to planning proposals, thus enabling LPAs to reduce drastically the number of bodies they specifically consult.

7.38 The General Development Order (Article 13(4)) requires an authority, in fulfilling its duty, to consult certain 'authorities, persons or bodies', and to allow them at least 14 days to respond. It requires them to take account of any such response, and forbids them to decide an application before the 14 days have elapsed. The intention was that the authority would go ahead if no reply had been received. Over the years the practice of waiting has unfortunately become ingrained. I suggest that the required consultation period be extended from 14 days to 21 days for Class A applications; but that if there has been no formal objection from a consulted party by the end of that period, the planning authority should decide the application without it. To achieve the hoped for improvement, however, local authorities must act on this. The present time limits under Article 13(4) are I suspect in many districts a dead letter. And if a condition is likely to meet the requirements of the authority which has been consulted, its terms should be suggested in the reply.

(d) Deemed consent
7.39 **Deemed permissions.** A Class A application which has not been transferred (see paragraph 7.11) should be deemed granted in the terms in which it is made at the end of 42 days from the receipt of the application by the authority, if the applicant has received no decision by that time. This period runs from receipt of a valid application by the local authority. The date of the relevant resolution or decision of a sub-committee or an officer would be treated as the decision, if made 3 days before posting, and duly recorded. Class A cases involving the approval of *reserved matters* should be subject to a similar time limit, but with a right of appeal in the event of the time limit being exceeded *instead of a deemed consent*. Permissions deemed to be granted on Class A applications should be subject to standard conditions. Amendment of the GDO will be necessary to provide for this.

7.40 Deemed permissions constitute a fundamental procedural change, but not as drastic as might at first appear. The same principle is implicit in purchase notices (Section 186(2) of the 1971 Act). The building regulations have a similar procedure. Section 65 of the Public Health Act 1936 (see also Section 4 of the Public Health Act 1961) states that if no decision is given within the prescribed period the local authority cannot subsequently take action for a breach of regulations. I realise that the deemed permission procedure is not new and has not always worked. It was abandoned in the 1930s after (it is said) causing chaos in the operation of the Restriction of Ribbon Development Act of 1935. And there is a danger that some councils will seek to play safe by issuing 'protective' refusals in simple cases on which they have failed to reach a real decision.

7.41 **Why deemed permissions are vital.** When my Interim Report was published, I doubted the practicability of deemed consents. Discussions with experienced local authority officers have convinced me that such a system can, with goodwill, be made to work and should result in savings of time and manpower substantial enough to justify the change. They much prefer it to any general relaxation of the GDO, a simpler but much less popular possible reform. It should be noted that the permission granted to development within GDO limits is also a 'deemed' permission, though without the need for any application. Deemed consents for Class A applications would, moreover, carry few risks, since these would be proposals which the planning officer himself had selected as minor and uncontroversial; and in the event of serious objections at the publicity stage, there would remain the option of transfer to Class B. Dark tales of chaos in the 1930s need not intimidate us.

7.42 The CBI, the TUC, several major professional bodies and some of our leading town planners in local government have all warned that a way *must* be found to clear the clutter of small, uncontroversial applications now clogging the planning control system. Deemed consent will not cure all the ills of planning, but it does offer a substantial and tangible improvement. No one has suggested any better alternative that meets the test of practicability. And this solution has the great virtue of being readily comprehensible and, I think, acceptable to most local authorities and to the public. I have, however, taken account of the strong opposition at present to deemed consent on applications for approval of reserved matters, and, accordingly suggest no change in the present procedure apart from the streamlining measures outlined elsewhere in this report (see para 7.137).

7.43 A system of deemed consents should not preclude the imposition of specific conditions where the need arises.

(e) Publicity for Class A applications

7.44 **Publicity requirements for Class A applications. Interested parties.** From the outset publicity must be simple, comprehensive, consistent in its form, and given quickly. But we need to match speed with greater certainty that those with a legitimate planning interest are given sufficient opportunity to object. All those who do object or make representations should be told as of right what decision the council finally reached, and its reasons.

7.45 **Telling the applicant.** A local authority, in acknowledging a planning application, should tell the applicant plainly what publicity is to be given to his proposal and what steps (if any) it requires him to take in this respect. Planning authorities should retain discretion as to the extent of publicity they stipulate, except where existing or new legislation requires specific steps (see para 7.47 below, Circular 74/73, S.26 of the 1971 Act). The authority will need to have the power to direct the applicant as to what publicity is necessary.

7.46 **Notification of parish councils, amenity societies and in local press.** Class A applications by their nature will not require as much publicity as Class B. There should be site notices or neighbour notification (see 7.49 to 7.52) in all cases. The planning authority would continue to notify parish councils.*

7.47 Any more extensive publicity would be at the discretion of the local authority, but I assume that the present voluntary practice of publishing lists of applications in newspapers and circulating lists to amenity societies and all councillors will (where it exists) continue. Councils who do not do so should seriously reconsider their procedures and should be encouraged to adopt this practice.

7.48 **Publicity for decisions.** Lists of A decisions, including permissions granted, should also normally be published in local newspapers and circulated to amenity societies.

---

*Local Government Act 1972, Schedule 16 paragraph 20.

7.49 **Site Notices.** In my Interim Report, I suggested the adoption of site notices as standard practice. These notices would need to be of uniform design and size, distinctive in colour, and written in plain, non-technical language.

7.50 Some people have seen difficulties in this. They have been haunted by the spectre of a single notice in the middle of a 100-acre site. That fear is groundless. Existing legislation already provides that publicity should be clearly visible to passers-by. This could be made universal. In any case, such a large-scale development would fall into Class B and attract the altogether wider publicity requirements set out below (7.60). In my view an application of this kind and size should always be advertised.

7.51 I still favour site notices for rural areas, where 'neighbours' may be difficult to define or may be some distance from the site. Here a prominently displayed and distinctively coloured notice should catch the eye of all who pass the site: a development of any consequence will quickly be news in the parish.

7.52 **Notification of neighbours.** In town, some development proposals, for instance at the rear of a building, may not much concern the passer-by, though they may affect the character of the locality for those living there. Moreover, the 'bush telegraph' generally works less reliably than in the country. For towns, therefore, I tend to favour compulsory notification of neighbours. 'Neighbours' by this definition would include those who live in or occupy premises opposite a proposed development. But circumstances will vary and it should be for the planning authority to determine whether neighbour notification or a site notice is the most appropriate (see diagram and definition of 'neighbour', Appendix II C i).

SECTION IV: CLASS B APPLICATIONS

(a) Period for decision

7.53 **Three months' limit for decision.** For Class B applications, the time limit within which the local planning authority must give a decision should be three calendar months. It should be possible to extend this with the agreement of the applicant. The period allowed for *consultations* on such applications should be 42 days.

7.54 At present a local planning authority is in theory bound to decide any application within two months of receiving it (GDO Art 7(3)). Class B cases will in general be more difficult, complex or controversial than most. They therefore demand a more generous time limit. Three months seems a reasonable period. It must, however, be treated in practice as a *maximum*. This would admit of only one exception—those cases where the authority requires an impact study. (I explain this requirement later.) I propose that a maximum of *six months* should be allowed for such cases. In all cases the applicant should be informed of the date when the application will be considered by the committee. If the decision is deferred he should also be told when further consideration of his application will be given. Knowledge *when* the decision will be made is as important to the applicant as is speed.

7.55 **No deemed consent for Class B.** Deemed consent is not recommended for Class B cases. Their likely scale, complexity or controversial nature makes it inappropriate.

7.56 **Reasons for failure to comply with time limit.** Though deemed consent cannot apply to B cases, local planning authorities must not feel able to infringe the time limit with impunity. They should therefore be bound to give reasons for failing to reach a decision in time. Some councils and one professional body who commented on this proposal were against it. The majority of comments from industry, most developers and many other local authorities, supported it. Besides, a significant number of councils do already give applicants their reasons for failing to meet existing deadlines.

7.57 Some councils have advanced 'shortage of staff' as a reason why they should not be obliged to explain delays. But if staff shortages in fact cause them to run over time, they should say so—with supporting facts. If a strict guillotine is to be applied to the comments of those consulted by councils, then the councils also should be seen to be subject to strictly enforced time limits.

7.58 Reasons given for a council's delay should, however, be specific, not generalised. For example, a sound decision on a substantial development proposal may require fresh traffic counts to assess its effect on surrounding roads and traffic flow. A sound decision on a proposed new shopping centre could well require careful and lengthy statistical analysis to establish its likely impact on existing shops. Such vague excuses as: 'This is an exceptionally difficult case requiring further consideration', will not suffice.

(b) Consultations
7.59 **Statutory right to consultations.** In addition to his right to be told reasons for a delay, a Class B applicant should also have a statutory right, when no decision is reached in time, to discuss his application with a senior planning officer or a member of the council's planning committee.

(c) Publicity
7.60 **Transfer cases.** Publicity already given to a Class A case need not be repeated if the planning officer transfers it to Class B. Some additional publicity, such as newspaper advertisements, may be required by the local planning authority.

SECTION V: IMPACT STUDY

(a) When applicable and time limit
7.61 **Impact study.** For *specially significant development Class B proposals* the LPA may require more information than the developer gives on the application form. In such cases, he will be able to submit an impact study and therefore the LPA should have the power to require him to do so. This power must be used sparingly (see para. 7.63), and selectively. Its purpose is to ensure that the applicant fully appreciates the environmental consequences of what he proposes and makes it clear to others. Moreover, in preparing it, he has a chance to improve his plans. This power should not normally apply to housebuilding.

7.62 The applicant should strive to produce an objective assessment of the effect of his proposals. A study which is a mere public relations exercise will fail in its object. For their part, the LPA and all other authorities must be willing to provide any information they have that can assist preparation of the statement. Rules should be made to ensure this.

7.63 **When to call for an impact study.** The LPA should almost never ask for an impact statement if the application seems likely to be refused. It may do so, however, in anticipation of an appeal, if the statement is likely to be valuable. In such cases, it must be made clear to the applicant that a refusal is contemplated. Here again there should be a strict time-table. The LPA should notify the applicant within 14 days of receiving the application that an impact study is required. The applicant should then be given normally 10 weeks to prepare the study. This would leave 3 months for the decision by the LPA (see para. 7.54).

(b) Content

7.64 **Content of impact study.** The study would describe the proposed development in detail and explain its likely effects on its surroundings. It would comprise a written report and whatever plans, maps, photographs, diagrams etc. would be needed to assist understanding. In particular, it should deal with the proposed development's effect on:

    (a) traffic, roads and public transport,
    (b) foul and surface water drainage,
    (c) publicly provided services, such as schools,
    (d) the appearance of the neighbourhood,
    (e) employment,
    (f) noise and air pollution.

Other aspects to be considered in the statement might include:

    (*g*) whether the development or its location constitute a hazard (e.g. fire risk),
    (*h*) whether it is likely to trigger off other development,
    (*j*) investigation of alternative sites.

7.65 **Model impact study.** The Department should publish a Planning Bulletin, perhaps on the lines of the former MHLG's Bulletins 1 and 3 on town centres, setting out a suggested form for impact studies. (I now understand that the Secretary of State has commissioned a separate investigation to consider whether such statements have a role in the British planning process, and, if so, what they should include and who should pay for them.)

(c) Publicity

7.66 **Publicity.** Where the local planning authority considers an application to have special significance requiring an impact study (para. 7.63), the proposal will need even more publicity. It should be prominently advertised in a local newspaper; and details of it should be posted on notice boards in public places such as town halls, public libraries and arts centres. It is not good enough to use only public notice boards inside buildings. Outside notice boards are often more widely read.

7.67 **Display and copies of impact study.** An impact study should be available for public inspection. The LPA should display a copy at its offices; it should remain on display until the application is decided, and any appeal from that decision also decided. Members of the public should be able to obtain a limited number of copies. The applicant should therefore be required to supply copies at a reasonable price within 14 days of a written request.

SECTION VI: MEETINGS

7.68 **General.** Consultations between applicants and local planning authorities can make an important contribution towards the speedy and expeditious processing of applications. I outline in the following paragraphs the forms of consultation needed. They apply predominantly to Class B applications, but may also be appropriate to certain Class A cases.

(a) Before decision

7.69 **Appearance before Planning Committee.** The Planning Committee should take the opportunity to interview applicants in suitable cases, particularly where there is a difference of view within the committee. Such a meeting should be open to the press while the applicant is present; and the committee should take account of (i) impact study, (ii) any objections to the development, and (iii) the applicant's oral representations.

7.70 Planning committees disagree with their officers more frequently than one might expect. An opportunity for the applicant to explain his case can therefore be of help.

7.71 **Section 52 agreements.** Section 52 of the 1971 Act (which has now been supplemented by section 126 of the Housing Act 1974) enables an applicant to carry out works which may overcome some technical objections, such as access. Planning authorities should be given clear directions to enter into such agreements wherever possible, instead of refusing permissions. They should also be prepared to enter into such agreements to deal with particular objections before an appeal (without prejudice to any other objections); time and effort involved would be well spent and will save much time at Inquiries (see 11.147–11.149).

7.72 **Practical limits to consultation.** In principle all consultation is useful. In practice, most district councils are at present quite unable to consult with every applicant. LPAs and the public must therefore 'ration' consultations to cases in which they are indispensable or are likely to be most productive.

7.73 **Meetings with planning officers.** Applicants must be able to discuss their difficulties with the LPA's officers. Government circulars have over the years often commended the virtues of consultation, but the practice of LPAs varies widely. Some planning officers stagger beneath a burden of excessive consultation, others begrudge almost all time spent thus, seeing it as time lost to positive plan-making.

7.74 **A sensible balance.** We need to preserve a sensible balance: to make it clear to the public that a planning officer's time is at a premium and he cannot be expected to act as the applicant's or the objectors' adviser: to make it plain to officers that they should encourage consultation whenever it offers real hope of a constructive outcome. No hard and fast set of rules can regulate this. Guidelines suggesting when consultations are or are not appropriate would be welcome, even if they serve only as reminders of the obvious.

7.75 **Independently chaired meetings.** LPAs may sometimes find it useful before deciding an application to arrange with the applicant to have a meeting with an independent chairman. Each party would then be able to put its case in its own words, thus helping the planning committee or sub-committee to reach a balanced, informed decision. Such meetings ought to be open to the public.

7.76 DOE Circular 142/73, para. 7, suggested this kind of meeting, but as far as I know no-one has yet tried it. I understand LPAs' reluctance to undertake this further burden; nevertheless I think some of them should at least experiment with it. If we are to move towards the much-needed spirit of greater co-operation in planning, such meetings would be a valuable step in the right direction.

7.77 **An 'Applicant's' Rule 6 statement.** When an LPA's officers meet an applicant, any additional information or evidence he gives them should be passed to the committee deciding the application. A convenient course may be for him to put it in a form similar to a 'Rule 6 statement'.

7.78 **Grounds of refusal.** In refusing applications, LPAs must be sure to distinguish between true grounds of refusal and any other objections they make to the details of the application. Most planning proposals raise difficulties which a process of clarification and modification can solve.

7.79 For instance, objections to drainage provision or the layout of service roads can probably be resolved often by a Section 52 agreement (see para 7.71). They should be set out not as grounds of refusal but as notes to the refusal. Applicants then know where they are and can try to resolve such difficulties by consultation.

7.80 The real grounds of refusal are likely to be more fundamental, for instance, that the proposal conflicts with an approved up to date development plan or is totally out of character with its surroundings. If there is going to be an appeal, it will help everyone, and save time, if right from the start everyone knows the real issues.

(b) After deemed or express refusal

7.81 **Deemed refusal: applicant's rights.** The one circumstance in which an applicant should certainly have the right to discuss his case with a senior planning officer was suggested in para. 7.59 above: where the LPA makes no decision within the three-month time limit for Class B applications. This amounts to a 'deemed refusal'.

7.82 This is of fundamental importance. My suggested longer time-limit for Class B cases is intended as a realistic one within which almost all can in practice be decided. Local authorities tell me that the deadline can be met. Where it is not, an applicant can reasonably ask the LPA's officers what is so special about his case, in addition to the statutory statement of reasons (see para. 7.56).

7.83 Such statutory meetings have another purpose. They may prevent unnecessary appeals from the deemed refusal. The LPA's failure to make a decision may stem from uncertainties which neither it nor the applicant can resolve. In such cases (which will be rare), he may prefer to hear about it so that he can quickly relocate his development elsewhere. In other cases, a face-to-face encounter may produce a solution.

7.84 **Applicant's right to be heard after refusal.** A person whose application has been refused should in due course, once the present delays have been removed, be given the right to meet the planning committee or the planning officer to discuss the reasons for the refusal. (I have already suggested a comparable right in cases of delayed decisions (para. 7.59).) This proposal seems at first startling. Yet some districts already in practice grant such interviews.

7.85 **Arguments for right to be heard.** This practice has considerable advantages: (1) it would encourage post-decision conciliation and discourage hopeless appeals; (2) the applicant can, at worst, be reassured that the committee have adequately considered his proposal; (3) the committee may sometimes be able to suggest to the applicant another way of solving his particular problem; (4) the meeting might sometimes produce a compromise; and (5) the act of conciliation would help to disarm some people's belief that in deciding planning applications local planning authorities act arbitrarily with no good reasons given.

(c) Exhibitions and public meetings

7.86 For at least some of the more important applications, a public exhibition and/or public meeting will be useful and worthwhile. It gives the applicant a chance to explain his proposals. The LPA can give its preliminary views and both can hear public reaction. But one basic distinction must be firmly made and understood; such exercises form part of the process of consultation, in themselves they decide nothing. The public right to be heard is not a right to veto or approve. The right of decision belongs to the planning authority.

SECTION VII: PLANNING APPLICATIONS – [A] OUTLINE AND DETAILED; [B] AMENDMENTS; [C] CHARGES

[A] OUTLINE AND DETAILED

(a) Outline applications and reserved matters
7.87 **Reserved matters.** When an LPA approves a planning application, it customarily defers consideration of detail not yet submitted Speed in deciding these 'reserved matters' when they are submitted for approval is quite as essential as speed in deciding the original applications. Indeed, delay at the 'reserved matters' stage often worries builders and developers more, because they are by then committed to a project.

7.88 Some of them have also expressed concern lest LPAs seek to use their power to reject details as a means of reversing an earlier decision now regretted. Such a practice is illegal. In almost all Class A cases there should be little or no dispute on approval of detail.

(b) Article 5 Direction
7.89 **Early details.** Where details of a development will be of special importance (for instance, on a key site in a conservation area), the LPA should exercise its existing power to call for more information and greater detail with the initial application (GDO Art 5(1), (2)).

7.90 This power to make an 'Article 5 Direction' allows the LPA to demand enough information for its consent to specify the character of the details in a general way, e.g. by stipulating certain materials. Since exercise of this power involves more work for both parties and tends to delay, LPAs should use it sparingly. (There is a right of appeal to the Secretary of State against a direction under Article 5(2).)

7.91 It could, however, with benefit be used more often in conservation and other sensitive areas as well as in town centres. It is a positive planning tool especially appropriate to cases where the content of a development seems likely to be acceptable if only its appearance is attractive and appropriate.

7.92 **Amenity society initiative.** An amenity society can usefully in certain cases take the initiative and ask the LPA to make an Article 5(1) Direction. Amenity groups should not, however, use this aggressively as a weapon against developers, seeking to delay or block an application by the extra burden a direction would impose. Its use should be positive: to encourage the developer to make an application which is likely to succeed.

7.93 **Transfer to Class B.** Any application for which the LPA issues an Article 5 Direction may have to be transferred to Class B, unless the Direction covers simple matters e.g. width of access. In other cases, irrespective of its size, it may arouse greater public interest than a simple Class A application. The LPA should make it clear to a Class A applicant that the Direction changed his proposal into a Class B one, with the differences of timetable and publicity that this implies.

7.94 **Time runs from completion of detail.** The timetable for such applications should begin to run only when the LPA has received the information required in the Article 5 Direction.

(c) New types of application: Outline, Hybrid, Detailed and Guideline

7.95 New types of application. At present there exist two types of application – 'Outline' and 'Detailed' – but the borderline between them is unclear. I suggest that future practice should recognise four types of application: 'Outline', 'Illustrative', 'Detailed' and 'Guideline'.

(d) Outline

7.96 Outline applications: Purpose. The purpose of an outline application is to establish whether, on a given site, buildings with the function and of the size proposed should be permitted. Outline applications should not concern themselves with what a development will look like. Indeed, Article 5(1) of the GDO only requires an outline application to include 'a plan sufficient to indentify the land to which it relates'.

7.97 Present position. The GDO adds, however, that applicants will sometimes need to submit 'such other plans and drawings as are necessary to describe the development'. And here the confusion arises. No one is certain whether these additions form part of the application or are mere illustrations of what it might or could look like. The situation could be made clearer by requiring that the plans and drawings establish the scale and impact of the development.

7.98 'Outline' to be strictly interpreted. I therefore suggest that it should be a strict rule that only the site plan should form part of the application. An applicant would be at liberty to submit other plans or drawings, but if he did so his application would automatically cease to be an outline application. Instead it would constitute an 'illustrative application'.

(e) Illustrative applications

7.99 There are many applications which the LPA can better assess if, for instance, details of layout and landscaping, and perhaps some indication of elevational treatment, accompany them. Such applications are neither truly 'outline' nor fully 'detailed'. An amendment to the GDO should recognise them as a separate type of application.

7.100 The plans should form part of the application and the present practice of having illustrative plans of uncertain status should be discontinued. The extent to which the permission will be tied to particular plans will be at the discretion of the authority and must be made clear in the permission.

7.101 Flexibility by LPAs in handling detailed applications needs to be balanced against the public's right to see constructed the kind of building the original application led it to expect, together with the kind of layout, character and scale of landscaping originally proposed.

(f) Detailed

7.102 Detailed applications. These would remain very much what they are now: approval of all building plans.

7.103 Flexibility in approval of details. Generally where the consent was to an outline or illustrative application and no Article 5 Direction was made, the applicant can reasonably expect detailed approval as a matter of course. This is why I recommend 42 days as the normal period for approval. Where an application has been transferred to Class B 3 months should be allowed.

7.104 Speedy decisions. All LPAs should hesitate before refusing approval of detail. No deemed permissions are suggested but the applicant can reasonably expect some flexibility in dealing with detailed approvals.

(h) Guideline

7.105 Guideline applications. The fourth type of application I propose is also new. It would serve to produce for an applicant guidance on likely permitted use in the future of a given site or area of land. Applicants would resort to it where no local plan gave sufficiently up to date or sufficiently detailed guidance. Guideline consent would not, however, commit the authority to approve any particular application.

7.106 Difficulties with outline applications. Outline applications no longer serve all the needs they were designed to. A prospective applicant should be able to ask the LPA for an answer in principle as to the use of a given site or the policies it will apply. The present procedure raises certain difficulties. For instance, lack of an Industrial Development Certificate may prevent an LPA from considering an outline application (other than under s. 72 of the 1971 Act, a special provision). An applicant can, it is true, to some extent get round this difficulty by submitting a layout of the site with roads, drains and sewers, simply in order to establish whether the LPA will accept this kind of development. But it is an artificial and cumbersome exercise. Where the law requires an office development permit, there appears to be virtually no method of obtaining the LPA's answer in principle.

7.107 Other difficulties. More is at stake, however. The Confederation of British Industry points out that its members need long-term planning policies to be clearly sign-posted to guide their expansion plans. But (quite apart from difficulties with IDCs and ODPs) an outline application inevitably raises immediate land-use problems – its effects on present road capacity and present employment levels, for instance. This is because an outline permission constitutes an immediate permission. An LPA cannot grant a 'delayed-effect' consent: in law such a postponing condition makes the whole consent invalid.

7.108 Need for longer-term commitment. Yet what many industrialists and others are seeking is not permission to develop here and now, but rather a clear indication of the LPA's intentions for a particular site for the future – an explicit public commitment in favour of certain kinds of development in (say) five or ten years' time. This absence of a full framework of structure and local plans makes this lack an acute one.

7.109 A practical answer. Some LPAs have met this difficulty by stating in a letter to the applicant their view that a stated use will probably be permitted. This does not, of course, commit the LPA to grant any specific application, and the risk remains that it will change its mind. But such a letter should in practice give the longer-term guidance industry says it needs. I do not think more can be expected.

7.110 Guideline decisions. I therefore recommend that this practice should receive statutory recognition in the GDO. The document expressing such Guideline decisions might be called a *'Future Development Certificate'*. It would state (to borrow the language of S.17(A) of the 1961 Land Compensation Act) what permission 'is likely to be granted', but would make clear that subsequent refusal of permission gives no right to compensation.

7.111 Premature and 'Isolated' applications. LPAs would also have power to give such a certificate in response to Outline or Hybrid applications. They could, for instance, do so where they considered the application premature, or on the grounds that they could not decide on the development of a particular site in isolation. Appeals from certificate would follow the normal planning appeals procedure.

7.112 Justification for Guideline process. Guideline applications and decisions would, admittedly, introduce yet another mechanism into an already complex planning process. But it would make long-term planning for vital social needs, such as housing or employment, that much easier and more effective. I therefore believe it is worthwhile.

[B] AMENDMENT OF APPLICATIONS

7.113 Local planning authority's power to amend applications. Inability to amend applications is probably one of the worst causes of delay at all stages. Sometimes, even though the local planning authority has approved the principle of the proposed development, it cannot accept the detailed plans. Local planning authorities should therefore have power, when considering an application, to grant a consent different from that asked for. But such variation in the terms of a consent should require the applicant's agreement.

7.114 Saving of time. This power to vary consents could save much time and effort. At present if an applicant asks consent for 20 houses and the committee would be prepared to give him 15, he must re-submit his application. Why should he need to go through the whole process again? Agreed amendments to planning applications would save both applicants and planning authority much time and trouble.

7.115 Amendment by applicant. Fairness and logic similarly demand that the applicant should have the chance to amend his application. Most authorities allow this, of course, because in the long run it promises to save them time and to prevent repetitious applications. But to restrain applicants from making amendments *ad nauseam*, there must be some conditions.

7.116 Conditions for changes. The following conditions are, I think, appropriate: (1) the development proposed should be of the same general nature as in the original application; (2) the amended application would only be valid after receiving the same standard publicity as the original application. This would only postpone the decision by the 21 days following the appropriate notification.

[C] CHARGING FOR APPLICATIONS

7.117 A charge for planning applications. My Interim Report suggested tentatively (para. 2.19) that local planning authorities should levy a money charge on all planning applications. This has provoked much discussion.

7.118 Arguments against a charge. The main argument against is the difficulty of finding a suitable scale of charge, both reasonably fair and not too complex to administer; such a charge could in theory relate to the floor space of the proposed development. Alternatively the individual should not have to pay to develop his own land. Control is for the good of the community who therefore should bear the cost of the planning process, the time and work involved in processing contentious applications. The system would be expensive and complex to run. Probably it would not justify its introduction.

7.119 System could be simple. I do however believe there is a strong case for introducing a stamp duty or similar standard charge. This could be at two levels: a standard of perhaps £5-£10 charge for Class A applications, and £50 for Class B. Such a standard fee would not be complicated or expensive to administer and would provide hard-pressed local planning authorities with a small (but no doubt welcome) extension of revenue. A sliding scale might yield significantly more and should be investigated. A more widely held view is that charges should be £5 for Class A applications, £10 for Class B. But then objection is made that revenue would scarcely cover check-in costs. Some exercises have been carried out and indicate that the benefits would be worth while. At least one leading property company strongly favoured a substantial charge. It will be for regulations to provide for appropriate adjustments in the case of transfers.

7.120 Income for local planning purposes. I stress that any revenue from such a charging system should go to the local planning authority and be earmarked for planning purposes, perhaps for the much-needed planning aid centres.

SECTION VIII: EFFECT OF NEW PROCEDURES ON APPEALS

(a) A & B and transferred cases.

7.121 Applicants should enjoy a right of appeal to the Secretary of State as follows:

Class A cases: (i) against refusal of consent;

              (ii) against conditions attached to an express consent.

Class B cases: (i) against refusal of consent, or conditions;

              (ii) on failure of the LPA to decide the application within the time limit, i.e. (a) within six months of receiving the application, if an impact statement is required (b) otherwise, within three months.

7.122 Amendments of GDO. The creation of automatic 'deemed consents' for Class A cases will still leave a need for a residual right of appeal against conditions attached to express consents. For Class B cases, the only changes in the law required would extend the period for decision from two months (GDO Art 7(3)) to three months, or six months in impact statement cases. Art. 16 may also require amendment as to other time limits, e.g. for submission of documents etc.*

7.123 Class A Cases. Class A application can only have one of the following four results:
(1) **Express consent** (to which the LPA would almost always attach conditions);
(2) **Refusal;**
(3) **Transfer.** (The applicant receives notice, within 28 days of the LPA receiving his application, of its transfer to Class B.)
(4) **Deemed consent.** (If none of the above (1), (2) or (3) occurs within 42 days, the application is deemed permitted.)

7.124 Possible appeal against transfer. Some planning officers might be tempted to transfer cases to Class B unnecessarily, thus causing additional delay and, in the absence of a decision, shifting responsibility on to the Secretary of State. If this happened on any scale, it might provoke demands for an appeal against transfer. Such an appeal would, however, be self-defeating; the appeal procedure itself would cause delay. I do not therefore recommend it.

* Articles 5, 6, 7, and 16 of the General Department Order 1973 are set out in Appendix IIBi.

(b) Costs on appeal from deemed refusal

7.125 In Class B cases there may be a tendency to take the line of least resistance, make no decision, and wait for an appeal. Sometimes the LPA will have good reasons for not deciding the application. These should then become clear in the discussion to which the applicant would have a statutory right (para. 7.59, 7.81).

7.126 In other cases, however, there may be no such good and convincing reason and delay in coming to a decision forces an applicant to appeal. If he succeeds, it seems only right that an order for costs against the LPA should follow as a matter of course.

7.127 Where, however, the LPA acted responsibly in delaying a decision, and explained its reasons to the applicant, the Secretary of State should normally award no costs.

(c) Reference by agreement

7.128 In a few exceptional cases, the LPA may want a decision to be taken by the Secretary of State. They will include applications which raise policy issues that the authority does not feel competent to decide, or which require long and detailed investigation better carried out on a national basis. This procedure should not of course be used by a local authority to avoid an unpopular decision.

7.129 The Secretary of State's existing power to call in cases for his own decision provides one way of dealing with such cases. But if an applicant and a local authority agree that the Secretary of State's decision is needed, they should be able to plan from an early stage with this in mind.

7.130 I therefore suggest a separate 'reference by agreement' procedure, activated by the LPA rather than the Secretary of State and applicable to a wider range of cases than those normally dealt with under the 'call-in' procedure.

7.131 The LPA should not, initiate this 'reference by agreement' until it and the applicant have satisfied all appropriate publicity and consultation requirements (para. 7.29).

SECTION IX: POLICY AS TO DESIGN CONTROL

(a) Should it be retained?

7.132 **Case for abolition.** Strong arguments can be advanced for abolishing aesthetic control by planning authorities over the design of proposed buildings. As I said in my Interim Report, such design control is an extremely subjective matter. Another stormy argument concerns the LPA's competence to sit in judgment on design questions. Why, it is asked, should lay members of a planning committee, or officers who are surveyors or land use planners by training, be able to decide the fate on aesthetic grounds of proposals drawn up by a qualified architect?

7.133 **Arguments for retention.** The temptation to recommend abolishing or streamlining the approval of details is therefore strong. I reject it, however, for the following reasons:

(1) **A useful tool.** Approval of 'reserved matters' relating to design goes far wider than those matters within the special knowledge of architects. For example, planning committees and officers are well qualified to judge questions of site layout and landscaping. A builder's layout often concentrates on maximum density rather than good planning; and it is also said that some highly experienced architects lack real understanding of

required standards of access and road design. There control over detail can be a positive planning tool: it can (and often does) objectively improve a development proposal.

(2) **'Deemed consent' inappropriate.** A system of deemed consents for design detail might at first appear attractive, but I conclude that it is not appropriate. Lack of objection to design detail tells the LPA nothing, since no publicity procedures exist for reserved matters. Nor do I suggest any (although I have suggested that interested parties may sometimes usefully ask the LPA at the outline stage for an Article 5(1) Direction).

(3) **'Illiterate' design.** Sometimes design proposals are visually illiterate. A strong case exists for retaining design control at least to prevent or improve such proposals.

(4) **Qualification no guarantee.** Architectural qualifications by no means guarantee that their holder will always produce, even in aesthetic terms, an acceptable design. Two decades of postwar development furnish only too many examples of buildings designed by qualified (and even illustrious) architects which have had a visually disastrous effect on their surroundings. In such cases design detail often either causes, or contributes substantially to, the visual damage.

(b) Delays

7.134 **Delays to house-builders.** House-builders, however, often have good reason to resent delays to their detailed applications. Control is in practice generally exercised by laymen, whose ill-founded pernicketiness may be out of all proportion to a detail's importance. Parkinson's Law applies here: the committee which swallows an outsize camel may strain inordinately at the gnat of detail.

7.135 **Use of specialist advice.** Councils should make much more use of outside specialist advice. The time has come to break down their traditional resistance to it (see also paras. 7.142 – 7.145 below).

7.136 **Unreasonable delays.** But that in itself will not necessarily reduce delays. Even in the 'best' areas, well-documented examples exist of unreasonable delays in dealing with design detail. The cost of these delays is often extremely serious, and the harm caused out of all proportion to the improvements to be expected from protracted consideration.

7.137 **Speeding approval of detail.** We therefore need ways of ensuring that all LPAs take swift decisions on design detail. I make two suggestions:

(a) The time limits for decisions on reserved matter of design detail should be 42 days in all cases unless a longer period is stipulated in the outline permission with reasons (see below), or the period is extended by consent. Clearly, there would be complicated cases in which consent ought only to be granted after careful consideration. The Secretary of State would take this into account in any award of costs.

(b) In most A and B cases there is no reason why the seemingly short period of 42 days should not be met. But the local authority (or the Secretary of State) is the best judge as to when this is impracticable for any good reason. No clear general rule can be laid down. For example, in impact study cases all the plans may have been discussed by the time an outline permission is granted, but a cottage in a conservation village may require reference to an Advisory Panel. I suggest that the law be amended to give

81

the planning authority the power to stipulate in a permission an extended period for approval of details, not exceeding 3 months for Class B cases and six months for impact study cases. All appeals on design detail should be transferred to Inspectors and dealt with by one of the architect members of the Department's inspectorate, almost always by written representations. He will have the power to amend the plans subject to appropriate publicity. If necessary the Inspector would hold an informal A type inquiry (see paras. 11.26 – 11.31) to agree his amendments.

7.138 **Appeals to the Secretary of State.** On matters of design detail appeals are and should in any event remain very much the exception. A successful appeal should almost always be followed by the award of appeal costs to the applicant, at least in cases where the refusal was not supported by objective specialist advice. I am afraid the award of 'damages' for delay to the development is not at present feasible.

(c) Local or National Design Guidance

7.139 **Local design guidance.** But we also need constructive measures to improve design standards, which the public often justifiably criticise. It would be wrong to give the impression that all LPAs are insensitive to design. On the contrary some have produced admirable design guidance. This may be of two kinds:

(1) **Design guides** set out overall design criteria, often for a given homogeneous area. They may indicate what kinds of design the LPA will not accept or, more positively, set out overall design criteria which it would like to see developers follow. These may cover such points as acceptable heights, densities and materials.

(2) **Design briefs** relate to a particular site, often relating to major sites to be comprehensively developed with the local authority's support, and may often be prepared jointly by it and the developer's consultants. The need for design briefs in development of 'Community Land' and large local authority projects is especially important. (Kent County Council's design brief for its Walderslade development is one of many examples.)

7.140 **Advantages of clear guidance.** A clear design guide or design brief enables an architect to design knowing what the LPA prefers. It should thus frequently save the time and effort spent on modifying a completed design in the face of criticism by a committee or its officers.

7.141 **Revision of Policy Note.** Central government can also help to obviate delays and misunderstandings. The Department issued its Development Control Policy Note No. 10 about a decade ago. It needs bringing up to date, and thereafter should be revised as policy changes demand. This is a matter of some priority to which I hope it will be possible to devote professional manpower. I make the following comments on its present text. It primarily addresses LPA officers indicating the factors they should consider when dealing with applications. If it said more about what design standards should be, applicants and their advisers would find it more helpful. I appreciate that it would be neither feasible nor right to dictate standards for the whole country. A policy note can, however, comment on the design guides so far produced, commending those which the Department considers examples worth following.

7.142 **Independent tribunal.** S.50 of the Town and Country Planning Act 1971 provides for appeals, on matters of external appearance and design, to an independent tribunal. Where they constitute the only issue I strongly suggest that the Secretary of State uses this procedure, at least on an experimental basis, as an alternative to the procedure recommended above (para 7.128).

7.143 **Design advice.** Quite apart from the need for an independent tribunal on design matters, there are of course such bodies as the Royal Fine Art Commission, whose advice to local authorities and applicants in formulating their proposals is invaluable.

7.144 **Conservation Area Committees.** These, however, are not as widespread nor as well used as they ought to be. Circular 61/68*, para 21 enjoined LPAs to establish Conservation Area Advisory Committees. Circular 147/74† repeated the plea. But so far in the 332 districts of England and Wales with more than 3,200 conservation areas, a mere 45 such committees have been established. This performance is lamentable.

7.145 **General advisory committees.** Some counties enjoy recourse for more general design advice to Architectural Advisory Panels, of which there are now some 50–60. Most are for counties, some for districts, but their coverage and the use made of them is patchy. Some counties have no such advisory committee, others several. Some committees advise on as many as 10,000 cases each year, others receive only four or five cases for their comments. At a time when planning control is under intense strain and suffers from scarcity of skilled manpower, LPAs could and should make more use of this valuable outside source of expert advice.

7.146 **Enhancement schemes.** The Town and Country Amenities Act 1974, Section 1 seeks to encourage schemes for the preservation and enhancement of conservation areas. We should also encourage LPAs to prepare such schemes for town centres and other areas of need or potential. The keynote should be positive conservation: a skilful mixture of preservation, sympathetic infilling, and improvement of surroundings.

7.147 **Need to implement Act.** The new Section 277 of the 1971 Act‡ which promotes such schemes has not yet been implemented because of economic circumstances. Any but a short deferment may, however, prove a false economy. Such schemes as it seeks to encourage are vital to the success both of conservation and of constructive public involvement. The Secretary of State should implement Section 277 as soon as resources permit.

7.148 **Details in local authority developments.** Regulations should provide for specified applications by local authorities for approval of details on sensitive developments to be made to the Secretary of State.§

SECTION X: LOCAL AUTHORITY PRACTICE AND PROCEDURE

(a) Generally: priority treatment

7.149 **Difficulties about priority.** My Interim Report recognised the unpopularity of giving some cases priority. There were two main features: that it would lead to queue-jumping, with all the resentment that can provoke; and that too many claims for priority would make the exercise self-defeating.

*Welsh Office Circular 57/68.
†Welsh Office Circular 220/74.
‡Introduced by Section 1 of the Town and Country Amenities Act 1974.
§cf Section 7 of the Town and Country Amenities Act 1974 which provides for corresponding regulations dealing with listed building consents.

7.150 **Existing priority treatment.** At the appeal stage, housing cases already receive some priority. Major industrial applications and appeals are also given priority (DOE Circular 30/72, Welsh Office Circular 68/72).

7.151 **Priority treatment should be exceptional.** In recent months, the numbers of applications have fallen: the problem now seems less urgent. This Final Report therefore seeks a system which works simply and smoothly. It demands that we keep exceptions to the very minimum. I therefore propose only two rare and limited circumstances for priority treatment. They are:

7.152 (i) **Hardship cases.** These are difficult to define, but I have in mind personal hardship, which could be physical or could be financial. Homelessness would constitute hardship; so might circumstances where refusal of a change of use of part of a building could force a business to close.

7.153 (ii) **Cases of major national importance.** This second priority category must include projects of national urgency, for instance, at the present time proposals for building an oil storage depot or the opening of a new coalfield with resultant gains to the balance of payments.

7.154 **Emergency treatment.** Such cases would be given continuous and absolute priority at every stage from the initial application onwards and including any appeal. I suggest that the district planning officer should have discretion to certify cases as being of exceptional importance requiring emergency treatment. Everything would be done to ensure a speedy decision, including perhaps some curtailment of time limits. Objectors in major cases who found difficulty in meeting these should receive financial and committee help to prepare their cases.

7.155 **Very much the exception.** But priority cases would be very much the exception. Some applications would clearly, whatever the LPA's resources, demand such treatment. These apart, the practicality of treating a given application as a priority case would depend on local circumstances: on the ability of the LPA's officers and committees to give genuine priority treatment. Some authorities dealing with thousands of applications a year may well be able, if the need arises, to give true priority treatment to 20 or 30 hardship or nationally important cases; the resources of another LPA may limit the number to single figures.

7.156 **Flexible system.** I therefore suggest a flexible system of priority cases. The GDO should be amended to provide for special treatment of these wholly exceptional applications, but it need set out no specific rules, leaving implementation to local discretion.

(b) Relations between counties and districts in handling applications

7.157 **Two main problems.** The handling of applications presents two main problems that are critical: (1) the division of responsibility between districts and counties; and (2) manpower.

7.158 **Division of responsibility.** Some critics assert that local government reorganisation has produced chaos in planning control. Paper work, they say, has snowballed and much time and energy been wasted in in-fighting between the two tiers. Such struggles are futile. We have neither time nor energy to waste in squabbles as to the niceties of who does what. We must concentrate on making the system work.*

---

*In some counties there are greater difficulties in arranging in development plan schemes the responsibility for local plans.

84

7.159 **Demarcation difficulties.** The Local Government Act 1972 did at least avoid the worst rigidities of the London reorganisation a decade earlier. Serious difficulties still arise in some counties. Former county boroughs sometimes find it difficult to accept that they no longer control strategic policy; some county planning authorities find it equally hard to remember that district councils now exercise extensive planning functions in their own right rather than by delegation. Sometimes clash of personalities is the cause rather than any lack of Whitehall guidance.

7.160 **Can good sense overcome difficulties?** These difficulties must be overcome. We can afford neither money nor manpower for duplication of effort or the building into the system of internal conflicts. Where there are delays there should be continuous re-appraisal of development control schemes to simplify them where possible and iron out unnecessary conflicts. Monitoring of delays (see para 7.30) should indicate when this is necessary.

7.161 **District Planning Officers' choice.** It seems right that the person responsible for making the distinction between county and district matters should have a discretion. Any attempt to lay down nationally a strict interpretation of paragraph 32 of Schedule 16 of the Local Government Act 1972 would be bound to fail. On the other hand, a district planning officer's interpretations should be written down so that he and his staff can apply them consistently.

7.162 **County policies.** Every development control scheme should either incorporate or refer to a 'statement of county planning policies', covering the matters regarded as 'county matters' for the purposes of paragraph 32. It should be the product of consultation between county and district.

7.163 **Publication.** I can see no reason why development control schemes, including documents relating to their interpretation, should not be published.

7.164 **Agency arrangements.** I would strongly support the advice given in DOE Circular 74/73. District councils, it urged, should handle applications involving such minor 'county matters' for the county on an agency basis. I know at least one county where this happens, and warmly commend the practice.

7.165 **Joint county/district groups.** Where, however, the county does not give districts the power to decide 'county matters', another practice which some authorities have adopted offers an alternative. Joint county/district groups meet to settle the disputes which must from time to time arise as to what is or is not a county matter. LPAs should however keep cross-consultation between county and districts on individual cases to the minimum.

7.166 **Public consultation.** I would urge that LPAs settle locally which authority should carry out public consultation, including consultation with other public authorities and undertakings. They should also take care to spell out the resulting arrangements clearly.

7.167 **Reserved matters.** When the county council has granted outline consent for a development, it should nevertheless normally be the district which decides the detailed application or settles any reserved matters. The impact of outline consent may be on the county as a whole; it is local people who have to live with the detailed design.

7.168 **Delegation to officers.** The terms on which an LPA delegates powers and functions to officers need setting out with clarity. I should like them to follow the practice I advocate in para 7.175 below.

7.169 **Individual tasks.** For the system to work efficiently, individual members of an LPA's staff also need to know how their tasks fit into the chain and the amount of time they have to perform them. Explicit deadlines and optimum times can help the efficient handling of applications.

(c) **Within authorities: Staff**

7.170 **A continuing shortage of planners.** We can expect no early and substantial increase in the number of qualified planning staff employed by local authorities. On the contrary, impending legislation on Community Land together with present economic difficulties will probably impose a heavier workload. LPAs cannot expect to fill all the many vacancies in the increased establishments resulting from reorganisation.

7.171 **Priorities in use of staff.** On the other hand, without substantially more staff directed to it, public involvement cannot continue at its present level. Something must suffer. Planning officers must try to balance resources against priorities. In this process plan-making and providing land for nationally important development must claim very high priority. It is now generally accepted that wherever possible professional planners should divide their time between plan-making and planning control.

7.172 **Using administrative staff.** Because of the shortage of qualified planners, LPAs may need to entrust more development control work to unqualified staff. (The TUC urged this course.) They will need special training for such tasks, and this can be provided as part of the wider staff training needed to implement the Government's proposals on land. There is also scope, for instance, in enforcement procedure, for greater co-operation with other Departments.

(d) **Within authorities: Meetings**

7.173 **Diversity of practice.** LPAs' diversity of practice in dealing with planning applications matches the surprising variety of ways in which committees and officers work. One explanation holds that this diversity reflects differing local needs and conditions. I am not convinced by the argument. Practice seems on the contrary frequently to be founded on mere habit or unquestioning tradition. I can discover no logical reason why the planning committee of one compact London Borough is unable to meet more than once every two months, whereas that of one district council in a far flung rural area manage without too much difficulty to meet once a fortnight.

7.174 **Code of practice.** Some variation is indeed needed to reflect local conditions. Nonetheless LPAs may be glad to have a national code of practice to guide them. I have been unable to find any reason why the practice of the more efficient authorities should not be followed much more widely.

(e) **Delegation**

7.175 **Delegation.** Similar divergences occur in the degree of delegation to officers and committees. Why should one council withhold power to make decisions even from the full planning committee, another delegate 70% of planning decisions to its officers? Members should be strongly encouraged to delegate decisions to officers or small sub-committees. It has been suggested that the decisions should be reported to the planning committee for critical appraisal, but not for review.

7.176 **Increasing acceptance.** The principle of delegation to sub-committees or officers is rapidly gaining general acceptance. The Local Government Act 1972,

S. 101, apparently prevents delegation to a single member of a planning committee. At least two members must make a decision. On the whole, I think this is sound. A committee can empower its chairman to make decisions subject to ratification.

7.177 Need for delegation. Except in London, councils almost everywhere now accept delegation. So do many professional bodies. We should encourage it further, but not force it on LPAs. Delegation of Class A applications is fundamental to this report. Planning committees should entrust them either to small sub-committees of two or three members or, better, to officers.

7.178 The corruption argument. The sole argument advanced against delegation seems to be that it lays members and officers open to suspicion of corruption. Yet many districts already delegate all minor matters to officers without any evidence of such suspicions causing trouble. It should be sufficient for decisions to be subject to systematic, critical review. This will ensure that delegated decisions are in accordance with the council's policy. Some councils may prefer to ratify the officers' decisions for a limited time after delegation while gaining experience of this procedure.

7.179 Whatever course an LPA prefers, the essential aim of delegation remains the same: to free most of the planning committee's members for its main task of deciding policy and handling major or particularly significant applications.

7.180 Sifting applications. Some committees deal with large numbers of applications, others with very few. This by itself is not significant. Some LPAs star or otherwise identify the controversial applications; the committee passes the rest 'on the nod'. There need be no single, standard procedure. It occurs to me, however, that decisions requiring mere formal approval might be grouped together and dealt with by a single resolution.

7.181 Concentrating on significant decisions. The principle must be that committees concentrate their time and attention on controversial or other important applications. Some district councils are obsessed with trivia. Local councillors are often under great pressure from constituents who expect them to take a personal interest in small planning applications.

7.182 Distinguishing the significant from the trivial. There are, of course, cases where a detail like the design of a bay window in a conservation area merits serious attention. If it has time to spare, the committee should look at these. They are not trivial. But some committees devote excessive time or give priority to trivial or detailed matters and keep house builders waiting for approval for large sites. That we should not tolerate. No managerial study is needed to cure it. All such planning committees lack is a commonsense set of priorities. Fortunately they are a minority.

(e) How planning committees should operate.

7.183 The lot of the elected member. The elected member of a local authority has in many ways the most unrewarding job in public life. Hours are inconvenient; his financial sacrifice in most cases considerable; active membership of the planning committee is in many districts almost a full-time job, making it difficult or impossible for him to pursue his normal work. For all this, he receives little recognition – only a barrage of criticism and complaints. Nevertheless if there are planning delays committees must meet more often (7.173).

7.184 Site visits. One complaint is that planning committee members seldom visit the sites of the proposed development which they are to consider. Elected members claim that they know the area. Site visits, they assume, are rarely necessary. I acknowledge that local knowledge may in many cases suffice; also that some planning committees (though very few) do make site visits whenever the case requires it. I must also accept that we cannot expect members to visit sites in other than exceptional cases. That would be impracticable. It does seem to me, however, that when members find it difficult to decide an application, a site visit would often be particularly appropriate and helpful.

7.185 **Admission of press: statutory requirements.** The Local Government Act 1972, Section 100, requires local authorities to admit press and public to meetings both of the full council and its main committees. They can by resolution exclude public and press from any part of the proceedings they consider confidential.

7.186 **Admission of press to other meetings.** At first I took the view that having the press present at all committee and sub-committee meetings would cause great difficulty. The presence of the press would, I thought, prevent members from discussing an application freely with their officers. Perhaps members would tend more to support an officer's recommendations merely to protect his prestige.

7.187 **Non-admission as an exception.** I still believe that in certain cases the press are better excluded. Where, for instance, the planning committee delegates Class A cases to two or three members, the intention is that they should deal very speedily with minor, unopposed applications. The presence of the press would hinder the informality and efficiency of such meetings.

7.188 **Presence of press beneficial.** In general, however, the presence of the press helps rather than hinders. Experience shows that planning committees can deal efficiently with even the more controversial applications with press and public present. Indeed in some respects an audience helps: it makes for a livelier atmosphere and a sense of urgency.

7.189 **Closed meetings: publicising decisions.** Where, however, a planning committee or sub-committee does meet in private, the public will often wish to know what it decided and also why. The local planning authority should move that information be made available both to public and press.

7.190 **Publication of officers' reports.** I have been encouraged to recommend that officers' reports in particular should be published after the closed meetings at which they are presented or even before the meeting. This is already the practice in some local authorities, and apparently works well.

7.191 **Press facilities.** Whether a committee or sub-committee meets in public or private, press and public may want to know what it is deciding. They have a right to know, and the local planning authority should help, not hinder, them in this. It should make available all ancillary papers needed for the proper understanding of the committee's discussions or decisions.

SECTION XI: REVOCATION OF PLANNING PERMISSION

7.192 There are complaints by the public that a wrong decision has been made and that they have not had enough notice of the application to make adequate representations. Mistakes do occur and revocation of permission is a remedy for it. But planning authorities are deterred because a revocation order may cause hardship even where compensation is paid. Further, the amount of compensation payable is often prohibitive.

7.193 Compensation may be claimed for:

(*a*) abortive expenditure, and

(*b*) loss or damage, including depreciation in the value of the interest in the land, as a result of the loss of planning permission.

7.194 Compensation will have to continue to be paid for abortive expenditure. Should it always be paid for loss of planning permission?

7.195 To put the problem in perspective there are only some 50 opposed orders a year (unopposed orders, thought to be in the majority, generally do not result in compensation). About five years ago it was estimated that payment for revocation and other compensation under the 1962 Planning Act totalled some £200,000 a year. But if no compensation for loss of development value is paid there may be many more revocation orders.

7.196 The reasons given for removing compensation for loss of development are:

(i) any loss in the value of an interest in land is purely notional;

(ii) a decision to revoke a planning permission should be made on planning grounds. The liability to pay compensation should not be a deterrent to the proper exercise of planning powers.

7.197 The arguments against are based mainly on anomalies and hardship which could result:—

(i) the loss suffered by those who had raised loans on the security of the value of their interest in the land with the benefit of the planning permission;

(ii) losses suffered by people who had bought land at an enhanced value through having the benefit of planning permission and who then faced a diminution in their capital investment;

(iii) liabilities for estate duty where an owner died after obtaining planning permission but before developing or selling the land and whose successors might have to pay estate duty on a high value which might be removed by a revocation without compensation;

(iv) planning permissions now lapse after five years if development has not commenced and so authorities have an opportunity to reconsider the matter when renewals are applied for.

Two reviews conducted by the Department in the last few years concluded in favour of no change.

7.198 I do not think that those arguments are overriding and cannot be met by skilful drafting and suitable exceptions. However, during the transitional period under the Land proposals* market value will still remain the basis for compensation and inconsistency will arise if it were removed in this one case. In the ultimate phase of the scheme when current use value is the basis for all transactions compensation for revocation will presumably no longer include the loss of development value.

7.199 Nevertheless, there may well be a case in the interim period for exclusion of compensation for loss of development value where a permission was granted through an oversight in a Category A application, or where the statutory or other publicity requirements have not been complied with and there is a risk of serious injury to the amenity of the neighbourhood. The order, however, must be made within a specified time of the date permission was granted, say 3 months.

7.200 I cannot express a concluded view on this in advance of publication of the Bill on Community Land, but commend it for consideration.

*'Land' Cmnd. 5730 HMSO September 1974.

ANNEX TO CHAPTER 7

TIMETABLE FOR PROCESSING APPLICATION

Class A applications

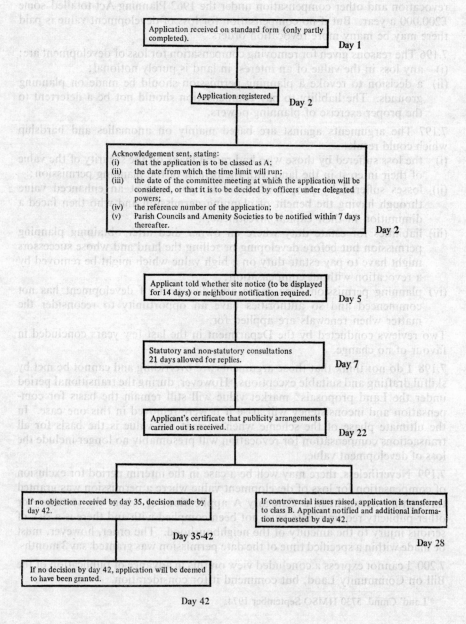

Application received on standard form (only partly completed).

Day 1

Application registered.

Day 2

Acknowledgement sent, stating:
(i)   that the application is to be classed as A;
(ii)   the date from which the time limit will run;
(iii)   the date of the committee meeting at which the application will be considered, or that it is to be decided by officers under delegated powers;
(iv)   the reference number of the application;
(v)   Parish Councils and Amenity Societies to be notified within 7 days thereafter.

Day 2

Applicant told whether site notice (to be displayed for 14 days) or neighbour notification required.

Day 5

Statutory and non-statutory consultations 21 days allowed for replies.

Day 7

Applicant's certificate that publicity arrangements carried out is received.

Day 22

If no objection received by day 35, decision made by day 42.

Day 35-42

If controversial issues raised, application is transferred to class B. Applicant notified and additional information requested by day 42.

Day 28

If no decision by day 42, application will be deemed to have been granted.

Day 42

90

TIMETABLE FOR PROCESSING APPLICATION

Class B applications

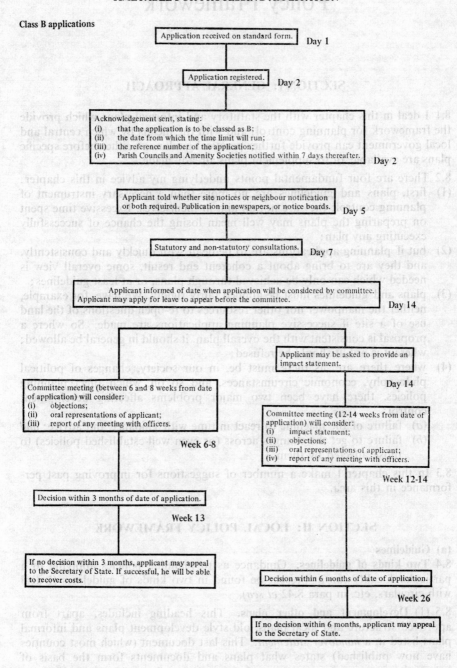

Application received on standard form. **Day 1**

Application registered. **Day 2**

Acknowledgement sent, stating:
(i)   that the application is to be classed as B;
(ii) the date from which the time limit will run;
(iii) the reference number of the application;
(iv) Parish Councils and Amenity Societies notified within 7 days thereafter. **Day 2**

Applicant told whether site notices or neighbour notification or both required. Publication in newspapers, or notice boards. **Day 5**

Statutory and non-statutory consultations. **Day 7**

Applicant informed of date when application will be considered by committee. Applicant may apply for leave to appear before the committee. **Day 14**

Applicant may be asked to provide an impact statement. **Day 14**

Committee meeting (between 6 and 8 weeks from date of application) will consider:
(i)   objections;
(ii) oral representations of applicant;
(iii) report of any meeting with officers. **Week 6-8**

Committee meeting (12-14 weeks from date of application) will consider:
(i)   impact statement;
(ii) objections;
(iii) oral representations of applicant;
(iv) report of any meeting with officers. **Week 12-14**

Decision within 3 months of date of application. **Week 13**

If no decision within 3 months, applicant may appeal to the Secretary of State. If successful, he will be able to recover costs.

Decision within 6 months of date of application. **Week 26**

If no decision within 6 months, applicant may appeal to the Secretary of State.

91

CHAPTER 8

Policy Framework

SECTION I: GENERAL APPROACH

8.1 I deal in this chapter with the statutory and informal plans which provide the framework for planning control; and with the means by which central and local government can provide further practical guidance – either before specific plans are available, or to supplement plans already made.

8.2 There are four fundamental points underlying my advice in this chapter:
(1) first, plans and guidelines are no more than a necessary instrument of planning control: they are not an aim in themselves. Excessive time spent on preparing the plans may well mean losing the chance of successfully executing any plan;
(2) but if planning applications are to be dealt with quickly and consistently, and they are to bring about a coherent end result, some overall view is needed which can only be achieved through plans, or at least guidelines;
(3) plans and guidelines must be applied fairly rigidly. We have, for example, neither the manpower nor other resources to re-open questions of the land use of a site if successive planning applications are made. So where a proposal is consistent with the overall plan, it should in general be allowed; where it is not, it should be refused;
(4) where there are, as there must be, in our society, changes of political philosophy, economic circumstances, and so on, which affect planning policies, there have been two major problems affecting development control:
    (*a*) failure of the machine to react in time with guidance and advice; *and*
    (*b*) failure to get the changes across (or even well-established policies) to those affected by them.

8.3 In this chapter I make a number of suggestions for improving past performance in this area.

SECTION II: LOCAL POLICY FRAMEWORK

(a) Guidelines
8.4 **Two kinds of guidelines.** Guidance as to planning policies applying to a particular locality can at present be found in two kinds of guidelines (I deal with circulars, etc. in para 8.42 *et seq*).

8.5 (1) **Development and other plans.** This heading includes, apart from approved structure and local plans, old style development plans and informal plans listed in a *handover statement*. This last document (which most counties have now published) states what plans and documents form the basis of planning control in the county. As they are approved, structure plans and the local plans which supplement them will largely constitute the guidelines.

8.6 (2) Guidelines for a particular locality or subject. Examples of guidelines for a locality include a "Proposal for the preservation and enhancement of a conservation area" (Town and Country Amenities Act 1974, s.3) and Informal Design Guide for a conservation area. Typical guidelines include design guides for residential areas such as that produced by Essex County Council.

(b) County Councils

8.7 Handover statements: county councils. To achieve coherent planning control, in the immediate future, all counties which have not done so should as to consultation with the districts (a) list plans and documents which ought to be used as a basis for planning control; (b) indicate to what extent each still applies; and (c) *State in each case the fundamental strategic policy the county expects to apply.*

8.8 District councils. Each district council should likewise produce a provisional statement of the main policies it expects to apply.

8.9 Filling the gap. The (to some extent unavoidable) delay in preparation and approval of structure and local plans leaves a gap. If handover statements are to fill it, they must (where they do not already exist) be available by mid-1975 at the latest.

(c) Local and Structure Plans

8.10 Towards a comprehensive and flexible system. Planning control in the immediate post-war years was difficult because of the absence initially of any development plans. Later when LPAs produced such plans, they tended to apply them too rigidly. Moreover, in many counties and county boroughs, by the time the Minister approved the plan it was already out of date.

8.11 Delays in plan making. Now the more flexible system of structure and local plans provided for by the Town and Country Planning Act 1968 is replacing the rigidities of the old system. Unfortunately (as pointed out in Ch. 3), in some places even structure plans will not be effective for another five years. Carrying the change completely and universally into effect will have taken at least 12 years from the date of legislation.

8.12 Importance of structure and local plans. These two types of plan form the twin bases on which planning control must rest. The new divided responsibility between counties and districts for both plan making and planning control adds a further complication. Any early change is, however, impracticable. We must devote our energies to making the system work as well as possible.

8.13 Need for speed. Speedy production of structure plans is crucial. Without them, district councils cannot complete local plans in the right context. Publication of local plans (produced as part of a programme agreed between district and county councils) should follow closely upon the structure plan's completion.

8.14 Local plans. These should, it is hoped, be ready almost everywhere within five years' time, and in most places considerably earlier. Schemes for the preservation and enhancement of town centres and other areas of special importance will form an important element in local plans.

8.15 Doubts about adoption procedure. I understand that no detailed firm procedure has yet been decided for the adoption of local plans. Will the county councils (as was widely assumed) simply certify that a local plan is consistent with the structure plan.

(d) Timetables for Structure and Local Plans

8.16 No statutory timetable. It is tempting to suggest a statutory timetable for the production of statutory plans. I resist that temptation. Experience of attempting to secure early production of plans by that means under the 1947 Act does not encourage such a course.

8.17 Continuous plan-making. Moreover, a statutory timetable might encourage the mistaken view that structure plans, once completed, need little or no amendment. A structure plan, if it is to serve effectively as a framework for planning control, cannot be static. On the contrary, most structure plans must constantly evolve with changing conditions. They therefore require ceaseless updating and modification. The modern approach to plan making sees it not as a finite but as a continuous process.

8.18 Need for a national programme. In some areas (though too few) the LPAs have made good progress in producing structure and, indeed, local plans. The development plan scheme which each county is required to prepare under s. 183(2) of the Local Government Act 1972 must include a programme for production of local plans. But these programmes vary greatly in form and in urgency.

8.19 Accordingly, although I reject the case for a statutory timetable, we urgently need a national programme for structure and local plan making; published by the Department, it would provide a yardstick against which LPAs could measure their progress. It should also help to concentrate the minds of the planners on those key issues that are the essence of structure planning.

8.20 Concentrating on key issues. A recent Departmental circular (98/74)* advised LPAs to "*concentrate on those issues which are of key structural importance*". Some counties still seem determined to prepare over-lengthy, elaborate and far too detailed structure plans. They miss the point of the whole exercise.

8.21 Dangers of too much detail. The points which should distinguish a structure plan from an old-style development plan are its brevity and its concentration on key strategic issues. Failure by LPAs to do this seriously threatens breakdown of the system and risks bringing structure plans into the same disrepute as the old-style development plans.

8.22 If a nationally produced and published timetable does no more than achieve compliance with the 'key issues' advice of the Circular, it will be amply justified.

(e) Applying the Guidelines

8.23 Presumption in favour of development. Where an up-to-date local plan exists, there should be a strong presumption in favour of any application which conforms with it. There should also be a presumption (though less strong) against an application which fails to conform. Thus conforming applications should usually gain the LPA's speedy consent.

8.24 "How to apply for planning permission". The quality of planning applications often falls below acceptable standards. When this occurs it can have a very significant effect on the time taken to process the application. It must be improved. We urgently need a simple guide "*How to apply for planning permission*". The Department has shown itself able to produce excellent booklets of this kind. It should produce this one with all possible speed.

---

*Welsh Office Circular 168/74.

8.25 **Local leaflets.** We urgently need also local editions or local addenda to such a booklet. This variant would add local and personal colour. It should, for instance, say who the district planning officer is, and outline his functions, and indicate to whom they should go for advice and assistance when they need it.

8.26 **Encouraging and preventing applications.** Such a leaflet should plainly state the realities of the planning control situation: e.g. that in this or that much treasured conservation area or village, the LPA has consistently refused all development applications and all appeals have failed. But it should equally add that elsewhere the authority will look sympathetically at good infilling proposals.

8.27 **Benefits.** I cannot usefully suggest a fixed set of rules for these local guidelines. I believe, however, that they have great potential – if kept short and simple.

(f) Filling the gap – Where no guidelines

8.28 **Old-style development plans.** These would be specified in handover statements (para 7.140). The inauguration of the new system of structure and local plans does not mean that we can automatically jettison the old development plans. Until the production of the new plans, each area will need to rely very substantially on the old. They, together with informal guidelines (prepared with full public participation) must fill the gap.

8.29 **Rigid application.** The public should be told, and must accept, that for minor or less controversial applications a reasonably up-to-date development plan will have to be applied with some rigidity. We must accept this for the sake of speed and certainty in the interim period before the production of structure plans.

8.30 **Not always out of date.** The old-style plans are not necessarily out of date. Some LPAs have brought them up to date informally, e.g. Hertfordshire in 'Hertfordshire 1981'. In other areas, both rural and sometimes urban, the old plans and old standards may still apply or at least be useful. But LPAs should indicate clearly which plans and policy statements represent their current planning policies, and why (see 7.140–2).

8.31 **Ad hoc planning.** During this transitional period there will often be no alternative to ad hoc planning where the old plans, even with the more up-to-date guidelines, do not provide a sufficiently clear policy framework for decision of applications with a major environmental impact or of long-term strategic significance.

8.32 **Call-in cases.** The Secretary of State will want to call in some cases for his own decision. In some major cases such as proposed oil refineries, hyper-markets and substantial housing developments in the countryside, the resultant public inquiry offers the most efficient way of securing a sound decision.

8.33 **Major local decisions with public participation.** In other instances even a decision of national importance may be better taken by the LPA after extensive public participation. Westminster City Council's approach to the future of Piccadilly in 1973 provides an example of this alternative. In choosing between this and the call-in procedure, LPAs should consult the Secretary of State as to which best fits a particular case.

8.34 **Public Inquiries.** In other major cases, refusal followed by appeal will ensure that a public inquiry considers the policy issues. Elsewhere the device of "reference by agreement" will achieve the same result.

8.35 All these procedures discussed in paragraphs 8.31 to 8.34 are elaborate but should provide policy guidance which can be used in preparation of statutory plans.

SECTION III: ACTION BY CENTRAL GOVERNMENT

Pilot Inquiries

8.36 **Advance policy decisions.** Sometimes what the circumstances really require is a decision on issues of planning policy in advance of decisions on specific applications. For instance where several competing applicants wish to build out of town or edge of town shopping centres, the sensible course is to decide first whether in principle the area needs one or more such centres.

8.37 I therefore suggest that the Secretary of State should sometimes appoint Pilot Inquiries to look at such policy issues in advance. This course would obviate repetitive inquiries into competing applications, all involving similar issues of principle.

8.38 **Circumstances of inquiry.** Such pilot inquiries might take place in a variety of circumstances. There might be simply one or more informal proposals for the kind of development in question; there might be one or more actual applications; or there might in other cases be one or more appeals from the LPA's refusal. In this last case, the broad issue of planning policy could be dealt with as a preliminary issue.

8.39 **Examination in public.** Such pilot inquiries *into* issues *of planning policy* would more appropriately use the "examination in public" procedure devised for structure plan inquiries. They would provide a much simpler alternative to the cumbersome Planning Inquiry Commission.

8.40 **Second-stage inquiries.** Once the Secretary of State has, with the help of the Pilot Inquiry, resolved the issues of planning policy, the field would be clear for ordinary local inquiries to consider the merits of any applications for particular sites.

8.41 **Powers and experience.** Section 282 of the 1971 Town and Country Planning Act gives the Secretary of State power which he could use to order such Pilot Inquiries. He would not need to do so more than occasionally. However, the Department's now considerable experience of holding examinations in public into structure plans should ensure that, where used, the Pilot Inquiry would prove a most effective method of resolving advance issues of planning policy.

8.42 **Clear up-to-date guidance** from central government is essential. Over the years the Department and its predecessor Ministries have published a plethora of circulars, bulletins and other publications relating to planning control. Some, of crucial importance, the Department has brought up to date. Others are obsolete and can only cause confusion. Guidance contained in some circulars is hedged with so many reservations and savings as to be capable of being read as meaning anything. It is very difficult to achieve a precision at the national level. But there are many circulars which have achieved this and best precedents must be followed. At least those writing circulars usually achieve greater clarity than legislators.

8.43 **Review of existing circulars.** The Department should first identify all circulars and other guidance which still apply, then consolidate them in a style which the public can readily understand. Development Control Policy Notes, which form the core of Departmental guidance, provide a good foundation to build on. Loose-leaf folders offer a convenient way of keeping such information up to date.

8.44 **Delays criticised.** Some critics claim that by the time the Department publishes a circular, the policy it deals with has changed. I doubt that. In many cases circulars command strict adherence for many years and gain the stature of rule of law. Circular 42/55 on Green Belts is a classic example.

8.45 **Need for prompt guidance.** Central government is not, however, always quick enough off the mark in giving guidance where it is needed. For instance, a change in government policy favouring the faster release of housing land took place in 1970. LPAs had to wait until 1972 for detailed official guidance on this (Circulars 102/72 and 122/73). It will both reduce delays and give planning a more stable basis if, in future, the Department communicates and explains more policies more promptly, even if this means less consultation in an attempt to reach a consensus.

8.46 **Need to reassure.** Formulating policy in a rapidly changing political and economic climate is not easy. Thus, even when policies remain unchanged, the public and LPAs need reassurance that an existing policy continues to apply.

8.47 **Early consolidation.** That is one reason why I most strongly suggest that the Department undertake a consolidation of published policy without delay. Now, when the pressure of applications and appeals is easing before the Community Land legislation takes effect, it has a golden opportunity to prune the obsolete, bring up to date what remains relevant, and put the whole into language the public can readily understand.

8.48 **No need to repeat consultation.** Much policy guidance demands previous consultation with local authorities. But where published advice is a restatement or digest of existing policies, the Department should not in the first place need to consult.

8.49 **Writing for the public.** DOE publicity is excellently produced but generally fails to reach a wider public. It is usually written to be read only by professionals. The Department should produce for the general public versions of the more important plans, policies and guidelines presented in a form they can understand.

8.50 One essential is a *regularly* published bulletin or news-sheet on planning. I urged this in my Interim Report as a shop-window on departmental thinking. I re-affirm this recommendation now. The Department should also publish important new circulars in shortened form for the general public. The Department itself provides first rate precedents for this.

8.51 **Desk Training Manual.** The Departmental Desk Training Manual prepared as a model for local authorities contains much valuable information based on long experience. It could be published for general use by LPAs and the general public.

8.52 **Need for planning control leaflet.** The Department has for many years used to good purpose a leaflet on appeal procedures. We urgently need a similar leaflet, equally clear and simple, on planning control.

8.53 **Lively and direct.** Some important professional organisations have pressed for publication of selected appeal decisions. These, however, tend to acquire the status of precedent – an approach foreign to planning. We need something livelier and closer to the Inspectorate and Regional Directorates, and more reflecting their views and experiences, than the cold letter of the decision on a particular site.

8.54 **Formula for a quarterly bulletin.** Some appeal decisions could usefully be published as illustrations of how the Secretary of State is applying current policy. But the main value of such a bulletin would be as intelligence from source, a direct indication from the Department of how it views the latest trends and events in planning. Statistics would teach one a little; explanations of circulars, sometimes of decisions, references to statements and questions in Parliament, dates of major inquiries, and topical news on (for example) the progress of structure and local plans – all these would be invaluable, and they are just examples.

8.55 **Clearing the air.** The public want above all to be assured that they know where they are in planning. Indirect, oblique or partial communication worries them. Regular and direct contact with the Department, such as this bulletin would provide, would clear the air.

8.56 **Forum for consultation needed.** The Department conducts extensive consultations on a wide range of subjects with local authorities, developers, the construction industry and some major amenity societies. But we lack a combined forum where they can all meet. The DOE needs regular face-to-face contacts with representatives of a wider public to keep its administrators in touch with everyday life, and perhaps also to dispel public suspicion that LPAs unduly have the ear of the Department.

8.57 **Planning Control Consultative Committee.** I therefore recommend the establishment of a Planning Control Consultative Committee, meeting regularly and drawn from, but not representing, all the interested groups I have mentioned. The membership could be changed each year to provide the Department with the greatest variety of views. The Development Control Review has brought forth many representatives of the public and private sectors, in addition to the Advisory Group, and their combined experience and interest should be allowed to make a continuing contribution.

8.58 **Failures of communication.** A thread of astonishment runs right through this report at the constant and serious failures of communication I have found. These occur even within the Department. But they are at their worst between central and local government and between both these and the public. There is no central body which brings representatives of all three together in one room.

8.59 **Encouraging consensus.** Selection would not be easy: the membership of such a standing committee should change constantly to keep up with changes in the interest groups it represents. However, one important lesson I have learned during this inquiry is this: once you overcome initial in-built suspicions, consensus on many issues is surprisingly readily achieved. It is on this potential for consensus that we must build.

8.60 **A composite view.** Some critics complain that almost all changes in planning policy in recent years have been sudden, jerky and to some extent too late. This criticism contains much truth. The Department diligently and lengthily consults many individual and disparate interest groups. What it lacks is a more rapid and composite reaction.

CHAPTER 9

Development Orders & Use Classes Order

SECTION I: INTRODUCTORY

9.1 Need to review. There are various reasons for doing so. *Firstly*, a relaxation of the General Development Order would have been one way of streamlining planning control. I reject that solution. *Secondly* there nonetheless remains a case for relaxation in special cases. I discuss it in detail later in the chapter. *Thirdly*, despite recent amendments, the GDO will require considerable adjustment to attune its procedures to changes suggested in this report. There also exists an undoubted need to clarify the terms of some of the permissions granted by the Order (e.g. Class XII), though I have not examined this in depth. *Fourthly*, some of the permissions may well be too generous, e.g. as to erection of garages in country areas. *Fifthly*, there is a clear case for tightening controls in areas of special environmental importance. This would be effected by Article 4 Directions and Special Development Orders.

9.2 Ending delays the priority. The sixth reason is important. We cannot, for economic and other reasons, reform the entire structure of planning control at once. Moreover, *tightening of controls means some delays*. The main object of this review is to cure them. We cannot have it both ways. Putting new controls into effect must therefore wait until the review's main task is achieved and planning control has become more efficient. But on some things we can make an immediate start. Preparatory work on revision of the GDO and extension of SDOs should begin at once. Implementation can be gradual.

9.3 Need to conserve. I hope, however, that it will prove possible to make one exception to this cautious approach. Control of demolition (as outlined in my special report of September 1974) demands early implementation. At a time when we have shed our empire and lost much of our wealth and power in the world, let us at least conserve our physical environment: the buildings, landscapes and townscapes which are still a cherished and tangible asset.

SECTION II: GENERAL DEVELOPMENT ORDER

9.4 Effect of GDO. The General Development Order* specifies classes of development which may be undertaken without the express consent of either the local planning authority or of the Secretary of State.

9.5 Recent revision. The Department revises the GDO from time to time. The last substantive revision took place in 1973, but introduced only marginal

---

*S.I. 1973, 31.

99

changes.   Perhaps inevitably, its ad hoc amendments have not improved the Order's overall clarity.

9.6 Major relaxation controversial.   Some professional bodies who commented on my Interim Report strongly favoured a major relaxation of the GDO.   But this was controversial.   It would, said some critics, 'turn the countryside into another Middlesex' and 'sanction the indiscriminate intensification of residential developments'.   Most local planning authorities favoured not relaxation but clarification.

9.7 Aesthetic impact.   Others expressed concern about the possible aesthetic impact of any major relaxation.   Wholesale extension of old cottages in rural villages could do grave damage, they warned.

9.8 Relaxation as remedy for delays.   Against this others have argued powerfully that a substantial relaxation of the GDO offers the best remedy for delays in planning control.   It could remove as many as 50% (or more) of all applications which, it is argued, deal with 'private rights'.

9.9 'A' and 'B' cases a better remedy.   I do not disregard this view but I cannot accept it entirely.   I hope, however, that my proposed division of applications into 'A' and 'B' classes will partly achieve the same objective.   One reason why I demur from the pro-relaxation views is that (as indicated in para 7.20) in practice the implied distinction between private and public interest is not always easy to apply.

9.10 Need for new major revision.   There is, however, a clear need, despite the 1973 review, for the Department to revise the GDO and at the same time look again at some of the provisions of the 1972 Use Classes Order.   One of the objects of revision should be to clarify exactly what development is permitted; another to review the conditions attached to deemed permissions under each class of the Order, which are not always now what circumstances and planning policy demand.

9.11 Explaining the GDO to the public.   The Department should explain the effect of the revised Order to the public simply and comprehensibly in a leaflet.

9.12 Needless applications.   At present many planning applications – some local planning authorities put it as high as one in four – concern development proposals which the GDO exempts from the need for express consent.   But planning authorities often treat them as applications and give decisions.   S.53 of the 1971 Town and Country Planning Act* allows planning authorities to determine whether a development proposal requires permission, but planning officers frequently allow the application to go through the ordinary consent procedure instead of saving time and money by considering whether the proposal in fact requires consent.

---

*There is a strong case for amending Section 53 to give a clear power to the local planning authorities to determine whether planning permission is required in *any* circumstances.   At present it does not enable local planning authorities to determine whether a proposal is covered by an existing permission: see Edgwarebury Park Investments Ltd MHLG (1963) 2QB 408.

9.13 **Clear and simple procedure needed.** This situation is unsatisfactory. In cases which are covered by a clear GDO permission a standard printed form should be used by local planning authorities in deciding this question. They could send it with an explanatory leaflet to applicants in suitable cases. Indeed, for many applications a simple printed postcard stating that consent by the GDO applied, together with an explanatory leaflet, would suffice.

9.14 **Relaxation of control.** In revising the GDO, we should provide for the immediate relaxation of control in some respects, which are set out in the following paragraphs.

9.15 **Industrial buildings.** These are covered by Class VIII which should be amended in order that:—

development within an existing industrial estate or premises should constitute permitted development, provided that:—

(a) it does not materially alter external appearance as viewed from outside the whole relevant premises;

(b) it complies with safety regulations; and

(c) an Industrial Development Certificate has been obtained (or is available) where statute requires it.

These extensions of permitted development should include 'bad neighbour' industry (special industrial groups as defined in the Use Classes Order).

9.16 **Possible amendments relating to changes in use.** I note in passing the following suggested changes:—

(i) The meaning of 'light industrial' in Article 2 of the Use Classes Order should be clarified by listing the processes it includes.

(ii) Changes from Special (bad neighbour) Industrial Use to General or Light Industrial Use should constitute permitted development. Class III of the GDO should be amended accordingly.

(iii) Changes from Light Industrial Use to warehousing should constitute permitted development, and Class III of the GDO should be amended accordingly.

(iv) Changes from warehousing to Light Industrial Use should constitute permitted development provided the buildings were completed at least five years previously. (This is to prevent evasion of IDC control.) Class III of the GDO should be amended accordingly.

9.17 **Other 'campus' developments.** By analogy with para 9.15 (a) above, development within the curtilage of other large sites, such as a university campus, could be made to constitute permitted development. The same condition as to external appearance would need to apply. This suggestion is tentative, however, and the need for a change less urgent.

101

9.18 Existing exemptions. I have considered many proposals for relaxing the GDO so as to permit development within the curtilage of a dwelling house. Local planning authorities have pointed out that a large proportion of planning applications concern proposals of that kind. Classes I and II of Schedule 1 of the GDO already exempt the vast majority of house extensions from the need to seek express consent.

9.19 Possible extension of tolerances. One obvious possibility is to double the specific limits in Paragraph 1 of Class I and to increase by 50% those in Paragraph 2. This would, for example, allow some householders to add as much as 230 cubic metres to their houses, and the permitted area and height for porches would increase to 3 sq. metres and 4.5 metres.

9.20 Arguments against relaxation. But such a relaxation, we must admit, could lead to some unsatisfactory development which would damage the amenity of the neighbourhood. It could only be accepted if we were to regard it as the price of freeing the planning control system from too much clogging detail.

9.21 Failing a courageous line of this kind, lesser changes were considered. For instance doubling of the limits in Paragraph 1 (a) has the disadvantage of permitting extensions to high density dwelling houses which would almost certainly have a substantial effect on local amenities, and could lead to substantial increases in occupancy. If one wished to be cheese-paring one could opt for increases of 50% rather than 100%.

9.22 An alternative, which was more attractive, and a little more discriminating, was to keep Paragraph 1 as it now stands subject to a doubling of the limits where a dwelling house is not less than 10 metres distant on either side from adjacent houses fronting the same highway and not less than 30 metres from any other dwelling house. Similarly, in the case of such a dwelling house one might allow development beyond the forwardmost part, provided there was no development within *20 metres* of the *curtilage of the highway*. But this could do damage in the countryside.

9.23 It is now clear, I believe, that the appropriate solution is a different one and I felt able to recommend that the tolerance under the General Development Order should not be substantially altered.

9.24 In revising the General Development Order attention should be focused on whether there are some existing permissions which should eventually be restricted.

9.25 Class I–XIV. It is clearly not possible to make changes here at the present time because of the inordinate length of time taken by many local authorities in deciding applications. But the permission for the erection of *garages* (under Class I), at least in the countryside, gives cause for concern. Class XIV, which permits works incidental to *improvement of highways* on land outside the boundary of the highway and, in effect, makes possible the demolition of old walls, is another difficult area.

9.26 In my Interim Report I suggest that in areas of environmental importance tighter control is justified.

9.27 I am still of the same opinion but *think it impractical to tighten controls until local authorities have proved able to comply with statutory time limits in an overwhelming majority of cases.*

9.28 There are several other specific proposals to tighten control. I only mention one, tentatively.

9.29 **Agricultural Buildings.** It is especially hard to suggest any additional administrative complications for farmers. It is not only that farming has to deal with great economic difficulties, but the importance of agriculture is increasing. At the present time the agricultural industry supplies 52% of the food consumed in this country. Its target is 75% and it must be borne in mind that 50,000 acres is taken every year from agricultural use for development.

9.30 Nevertheless, it is pointed out that the pattern of agriculture is changing. Farming is now an industry, and it often uses prefabricated buildings which mar the countryside. Certain agricultural buildings are already subject to control*.

9.31 My advice would be to amend Class VI of the GDO to exclude:

(a) buildings within 100 metres of existing buildings;

(b) intensive building groups although for the use of livestock are not requisite for the use of land for agriculture.

SECTION III: SPECIAL ENVIRONMENTAL AREAS

9.32 **Tighter control in special environmental areas.** It is essential that there should be specific recognition of special environmental areas in which tighter control procedures should be applied. I consider the nature of these areas and the methods of control in the following paragraphs.

9.33 **Areas of national and local importance.** Special environmental areas can be divided into those of *national importance* (national parks, areas of outstanding natural beauty, the proposed heritage coasts and the more important conservation areas) and those of *local importance* (other conservation areas and other areas of town or country identified in the development plan or policies).

9.34 **'Nationally important'.** By 'nationally important' I mean first those areas of countryside which receive special recognition for their landscape quality. These are national parks, areas of outstanding natural beauty and the proposed heritage coasts as defined in the Countryside Commission's Heritage Coasts

---

*Class VI of the GDO covers agricultural buildings so long as:

(a) the ground area of the total building does not exceed 465 sq. metres;

(b) the height does not exceed 3 metres within 3 kilometres of the perimeter of an aerodrome, nor 12 metres in any other case;

(c) no part of any buildings is within 25 metres of the metalled portion of a trunk or classified road.

Report of 1970. These three types of areas differ in the nature of the landscape included within them, in the procedures adopted for their designation or definition, and in any special arrangements made for their administration. However, all three types are identified only after a procedure involving the Countryside Commission who seek to secure nationally comparable standards in deciding whether a particular tract of landscape should be included in one of these classes, and in delineating the boundaries with the help of local authorities and others. 'Nationally important' also includes conservation areas of outstanding national importance.

9.35 A ready-to-hand test of which conservation areas are 'more important' already exists in the lists of those which the Secretary of State recognises as of 'outstanding national importance'. At present some 150 conservation areas appear on this special list; more than 3,300 other conservation areas have been designated. There should, in my opinion, be more of both categories.

9.36 **'Locally important'.** By 'locally important' I mean those other tracts of countryside or areas of towns which have a distinctive environmental quality which has been recognised in development plans or policies as meriting special control policies. The remaining conservation areas fall into this class, so too do many landscape areas, sometimes formerly classified as of great landscape value, which are being identified in the county structure plans; and perhaps also Areas of Special Scientific Interest. All these areas are important, but more so to the local community than to the nation at large (although, of course, collectively they are a national asset of great importance).

9.37 I have not included green belts in either category because the objective of development control in green belts is primarily to limit the quantity rather than to enhance the quality of development. Development control in these areas is operated with the purpose of checking urban sprawl, keeping existing settlements apart or retaining the character of certain special historic cities (e.g. Oxford), and green belts are therefore fundamentally different from the other special areas, national or local, referred to above.

9.38 **Need for tighter control.** In both nationally and locally important environmental areas a basic purpose of development control is to secure that new development, where appropriate, is in accord with the quality of the area. Evidence submitted indicated considerable dissatisfaction with the effect of GDO permissions and a number of local authorities seeking Article 4 Directions to restrict such permissions.

9.39 On the basis of this and of advice given to me by the Planning Boards of two national parks, I believe that the lack of control over development, arising from exemptions under the GDO, can cause harm to the landscape or to the character and appearance of these areas. The Planning Boards draw attention to such eye-sores as prefabricated garages, the painting of exterior walls in vivid colours, the use of land for camping, the siting, design and external appearance of agricultural buildings, insensitive installation of street-lighting and design of road improvements, overhead electricity lines and such structures as sub-stations and booster stations.

9.40 I conclude that there is good reason to question the degree of protection which can be given to special environmental areas so long as there is no control over the permissions granted automatically for such developments under Schedule 1 of the GDO.

9.41 **Leisure Plots.** In passing, I would however like to make one specific recommendation. There is evidence from at least one county of a recent practice of selling leisure plots on the assumption that a planning permission is not required. This naturally leads to serious objection from the public, as in practical terms a weekend invasion results and substantial intensification of use of land takes place. Clearly this should be made subject to planning control. Section 22(3) of the 1971 Act should be amended to provide (for the avoidance of doubt) that a change in the use of a separate plot of land from agricultural to a 'leisure' purpose would constitute development.

SECTION IV: THE WAYS IN WHICH TIGHTER CONTROL MIGHT BE EXERCISED

9.42 I now turn to the methods which might be used to achieve tighter control:

(1) in special environmental areas of national importance the decision to adopt tighter controls should be a *national responsibility*, but of course the controls should be operated by local planning authorities;

(2) in locally important special environmental areas, the decision to seek tighter control should *rest with the local authority* but this decision (which involves a withdrawal of rights enjoyed previously and elsewhere) should be subject to Ministerial approval.

9.43 The methods of tightening control over the developments covered by Schedule 1 of the GDO are:—

Special Development Orders,
Local Development Orders (a new concept),
Article 4 Directions.

9.44 **Special Development Orders.** The 1971 Act provides (S.24(3)): 'A development order may be made either as a general order applicable (subject to such exceptions as may be specified therein) to all land, or as a special order applicable only to such land as may be so specified'. Special Development Orders can thus be used to tighten or relax control in particular areas. They come into force only after being laid before Parliament.

9.45 SDO's may be particularly appropriate to provide uniform control for extensive areas under the responsibility of several local authorities. It would be preferable to separate Article 4 Directions promoted by the different authorities. This is particularly relevant to areas of outstanding natural beauty, since 27 out of the 32 such areas cover territory in more than one district council, and 11 also straddle county council boundaries.

9.46 There are at present 4 SDO's, for New Towns, Ironstone Areas, Atomic Energy Establishments and Landscape Areas. The Landscape Areas SDO (LASDO) is the most relevant in the present context.

9.47 **The Landscape Areas SDO.** Made in 1950, this provides that development for the purposes of agriculture and forestry which is permitted under the General Development Order (Classes VI and VII) shall in certain areas be subject to a condition enabling the local planning authority to control the design and external appearance (but not the siting) of buildings. The areas covered comprise most of three national parks, i.e., the Peak Park, the Lakes and Snowdonia*. The Order requires 14 days' notice in writing to be given to the local planning authority, including a short description of the proposed building or extension, the materials to be used, and a plan of the site. During that period the planning authority may require a planning application to be made.

9.48 Since the aspects of control which will deserve particular attention in national environmental areas will be the design, external appearance (and also siting) of development, the LASDO is a useful model to study. The experience of those who have operated the LASDO suggests that the Order is a useful procedure which could be adopted more widely, whether or not a notification procedure were used. However, I consider it is deficient in not giving control over siting. It would, of course, be open to Parliament to agree to an SDO for nationally important special environmental areas covering many more classes of Schedule 1 than are covered by the LASDO.

9.49 **Local Development Orders.** The Interim Report canvassed the idea of giving local authorities power to make local development orders to extend the scope of the GDO for a whole or part of their area. I think local authorities would be most unlikely to make use of such a power; after all, they can always achieve additional freedom by a liberal policy towards the granting of planning consents.

9.50 Alternatively, an LDO might be used to restrict development in high quality environmental areas. I agree that it is important for local authorities to have the requisite tools to protect places of environmental quality in their areas. However, this can be achieved by the greater use of Article 4 Directions. It seems unlikely that any greater power would be given to local authorities to adopt restricting LDOs than they have to make effective Article 4 Directions. Accordingly I see no advantage in introducing LDOs.

9.51 **Article 4 Directions.** Under Article 4 of the General Development Order 1973, a local authority may make a direction restricting development in any of the classes in Schedule 1 to the Order, or any particular development in any of those classes, by requiring an application. Under Article 4(3) a local authority can make a direction in respect of a listed building without the Secretary of State's consent, and likewise for Classes I–IV of Schedule 1 if the development would threaten amenity, but in the latter case such a direction would lapse after six months unless confirmed by the Secretary of State. Because local circumstances vary so much, I consider there is little purpose in setting out a model Article 4 Direction. Nevertheless, the ability for local authorities to make such directions to control development locally, and perhaps especially in conservation areas, twilight and stress areas of cities is crucial. The degree of remaining

---

*The reason for this partial coverage is that the LASDO was made before any national parks were formally designated. The Order does not even coincide with the boundaries of the three parks affected and extends outside their boundaries in places.

Ministerial control should be gradually relaxed; this would depend on whether local authorities are able to speed up controls, and the effect of other forth-coming legislation on resources.

9.52 **Need to change basis of compensation.** Section 165(1) (b) of the 1971 Act, which provides for compensation when an Article 4 Direction is made, seems to be heavily weighed against the use of the method. Its repeal or replacement of wording restricting compensation to actual damage is of great importance if the procedure is to be more widely used. This change of law may, however, have to wait for a suitable legislative opportunity in connection with other compensation reforms. There is a case for special treatment of the cost of providing agricultural building acceptable in local landscape and grants or fiscal advantages may provide equally effective solutions (in respect of both SDO's and Article 4 Directions).

9.53 **Conclusion.** Existing powers (SDOs and Article 4 Directions) are wide enough to provide the necessary control for special environmental areas and should be more extensively used. I do not think any new powers are required, but the existing compensation provisions should be reviewed.

MEANS OF SECURING ADDITIONAL CONTROL IN SENSITIVE AREAS

CLASSIFICATION	TYPE OF AREA		SDO OR GDO	ARTICLE 4
National environmental areas	1. National parks 2. Areas of outstanding natural beauty	landscape category		option retained
	3. Heritage Coasts Conservation areas of national importance		SDO	
Local environmental areas	Other conservation areas		GDO	more liberal use of Article 4 (perhaps especially after local plan approved)
	Local landscape areas			
Other town and country areas	the rest of the country		GDO	option retained

CHAPTER 10

Public Involvement

SECTION I: GENERAL

10.1 Role of public involvement. Other chapters of this report give substantial coverage to many aspects of public involvement. Nonetheless, it is a topic of universal interest. At virtually every meeting arranged in connection with this review, public involvement in some form or other was one of the first and most frequent topics raised. I therefore devote a separate chapter to it, which provides the background for more specific conclusions and recommendations elsewhere in this report.

10.2 Definitions. In this chapter it will be convenient to use the following expressions:

(a) **Public involvement,** which covers both public participation and public consultation.

(b) **Public participation,** which means taking an active part – from the outset – in the formulation of development plans and the making of major planning decisions of strategic importance.

(c) **Public consultation,** which means giving the public an opportunity to express views on planning applications.

(d) **Interested parties.** The public are often described as 'third parties' (the owners or the tenants of land in respect of which an application has been made being known as 'section 29 parties' or, alternatively, as 'interested parties'). I use the expression 'interested parties' in relation to all the participants, other than the applicant and district and county councils.

(e) **Individual rights.** I have already dealt with this question in Chapter 7, paragraphs 7.18 to 7.21, but the text of Circular 77/73* merits quotation. It says: 'Planning is concerned to ensure that in the development of land the public interest is taken fully into account. Its objective is not the safe-guarding of private property rights as such; nor in particular, to protect the value of individual properties or the views to be had from them. There are, however, occasions when the public interest may require that the interests of those immediately affected by even a comparatively minor proposal should be taken into account as a planning consideration'.

10.3 Arguments for Public Involvement. The practical help the public can give in planning control has lately assumed a new and very considerable importance.

*Welsh Office Circular 149/73.

109

(1) **Changes in Local Government.** The elected member now generally represents many more constituents spread over a far wider area. He cannot now be expected to know in detail all relevant circumstances in every locality. The public has more detailed, first-hand knowledge and can be of vital importance in reaching sound decisions.

(2) **'Community Land'.** The proposed legislation on community land will involve local planning authorities very much more in acquisition and development of land. The reactions of interested parties will assume a new importance. There may often be no-one else ready to draw attention strongly enough to the possible damaging effects of a proposal to which the local authority is a party.

(3) **Amenity societies.** Local and central government can profit from the special expertise of amenity societies and from the voluntary efforts of the public.

(4) **Public confidence in planning.** In many ways, therefore, the public can now offer information and points of view *not otherwise available*. Confidence in planning will be strengthened if the public feel they have the opportunity to make their contribution at an early stage.

10.4 **Arguments against public involvement.** The main difficulties in this area arise from a real or apparent conflict of interest between on the one hand the proposed developer and the planning authorities (even though these two may have opposing objectives); and on the other hand ordinary people who would be affected by the development (and who again may have opposing views about it). Because planning is a complex technical process, conflicts may arise through lack of understanding on either side: ordinary people may not appreciate the complexities, but the 'professionals' (developers or planning authorities) may not be sufficiently in sympathy with the justifiable fears of the public. Those against public involvement argue:

(1) that some members of the public, perhaps inevitably, lack sufficient understanding of how planning control works;

(2) that in particular they may fail to understand which are valid or relevant grounds on which to base objections to a development proposal;

(3) that they often find it difficult to understand what plans and applications are really saying;

(4) that they add to the work of planning officers, of elected members and central government;

(5) that people do not understand the limits set by statute and national policy to a local planning authority's freedom to decide applications or impose conditions as it wishes. They are, however, not alone in finding such matters troublesome.

10.5 **Complaints from the public.** These are often overlooked. The faults are not necessarily all on one side, however. The more frequently-voiced complaints by members of the public about shortcomings in public involvement include:

(1) Too little notice is given of development proposals. By the time the public are aware of a proposal, either no time or too little remains for them to make effective comments or objections.

(2) Information is difficult to get at, whether contained in public registers or elsewhere. Plans cannot be produced when asked for.

(3) No-one explains to them what effect, if any, their representations have had.

(4) Elected members do not always sufficiently understand the function of public involvement in planning, or in some cases, of the planning system itself.

10.6 **Proper function of public involvement.** It is, therefore, important that the proper function of public involvement should be clearly understood and not exceeded. It should assist elected members and central government by giving them information and other help they may need, but should not impinge on their prerogative of decision-making.

10.7 In order that it may continue and become increasingly useful, public involvement must be:

(1) relevant: i.e. limited to planning considerations affecting the matters for decision;

(2) more efficient: this will be achieved gradually as the public learns more about planning, and planners learn how to involve the public more effectively;

(3) constructive and selective: whilst anybody likely to be adversely affected by a proposed development should have an opportunity to make a representation, those who object to all development all the time, everywhere, can do great harm by discrediting public involvement.

SECTION II: PUBLIC CONSULTATION

10.8 **Early consultation is best.** All forms of public involvement including consultation about planning applications should take place at the earliest possible opportunity.

10.9 **Statutory publicity.** Section 26 of the 1971 Act requires the publication of notices of applications in a wide range of 'bad neighbour' cases, such as those where it is proposed to build public conveniences, scrap yards, high buildings or motor-racing tracks*. The General Development Order prescribes a form of notice which must be advertised by the applicant in a local newspaper of his choice. Paragraph 20 of Schedule 16 of the Local Government Act 1972 deals with notification of parish and community councils. The 1971 Act and the Town and Country Amenities Act 1974 cover publicity in conservation areas. Statute now recognises public involvement: it has become an integral part of the planning process.

---

*See Article 8(1) of the General Development Order.

10.10 **Further publicity for applications and decisions.** I have already indicated in paragraphs 7.29, 7.30 and 7.48 the need for *site notices* or neighbour notification for all applications, and for the giving of publicity to decisions.

10.11 **Neighbour notification.** This method of notifying the public is strongly supported: more than four-fifths of all councils say they use it, and many consider it more effective than site notices in highlighting controversial proposals. However, it is regarded by some as an incitement to neighbours to complain about each other and some people who make representations are upset when the local planning authority approves an application despite their objections.

10.12 **Who is a 'neighbour'?** One or two of the comments queried the definition of 'immediate' neighbours, as complaints may arise when some, but not all, nearby owners are notified. This point was conveniently answered by 'the Procedure for Notification of Surrounding Residents', issued by one district (see Appendix II Ci).

10.13 **The role of the parish council.** Parish councils (community councils in Wales) are entitled to be consulted on planning applications. (See para. 7.46.) A detailed note on these councils is in Appendix II Cii. It is unfortunate that many large urban areas have no such bodies to represent them. It is beyond the scope of my review to recommend how this omission should be remedied, but the creation of neighbourhood councils may well fill the gap.

10.14 **Public access to registers.** If public consultation is to be effective, and the public is to accept a speeding up of the planning decision process, they must have very much better access to registers of planning applications.

(1) **Duplicate registers.** I understand that there is no insuperable reason why the new and larger district councils should not display details of applications in several duplicate registers at convenient places in their areas. Anyway, Article 17(8) of the General Development (Amendment) Order 1974 enables that to be done.

(2) **Hot lines to local authority offices.** District councils should provide at least lists of applications in convenient local places with direct telephone links to the register.

(3) **Open at lunchtime and evenings.** Registers should be accessible during weekday lunch-hours and on at least one evening each week.

(4) **Explanations to hand.** If possible, a member of the planning office staff should be available to explain entries in a helpful and sympathetic way. Many authorities already see that this is done.

(5) **Help with staffing.** Where a local planning authority has staffing difficulties, but is on good terms with a local amenity society, volunteer help in manning the register might be the answer.

(6) **Application plans.** The legislative changes suggested in paragraphs 11.30 – 11.40 will, if adopted, establish beyond doubt the right to copy plans.

MAJOR APPLICATIONS

10.15 Major applications. In Chapter 7 I suggested that, in addition to consultation procedures on these lines, there was also scope for special publicity arrangements in the case of major Class B applications (7.66 and 7.67). The applications I have in mind are those concerning areas of national or regional importance, and I suggest that exhibitions or meetings should be held before the application is made (except where they are initiated by an interested party when the meeting will come later).

10.16 Meetings. Several kinds of meetings are possible:

(1) Called at the initiative of an applicant,

(2) Organised by the council or its officers,

(3) Initiated by those affected by the application, by the parish council or an amenity society.

10.17 Exhibitions. Exhibitions could be linked to public meetings and should, if possible, take place on neutral ground (see paragraph 10.49 dealing with urban study centres).

Direct participation of local societies in the work of local authorities

10.18 Co-option to committees. I have dealt in Chapter 7 and in 10.3(3), with the need to consult amenity societies on planning applications in some cases. Local authorities should also consider arrangements for enabling members of such bodies to contribute directly to the consideration of planning issues by co-opting them to serve on committees. I know this would not always be acceptable but precedents for making such arrangements already exist (for instance the London Borough of Lewisham's planning committee) and co-option of interested outsiders is, of course, the invariable rule with education committees.

10.19 Terms of co-option. It may be argued against this suggestion that such bodies are often partisan in their point of view, and that the duty of actually deciding issues should rest with elected councillors responsible to the community as a whole. However, where co-option takes place, elected representatives are in a majority, and co-option of members of such bodies seems to me a valuable way of enabling them to contribute directly to the work of the local authority, provided that the record of those bodies does not indicate a general bias in approach and that co-option is understood to be conditional on the co-opted member taking a broad view and not simply acting as a delegate to a sponsoring body. This practice might also help the applicant as he would seek to satisfy a single co-ordinated body.

LOCAL GUIDANCE

10.20 (*a*) Planning Design Guides and Planning Briefs are already provided by many local authorities. They are badly needed for many purposes.

    (*b*) A presentation of local planning policy and planning control method is lacking in many districts, although some areas have produced excellent guides.

10.21 For example, I have seen several linked four-page guides produced by a district council in the South East. Each leaflet is about 1,600 words long. One is entitled 'Have you come to see the Plans List' and has the following headings:

(1) The powers of the District Council

(2) What is development?

(3) What requires permission?

(4) How is permission obtained?

(5) What factors are taken into account in the consideration of an application?

(6) How do I know that an application has been made?

(7) How can I make my views known?

(8) What is best, an individual letter or petition?

(9) What if it spoils my view or causes me financial loss?

(10) Can I make representations about what my neighbour wishes to do?

(11) What if I disagree with a decision of the council?

10.22 **Other Leaflets.** Two other leaflets equally commendable are on:
(a) 'Extending your House",

(b) 'The Green Belt in your District'.

10.23 Leaflets like these should also give general information such as the addresses of planning offices and information centres and the times when they are open.

10.24 **Information Sheets.** Some authorities find it worthwhile to publish information sheets on major development proposals (including roads), progress of local plans, on conservation areas and the listing of buildings, etc. The relevant information can often be given on a single sheet.

10.25 There may be occasions, however rare, in which these sheets should be circulated to all householders. (Some councils already issue news-sheets on planning and all other subjects to householders.)

PLANNING INFORMATION AND ADVICE

10.26 **Information and advice centres.** Local authority information centres and independent planning advice centres can play a particularly important role in helping both applicants and the general public. These centres would fulfil distinct but complementary functions; the need for the former is generally accepted, but there are so far few, or no, examples of the latter.

10.27 **Pioneer examples.** There are only a few local authority information centres which concentrate on planning. A government research station has investigated these centres, and a description of them is printed in Appendix

II Ciii. The pioneering work of Leeds, Winchester, Lambeth and Kensington in operating planning information centres at or near their planning offices should be followed. Such centres should be suitably located, appropriately manned and advertised. Local authority information centres would inevitably be expected to deal with non-planning activities.

10.28 **Case for planning information and advice.** The arguments for having planning information and advice readily available are that:

(1) planning is a complicated subject, and the ordinary layman is entitled to receive at least some initial advice on any work he proposes to do on his own property before having to turn to professional advisers;

(2) if potential applicants can discuss the circumstances and details of the proposed development, the quality of the application will be improved, the decision process will be simplified, and there should be fewer abortive applications, refusals and appeals;

(3) the general public, concerned with aspects of proposed developments, require detailed, expert, unbiased explanations. They also need an easily approachable contact to whom they can explain their view, knowing that these will be taken into account when the decisions are made. This is the kind of help most often lacking at present.

10.29 **What kinds of information?** Information may take the form of:

(1) explanatory literature and planning forms, general advice on completing forms, and information about the progress of current applications, dates and agenda of planning committee meetings, applications received, council decisions, etc.;

(2) records, maps and planning histories of specific properties made available for consultation;

(3) general information, such as interpretation of local plans, and discussion of legal aspects (e.g. whether planning permission is required);

(4) answers to specific enquiries, referring to particular applications, which can only be dealt with by the officer in charge of the file.

10.30 **Independent Planning Advice Centres.** An independent national system of advice centres should be set up to help applicants and objectors alike, but should in no way detract from (or compete with) the service which local authorities provide for the public.

10.31 **Planning Aid.** There is a strong case for the introduction in due course of a Planning Aid Scheme, similar to the Legal Aid Scheme for those who cannot afford professional help*. It might be funded on a £1 to £1 basis up to a prescribed limit, but aid would only be available where a Planning Aid Committee certified that it was reasonable to give such assistance. Alternatively, costs of the scheme could be met partly by assessed contributions, according to income. In all cases funds for such aid should be provided by central government.

---

*The Town and Country Planning Association are already operating a scheme of this kind. I am impressed by its work and judge it most important to give it encouragement and assistance. This would, at least, be a good start.

10.32 **Independent Administration.** Any planning aid scheme should, like the legal aid scheme, be administered by an independent professional body such as the Royal Town Planning Institute, the Royal Institution of Chartered Surveyors or the Royal Institute of British Architects.

10.33 **The Cost of Aid.** The cost of such a scheme should be at least partly met (albeit indirectly) by charging for applications (see paragraphs 7.117–7.120).

VOLUNTARY ORGANISATIONS AND STATUTORY BODIES

10.34 **British Environment Council.** Such national and regional voluntary bodies as the Town and Country Planning Association, the Civic Trusts and Council for the Protection of Rural England have done impressive work over the years both in interesting a wider public in planning and associated topics and in presenting the views and suggestions of a more enlightened public to central and local government. Yet we still lack a strong, central, impartial co-ordinating body provided with adequate funds from public sources. I recommend that attention be given to the creation of a British Environment Council. Even if funds are not immediately available, foundations for it should be laid immediately.

10.35 **Grant aid to date.** The Department has so far made grants on a £1 for £1 basis to the North West Civic Trust (up to £10,000 a year), the Civic Trust for the North East (up to £5,000) and the Yorkshire Council for the Environment (up to £6,000 this year). Neither the TCPA nor the national Civic Trust as such receive grant aid. The TCPA has submitted a request for a substantial sum to expand its pioneering and most valuable planning aid service. It deserves immediate cash support from government funds. Comparatively small sums are involved and much is at stake.

10.36 **Longer-term needs.** In the long run, if the public wish to participate in planning and to retain and enhance the physical environment and to secure speed and efficiency in planning control, they will have to be willing to allow central and local government to spend public money on a scale bearing some comparison with that given to the Arts.

10.37 **The Countryside Commission,** with its modest budget, acts as a guardian of the countryside, but there is no similar central body to provide an equivalent service for our cities.

SECTION III: PUBLIC PARTICIPATION

10.38 **Publicity for plan making and B applications.** The 1971 Act makes various statutory provisions for publicity. Section 8 deals with publicity in the preparation of structure and local plans. These procedures are outside my terms of reference. Nonetheless, I refer to them, as public participation in local plan making and public consultation on Class B applications tend to give rise to the same kind of problems.

10.39 **Choosing the right methods.** At present funds are limited; if money is to be spent on public involvement the right method must be carefully chosen. Local planning authorities' attempts at public involvement have often failed because they chose the wrong approach for the particular circumstances or a particular 'public'. The appropriate methods must depend partly on the degree of active interest found in those the planners seek to involve.

10.40 **Need to reach the 'non-joiners'.** Planners should beware of ignoring, or making assumptions about, the attitudes of neighbourhoods which ordinarily display little interest in civic affairs. They must not write off the 'non-joiners': people who belong to no societies, shun public meetings, never reply to questionnaires and do not take local papers. These people have a right to be consulted. Moreover, they may react sharply if development takes them by surprise.

10.41 **Every household.** In some cases where a particularly significant B proposal affects a public which clearly includes this 'non-responding' element, the only effective way to reach them is by distributing to all households a single, small information sheet giving details of what is proposed (see paragraph 10.24 above). Door-to-door or sample surveys of public opinion are suggested as on alternative.

10.42 **Early involvement vital.** I have stressed elsewhere that public involvement must take place early to be effective. For most planning applications, this means the public participation process should begin just as soon as the local planning authority receives them. But for some major or particularly significant Class B proposals, it should begin earlier. The process needs to be in effect 'participation' rather than 'consultation'. The public needs to feel it can make its views felt before either developers or the local planning authority is fully committed to particular proposals. Here the involvement process – publicity, exhibitions, meetings and, sometimes, door-to-door leaflets and surveys (if there is money for them) need to start at the pre-application stage.

EDUCATION

10.43 **Key to success.** Education is the key to efficient and effective public involvement. The Skeffington Report ('People and Planning' 1969) made various recommendations about education, but I understand that the response has been negligible. I believe there is scope for greater collaboration between local education and planning departments.

10.44 **National effort.** There is a need to provide at national level for education about planning in school curricula, evening class programmes, adult education institutes and universities.

10.45 **Material for local societies.** Central and local government should supply national and local amenity societies with suitable material, i.e.:

(i) background texts for lectures, slides and films,

(ii) material for exhibitions, e.g. models, photographs and plans.

10.46 **Need for research.** We need much more research: both to discover how and to what extent local authorities seek to involve the public, and to measure which of their methods are most effective. We particularly need a clear picture of the techniques and approaches of the most successful local planning authorities in this field. There is also some need for cost/benefit analysis of the different methods employed.

10.47 **Departmental research.** The DOE in association with certain local authorities has commissioned a substantial programme of research into participation in connection with structure and local plans*. I welcome this, but I think it should be extended to include participation in development control. I also recommend that publicity should be given to this programme so that those interested can contribute ideas and so that the benefits of the programme as they occur become more widely known.

10.48 **Amenity Societies: information and training.** Amenity groups should themselves be better informed about planning and development control. This can be achieved:

(1) by meetings with central and local government;

(2) by giving the national and regional amenity societies (Town and Country Planning Association, Victorian Society, Georgian Group, Society for the Protection of Ancient Buildings, Ancient Monuments Society, etc.) sufficient funds;

(3) through established local amenity societies giving help to new local societies and explaining when and how to intervene in the planning process.

10.49 **Urban Study Centres.** The proposal to establish 'Urban Study centres' deserves support. These would be permanent centres on neutral ground, for meetings between the planners and the public, and would provide a venue for exhibitions and 'community forums'.

SECTION IV: THE PRESS, RADIO AND TELEVISION

10.50 **Towards a better coverage.** We must find ways of securing greater, and perhaps more thoughtful, coverage of planning by local press, radio (including local radio), television and documentary films.

THE PRESS

10.51 **Task of local press.** The local press is obviously important. It informs the public about 'proposed developments' and gives them the opportunity to make their views known.

---

*This programme was commissioned in 1972. It comprises 5 subjects which involve monitoring and evaluating various aspects of participation in the structure plan process, with particular reference to Merseyside, Teesside and Cheshire. The local authorities concerned are co-operating in the work which is being carried out by research staff of the Universities of Surrey, Liverpool, Sheffield and Salford.

10.52 **Circulation of local press.** Over 700 local papers are published in England each week, together with a further 180 which are distributed free of charge. The total circulation of the local press is apparently about 19·2 million copies per week to 14 million households. Most households are therefore likely to receive at least one local paper, and a substantial proportion two or more.

10.53 **Local press coverage of planning.** During a six-week period in May and June 1974, staff of the Building Research Station studied the coverage given to planning by local press throughout England and Wales. They looked at some 200 cuttings from about 100 different newspapers.*

10.54 The most common way of publishing planning applications proved to be in the form of a selection from the full list, usually covering a period of one week. 36% print the full lists free, while some print the full lists in the form of an advertisement at the Council's expense. Some selections of applications could be 5 or 10 lines at the bottom of a page; whereas a new controversial development might be given full page coverage with photographs and maps.

10.55 Most planning authorities provide the local press with the full list of applications for a given period. Planning officers generally consider that the local press is one of the best means of communicating planning proposals to the public and would like to see full lists published. There is some evidence that, since April 1st 1974, full lists of applications are more frequently published.

10.56 Next to the lists of applications, the most common form of press coverage of planning matters was found in meetings of planning committees and of the council. Reports usually follow the making of the application and the discussions of the planning committee. The amount of space newspapers give normally depends on the size of the development. New roads or town centre developments often get full page coverage.

10.57 Reports on appeals and inquiries also feature largely: they are always given considerable coverage.

10.58 The cuttings also included letters to the editor on planning matters (invariably the majority of letters were criticisms of the local planning authority or of developers), reports of the parish council meetings and editorial comments on planning.

10.59 **Attitude of local planning authorities.** As a result of a survey† it was established that the reaction of the local planning authorities to the amount of publicity given by the press is mixed. The majority (71%) say that the press gives sufficient publicity. Some consider that printing the lists 'stimulates public participation' and that lists in the press 'have greatly improved awareness of the system', but others say that the importance of 'publicity in the form of lists in the local paper is over-emphasised'.

---

*For a detailed breakdown of the content of these cuttings see tables 1 and 2, Appendix II Civ.

†For details as to survey on the role of the local press as seen by planning officers see Appendix II Civ.

10.60 **Editorial or Advertising.** A distinction needs to be made between coverage given in advertisements paid for by the local planning authority, and editorial coverage (whether news, features or comment), which is free but dependent on the varying amount of space and competition from other items. Generally speaking, it seems wiser not to lay down hard and fast rules but to leave the 'mix' to local circumstances. But clearly mandatory publicity requires *paid* advertising to ensure publication (though it should not, just because it is an advertisement, become unintelligible to the public – see 10.61 below). The ideal coverage is for important development proposals to feature in both advertising and editorial columns. With a major or controversial proposal, this will normally happen. A 'small ad' never stopped a reporter from writing a story; on the contrary, it sometimes stimulates him to do so.

10.61 **Advertisements of planning applications** must be intelligible and accessible to newspaper readers. They should:

(1) be worded in plain, non-technical language;

(2) enable the reader to understand the general location and nature of the proposed development without reference elsewhere; and if possible

(3) have a layout which makes them distinctive;

(4) not be lost among a mass of other public notices. They should be placed on pages which are widely read.

10.62 **Closer contact.** Local newspapers would be able to give a much better service if more district planning officers were in close touch with editors. Another improvement would be to make more use of the experts. An increasing number of planning and environment correspondents write in the national and specialist press and there are local planning issues which deserve their coverage and comment. Some local newspapers now also give to one of their reporters a special responsibility for planning topics and this can also make for better understanding and coverage.

10.63 **Television.** Surprisingly, television has so far taken far less active interest in planning than might have been expected. Interest is growing, however, and I understand that some time later in 1975 a complete film of a local inquiry will be shown.

10.64 **Regional television.** It would be well worthwhile for regional television sometimes to show films or live coverage of committee meetings. Some channels have done so. The practice, if continued with some degree of regularity, might succeed in 'opening up' the planning process.

10.65 Besides showing whether elected members are using their time to the best advantage it would allow the public to see how officers present reports on planning applications. (I have witnessed some examples of how this is done in London and was most impressed by the clarity and expertise of presentation.)

10.66 **Radio,** especially local radio, is important as it provides amongst other things a forum for amenity societies. Programme directors seem to be well aware of this.

CHAPTER 11

Appeals

SECTION I: THE PRESENT POSITION

11.1 **Delays.** In 1973 the delays in dealing with appeals were probably a main reason why this Review was thought to be necessary. That particular crisis has eased. In England alone, the number of appeals pending was 17,034 in October 1973 when I was appointed. It rose to just under 18,000 in February 1974 and has fallen to 14,053 in December 1974. An increase in the numbers of Inspectors and improved management methods, as well as a fall in the number of appeals, have helped to reduce the pressure. This is to the credit of the Inspectorate but it does not alter the fact that the appeal procedure still takes far too long and that radical improvements are needed. Fortunately, the easing of the pressure has now given us a little breathing space in which to re-appraise the whole system.

11.2 **Speedier appeal decisions.** As with other aspects of planning control, so with the appeal system, conflict may arise between my two objectives: maintaining and improving the quality of decisions and cutting the time it takes to reach them. The conflict is more apparent than real. A planning decision which takes too long to reach is often, because of that, a bad decision, whatever its content. Moreover, there is no real reason why the present system could not be adapted so that it would operate well *and* with reasonable speed.

11.3 **The quality of decisions.** There is far less complaint about the quality of decisions than there is about the time which it takes to arrive at them. Consequently, although I have not forgotten my other objectives of improving the quality of appeal decisions, this chapter is devoted very largely to a consideration of possible methods of speeding up the procedure.

11.4 **Criticisms of the appeal system.** Some criticisms have, however, been made of the appeal system itself; people complain of the court-like formality at Inquiries and the extent to which the essentially administrative process of appeal has become too legalistic and cumbersome. There are now doubts as to whether the highly developed quasi-judicial system of appeals, however popular with some members of the public, need be retained in its entirety. I have borne these doubts in mind.

11.5 There are also complaints that the presentation of Inspectors' conclusions and the Department's decisions sometimes fall short of the very high standard of clearly-explained reasoning normally expected of judicial decisions. While this may happen in individual cases, I do not consider that this is a major problem. In decisions of this kind reasonable brevity and speed are more important than style.

11.6 **Rights of the Individual.** There is, finally, some conflict between the need to cut delays and the natural anxiety to protect the rights of the individual and the interested parties. I have endeavoured to resolve it fairly.

11.7 The two questions to be asked are:
(*a*) should the present form of 'Inquiries' be radically changed?
(*b*) are we over-sensitive about the protection of the rights of the individual?

11.8 **Examinations in Public.** It might be possible to substitute for Inquiries a form of 'Examination in Public', on the lines of the procedure for examining structure plans. But 'Examinations in Public' were designed to deal with broad issues arising under such plans. A procedure of this kind would have to be adapted to deal with specific planning problems and to ensure the protection of individual rights. The result would be something very similar to the existing procedure under a different name.

11.9 As to individual rights, the balance is now just about right. I think the same *balance* should and can be maintained, although a readjustment is needed in the way in which it is attained. There is a case for stricter discipline at an Inquiry, for all parties, including interested parties. At the same time there must be more *publicity* at the pre-inquiry stage. The point is, that while maintaining the proper balance, we have to ensure that the time taken over appeals, at all stages, is reduced to an acceptable level.

11.10 There is no need to change the whole system, but we would be justified in experimenting to find out whether a change of approach (and some short cuts) can be introduced without impinging, in practice, on individual rights.

11.11 The recommendations in this report reflect this general conclusion. They are designed to shorten the overall time taken to decide appeals while providing for more publicity before the Inquiry. Unless action is taken on the lines which I recommend, the Government will have to face the dilemma of either accepting planning delays or sacrificing individual rights.

SECTION II: THE RIGHT TO APPEAL

11.12 **Three approaches to the problem.** There are three directions from which this problem can be tackled. First, to restrict the right to appeal in some way, so reducing the actual number of appeals; second, to improve the procedure for dealing with the appeals once they are made; or, thirdly, to transfer some appeals to a different appellate authority. There is, however, a real danger of suggesting procedural changes which would save time at one stage, only to cause additional delay at another. In trying to avoid this, I have inevitably had to make some compromises.

11.13 **Retain the right of appeal.** I have received considerable support for the idea that the right to appeal should be retained as a matter of principle. (Indeed, I have had suggestions that a new statutory right should be introduced to enable third parties to demand an appeal where planning permission has already been granted.) Such opposition as was expressed came largely from those who pointed out that repetitive appeals concerning the same site could be annoying and expensive.

11.14 (*a*) **Power to refuse to entertain an appeal.**   Section 36(7) of the 1971 Act does not restrict the right to appeal; it does, however, give the Secretary of State the power to refuse to entertain an appeal in certain cases.   This power has never been used.

(*b*) The background to the Town and Country Planning Act 1947 explains this. An identical sub-section was enacted then.   It was then thought that a permission would almost always be granted or refused in accordance with the Development Plan allocation; an assumption which was based on the practice under the Town and Country Planning Act 1932.

(*c*) There was, therefore, apparently no intention to confer a wide ranging right to question a decision based on a Development Plan.   Appeals were intended for cases where conditions might have changed or there were special circumstances which warranted a review.

(*d*) Apparently the original intention of the draftsman was to enable the Minister to refuse to entertain appeals if the decision of the authority complied with the Development Plan.   This certainly was not clearly expressed, but was anyway doomed to fail because it took about three years from the 'appointed day' for the 1947 Act before even the first Development Plan was approved. Most Development Plans took much much longer than this to complete.

11.15 **Power to direct written representations.**   It is difficult to turn the clock back, but something of the original intention is worth retaining.   We could achieve this by giving the Secretary of State the power to exercise his discretion whether the appeal should be determined by an Inquiry or the more economical written representation method.   He would no doubt exercise that authority sparingly as the climate of public opinion has changed so much since 1947.

11.16 **Restriction of right of appeal.**   I have received some suggestions that the right of appeal should be restricted to certain persons (e.g. the owner of the premises) or to certain grounds of appeal (e.g. that the decision appealed against is contrary to national policy).   I do not regard any restrictions of this kind as practicable.

11.17 **Transfer to other tribunals.**   For more than 5 years the Secretaries of State have been transferring what is now a large proportion of appeals (75% in England and 65% in Wales) to Inspectors.   It is sometimes suggested that this process could be carried further and that for some kinds of appeal a different appellate body should be found.   For example, since most planning decisions are now made by district councils, appeals against some or all of them could lie to the county council; alternatively, appeals of purely local interest could be dealt with by local tribunals set up for the purpose (whilst enforcement appeals raising only legal issues might be heard by the Lands Tribunal or County Courts).

11.18 Each suggestion of this kind is open to some objection, one sound one being that transfer of appeals to another tribunal would not cut delays.   My principal reason for rejecting all such suggestions is that the existing system is sound and that the Inspectorate who operate it enjoy well-deserved esteem.

11.19 **Keeping, but improving, the present procedure.** I therefore recommend that all appeals, except insofar as they are, under the existing statutory arrangements, already decided by Inspectors, should continue to be decided by the Secretaries of State themselves. Efforts should be concentrated on:

(*a*) continuing to recruit the right type of Inspector;

(*b*) speeding up the appeal process (as its slowness is the only persuasive reason why the alternative tribunals are suggested).

11.20 **Publicity arrangements.**

(*a*) **Notification to interested parties.** At present local authorities notify people who might be interested of any pending appeal. Generally I have had no significant complaints regarding these procedures and they should continue for both written representations and Inquiries.

(*b*) **Site notices** are at present always exhibited for 14 days prior to the Inquiry if the appellant has control of the land. In future these should be made compulsory in all cases, for 28 days in Class B, and 14 days in Class A.

(*c*) **Lists of appeals.** I also suggest that the publication of lists of appeals (and their results) in local newspapers should be encouraged. Many authorities do this already.

(*d*) **Major cases.** This may not be sufficient in very controversial cases, and in these there should be a statutory power to require the appellant to insert an advertisement of a kind which would attract attention.

11.21 In certain cases where 'bad neighbour' development is involved there is a statutory requirement for the application to be advertised (under Section 26 of the 1971 Act). If this has been overlooked but a refusal was issued, the Secretary of State should have the power to accept the appeal if there is equivalent publicity at that stage.

SECTION III: CLASSES 'A' AND 'B'

11.22 **Categories of appeals. All appeals should be divided into two classes** to correspond with Classes 'A' and 'B' (see Chapter 7 paragraph 7.3). Class A appeals should comprise all 'small development appeals' and in particular appeals from refusals of permissions:

(*a*) all simple cases;

(*b*) appeals relating to development which, within specified limits as to size, conform to an approved up to date development plan;

(*c*) appeals relating to development only just exceeding the limits permitted by the General Development Order;

(*d*) appeals against a refusal to approve details under an 'outline' or 'illustrative' Class A application (7.96–7.97).

All others will fall in Class 'B'.

11.23 Class A applications would almost always on appeal be dealt with by Class A appeal procedure, though I appreciate it would not be possible to treat automatically as a Class A appeal every case in which the proposals conform to a local or similar plan (see paragraph 7.3).

11.24 It would be for the Department to stream appeals into the two classes A and B (and this would probably be done by the Case Officer).

11.25 The new classes cut across the existing categories:

(a) 'Secretary of State cases'; and

(b) 'Inspectors (or transferred) cases' (see paragraph 5.9); and indeed across another possible classification, such as:

(i) 'Local Inquiry cases'; and

(ii) 'written representations cases' (see paragraph 5.20 et seq.).

11.26 **Simpler Procedure for Class 'A' Appeals.** Smaller, less controversial cases (i.e. most appeals which would come in the proposed Class A) can be considerably simplified and speeded up and they could well be conducted in a more informal atmosphere. I recommend that the Inquiries Procedure Rules should be amended to provide for informality in Category A cases. The changes I propose are as follows.

11.27 **First,** in most cases neither party should be obliged to provide a Rule 6 statement.*

11.28 **Second,** the preparatory paperwork should be cut to a bare minimum. The Inspector's file need contain no more than a copy of the application, the plan, the grounds of refusal and notice of appeal, and the standard regional brief (which is a printed document).

11.29 **Thirdly:**

(1) There should be a wider choice of venue. A village hall could be used or a room in the district offices or even in a local public house. (A suggestion that in some cases the inquiry should be held in the appellant's home cannot, I fear, be accepted as this may be thought to prejudice interested parties.)

(2) The procedure should be most informal. I would rely on the authority of the Inspector to create the right atmosphere. Parties might sit round a table and remain seated.

(3) There would be no legal representation for either side and normally the Inspector would ask questions of the appellant or his representative (e.g. a local surveyor) and of one representative of the local authority, i.e. someone from the planning department.

11.30 **Finally,** I recommend that in a transferred inquiry case the Inspector should be entitled to give a decision on the spot, although his reasoned letter of decision would follow in all cases. There will thus be substantial procedural advantages. Provided it is known that a simplified procedure will be used for 'A' appeals, much time will be saved at all stages and especially in the preliminary stages (i.e. before the file is sent to the Inspector).

11.31 **Rules of procedure.** It follows that the Rules of Procedure should be amended in respect of 'A' appeals. They will then provide that although in

---

*Rule 6 of The Town and Country Planning (Inquiries Procedure) Rules 1974, No. 419 is set out in Appendix III vi.

most cases neither party would need to produce a Rule 6 statement, in some cases the Department could ask for a brief Rule 6 statement from the local authority. The underlying intention is to stream into the 'A' class cases in which an assessment of the merits can be made on a site view with minimal reference to policy.

11.32 **Class A Written Representations.** It would also be possible to apply the procedural limitations as to documents which would be required, to written representations in Class A cases. This would restrict all the preliminary procedures to putting on the file the grounds of refusal and appeal and representations, if any, from interested parties. The timetable set out below in paragraph 11.108 would not apply and all these cases would be transferred to Inspectors. Clearly, this procedure (i.e. without further pleadings) could be used only where the decision was a matter of common sense rather than application of a general policy; and the consent of both the appellant and local authority would be required. The saving in time would be very substantial. The whole procedure might take as little as about two months.

11.33 **Priority cases.** The giving of priority to some applications or appeals is an unpopular measure. It is, however, recognised that certain cases (principally those concerning industry, minerals or housing) must be given priority. It would be a tedious complication if all appeals were classified according to their contribution to the national economy. There are, nevertheless, some appeals (and compulsory purchase orders) to which an emergency approach is appropriate.

11.34 **Supposed snags.** It has been put to me that a priority system based on such considerations is unworkable because the parties will not themselves keep pace with an accelerated timetable and that those with limited resources will be debarred from playing an effective part in the appeal. I do not think so. My experience is that in such cases the main parties, if under pressure, get ready within the prescribed time. If it is really unavoidable, the Inspector can always adjourn the Inquiry, an event which I think in practice would be most unlikely.

11.35 **Interested parties,** may need help in these high priority appeals. I deal with planning aid in paragraph 10.31; and if there is one category of cases in which financial aid should be given to interested parties straight away, it is those where an Inquiry is to be held within a few weeks from the date of receipt of notice of appeal by the Department.

SECTION IV: METHODS OF DEALING WITH APPEALS

11.36 The division between 'transferred' cases and 'Secretary of State' cases should be maintained and in both types of cases it should be possible to proceed either by written representation or by local public inquiries.

11.37 **Transferred Cases.** I was inclined to doubt whether the quality of decisions in transferred cases is as constantly reliable as in the Secretary of State cases. It appeared that in transferred cases there was a greater percentage of refusals. In the last 5 years the average of Secretary of State cases allowed was 29·6% and average of transferred cases allowed was 20·5%. It may be that Inspectors felt more bound to say what they believed was expected of them, rather than free to use their own judgement when it conflicted with local authority opinion. This would explain a tendency for decisions on transferred cases to accord with the local authority's view. But in 1974 the success rate in transferred cases was marginally higher (by 1%) than in the Secretary of State's cases. In any event, no detailed conclusion can be reached on the basis of the figures, without information about the subject matter. It is, however, reasonably safe to conclude that transferred case decisions are on the whole as reliable as the Secretary of State cases.

11.38 **Investigation needed.** Nevertheless, whilst I am inclined to favour the transfer of more categories of cases to Inspectors, the reasons why there was an apparent bias in favour of local authorities' decisions should first be investigated. It may well be that in smaller cases there is less scope for departure from the local view.

11.39 **Transfers: present position.** The categories of cases which can be transferred are specified in Appendix III (ii). They are quite extensive. For instance, appeals relating to housing development up to 2 hectares (4·94 acres) or 60 dwelling houses or change of use to the floor of 500 sq. metres (5,381.555 sq.ft.) can generally be dealt with by an Inspector subject to the investigation which I have suggested in paragraph 11.38. I can see no reason why the Inspectors' jurisdiction should not be doubled. If and when this is implemented, the results should be constantly monitored to ensure that Inspectors' decisions show the same consistency as those made by the Secretary of State.

11.40 **Anxiety over increase of transferred cases.** Some local authorities and one of the local authority associations have expressed some disquiet about the extension of Inspectors' jurisdiction. This is why I place much emphasis on the importance of keeping and recruiting Inspectors of sufficient calibre to make further transfer of jurisdiction possible.

11.41 **Written representations.** Despite the disadvantages outlined in paragraph 5.21, I am in favour of an increased use of written representations instead of inquiries. (I deal in greater detail with procedures in paragraphs 11.104 *et seq.*)

11.42 Originally, written representations were introduced as a simpler and speedier form of appeal. On average they take 40% less time than cases which go to inquiry and the procedure tends to be cheaper and easier. If the inquiry procedure is simplified for Class A cases, then the parties will sometimes prefer that course. But for many other cases written appeals will still be best, provided the set time table is observed and enforced (see para. 11.108). The Department naturally wish to make the maximum use of written representations (Circular 142/73 paragraph 14), and the appellant is asked to indicate on the appeal form whether he is willing to use them. The Department provide some help in their publication 'Planning Appeals – A Guide to Procedure', which is sent to all appellants with the appeal form. Inclusion in this booklet of more extensive guidance on the differences between written representations and local inquiries would be extremely helpful.

11.43 Guidance for the appellant. It is explained to the appellant that the procedure for written representations is normally faster and less expensive. The advantages of personal and direct contact at an Inquiry, including the opportunities for cross examination should, however, also be pointed out.

11.44 Written represenations are especially suitable where there has been a previous appeal and where the grounds for appeal are essentially unchanged, but not where there are substantial objections by interested parties. The practical advantages of written representations diminish rapidly where the interchange of correspondence becomes complex.

11.45 Limitations of written procedure. An effort must be made to enable interested parties to 'write in' and comment on the representations made by the appellant and the local authority. To this end the procedure is already changing and the appellant's and the local authority's statements are put on deposit in the local authority's offices for public inspection in some instances. (Circular 71/73*).

SECTION V: THE INSPECTORATE

11.46 Inspectors. The status and career structure of the Inspectorate should be maintained and improved. The Department should offer sufficient inducement to attract a greater number of private practitioners thus ensuring a wide range of background experience. Even greater reliance will have to be placed on Inspectors in the future and the quality of decisions must be maintained.

11.47 The status of the Chief Inspector should be given full recognition in conventional Whitehall terms. It would be beyond my terms of reference to suggest how this could best be done, especially as I recognize the vital role played by Regional Directorates and others in the planning appeal process.

11.48 The career structure of Inspectors may well need to be reviewed. I make no recommendations as to that. I would only say that the aim must be to continue to attract men of high calibre generally, and increasingly to attract those who are professionally qualified. It must be remembered that a growing number of cases are of sufficient national importance to demand well above average ability.

11.49 Inspectorate to remain within the Department. No case has been made out for the transfer of the Inspectorate to the Lord Chancellor's Department and there is every reason why the Inspectorate should remain within the Department.

11.50 Training. Recruitment of the right people, though vital, is not enough. Adequate training is also essential. The Department should revise arrangements for the training of Inspectors, drawing on legal as well as planning expertise to train them in decision making. (Of Inspectors now making decisions, 50–60% have been doing so for less than 2 years.)

---

*Welsh Office Circular 134/73.

SECTION VI: REPORTS AND DECISIONS

11.51 Inspector's reports. It may well be that Inspector's reports are (apart from the findings of fact and conclusions) unnecessarily detailed, that their examination within the Department is too elaborate, and that there is super-fluous consultation with other Departments in some cases.

11.52 Inspectors should feel freer to use their discretion in deciding what needs to be included in a report. For instance, it is tempting to suggest that all Inspector's reports should be shortened by cutting down (or out) the summary of evidence and arguments of the principal and interested parties.

11.53 In Secretary of State cases the temptation to cut drastically the reporting of evidence and arguments must be restrained. Regional Directors rightly feel that they need to have a comprehensive report of what happened at the Inquiry; Inspectors can still avoid unnecessary detail and should use their discretion in favour of brevity. If a report is clear and the content right, neither the public nor the Courts will demand perfection of style or the precision of a Chancery draftsman. Speed is more important.

11.54 Decisions. Those who deal with decisions should not feel bound to go into every detail lest its omission should be misinterpreted as lack of thorough-ness. The Department has already achieved much by shortening decision letters on transferred cases. This is good, but even greater effort should be made to help Inspectors in all cases by illustrating to them, with examples, the importance of brevity in recording the evidence and arguments.

11.55 Findings of Fact and Conclusions. One cannot easily draw a clear dividing line between findings of fact and conclusions (especially where opinions on policy have to be dealt with), but a distinction between arguments on the one hand and conclusions on the other is more easily understood and is important. The decision branch should concentrate on the content of Inspector's Findings of Fact and Conclusions; they should consult other officers of the Department (or other Departments) sparingly.

11.56 Overruling Inspectors. The present practice whereby Inspectors are over-ruled by the Secretary of State only in exceptional circumstances and only for a very clear policy reason is sound and popular, and this in itself is a fact which suggests that time can be wasted in over meticulous examining of their reports.

11.57 Independence of the Inspectorate: constant briefing and training. The existing independence of the Inspectorate should be maintained. This inde-pendence of the Department is one of the many reasons why the Inspectors enjoy high regard and respect. The Department take meticulous care to pre-serve this independence, but nevertheless they do need prompt and constantly up-dated guidance on policy and should be ready to respond to it.

11.58 I understand and respect the concern for the independence of the Inspectorate. I see no harm and much value in encouraging direct contact between Regional Directorates and the Superintending Inspectors, as the latter do not take Inquiries or make decisions. Administrators should gain by being better informed about the flow and content of pending appeals and the Inspec-tors would gain insight into the thinking on policy.

11.59 **The briefing of the Inspectorate** is carried out almost entirely in writing. The result is that the process of briefing over a period of time tends to consist of a series of written statements announcing apparently abrupt changes of policy. Yet in practice policy does not often change in this sudden fashion; far more often it evolves in a continuous process. Present practice being what it is, the Inspectorate is unable to sense this process at work. Hence the need for closer contacts between Superintending Inspectors and administrators.

11.60 **Policy guidance to be made public.** There is no reason why written policy guidance given to the Inspectors should not be made public. I do not think, however, that this should apply to 'regional briefs', which are normally inserted in the Inspectors' files. These merely contain a summary of published information of a strategic nature and if the parties were supplied with it they would be likely to feel that they should cover it in evidence. This would be quite unnecessary in most cases.

SECTION VII: GUIDANCE

11.61 My recommendations on Planning Control have referred to the need for guidance on policy. These recommendations are contained in paragraphs 8.42–8.60 and apply with equal force to Appeals.

11.62 **Publicity for success rates.** It is in the interests of appellants themselves, especially in small cases, that they should have statistical and other information on their chance of success and how they are most likely to achieve it.

11.63. Planning Advice Centres are badly needed to give further help and, if they head off many appeals which never had a chance of success, they may well almost pay for themselves. For the time being a well produced leaflet kept up to date may have to suffice.

11.64 Local authority officers should be encouraged to give a prospective appellant frank and objective advice, or at least direct him, when appropriate, to professional advisers who can help either in presenting, or advising against, an appeal.

11.65 **Local authorities** must also be guided and encouraged to consider an application carefully before refusing permission in categories of cases where there is a high percentage of success on appeal (e.g. change of use to bingo halls). Where some types of case are concerned, this need mean no more than reminding local authorities that they should apply the policy set out in Development Control Notes.

11.66 It may also be useful for the Department to give wider publicity to the proportion of appeals allowed district by district. There are no statistics available showing percentage of appeals from particular districts compared with the national average (of about 20%). They may be quite revealing.

SECTION VIII: GROUNDS OF REFUSAL AND APPEAL

11.67 **Grounds of appeal** should be explicit and well-considered, excluding anything which is not absolutely relevant. Grounds of appeal at present may consist of nothing more specific than a denial of the local authority's case.

11.68 In B cases grounds should be given in full from the outset, and the appellant should be restricted by the rules so that he cannot introduce further grounds without leave from the Secretary of State. Such leave, if given, would carry with it an order for costs.

11.69 This would make a contribution towards ensuring speed and would simplify the making of decisions.

11.70 **In A cases,** it is difficult for *all* appellants to be brief, relevant and explicit. It is inevitable that some grounds of appeal should fall short of the best standard; but this situation should not be too difficult to accept as the issues are normally simple. Well drafted grounds of refusal are, however, a help. The appellants should, however, be given guidance in the Appeals booklet as to which cases are likely to fall into class A.

11.71 **Grounds of refusal** lacking in substance should be strongly discouraged and greater efforts should be made by the parties to resolve objections before the Inquiry. Local authorities must understand that they are expected to be explicit and frank in their grounds of refusal and Rule 6 statements, and that they should identify objections which can be resolved by negotiation, by Section 52 agreements, by conditions or in any other way. The Department and the Inspectorate should give a *strong* lead in this respect.

11.72 It is very important that on appeals from outline applications local authorities should be discouraged from raising objections relating to matters which can be reserved for detailed approval. (See para. 7.87–7.88)

SECTION IX: PREPARATORY WORK AND MANAGEMENT

11.73 **Every appeal goes through three stages:**

(i)   preparatory work carried out by the Administrative Division of the Inspectorate;

(ii) inquiry or in written cases a site visit;

(iii) decision by the Inspector or the Secretary of State.

11.74 **Delays.** These three stages are described in some detail in Chapter 5, para. 13–28 and it is pointed out that most of the delay occurs at the preparatory stage: in 1973 stage (i) (from receipt of appeal to start of local inquiry) occupied 66% of the whole period in Secretary of State cases, and 83% of the time in Inspectors' cases. Similarly, in written representations cases by far the greater proportion of time was between the receipt of the appeal and the date of the site inspection.

11.75 **Changes in administration needed.** The staff of the Administrative Division use methods which have evolved over many years. It has been forcibly put to me that an independent management study is needed. This should be carried out, as soon as funds permit. However, it is clear even without this, that some alterations are needed with regard to relations with the public.

11.76 Avoidable delay is often caused by failure on the part of the appellant or the local authority to comply with various procedural requirements; often the documentation is incomplete or inaccurate, and the timetable is not observed.

11.77 **Attitude of the Department.** The Department's benevolent attitude to the parties may be partly to blame. The attitude of the appellant is more easily rationalised. It is his appeal: he stands to lose most if his case is not fully presented. There are limits too to the pressure that can be put on local planning authorities to speed up the presentation of their cases. They frequently cite factors such as staff shortages to explain delays sometimes, no doubt, with justification.

11.78 **A firmer control.** On the whole, probably too many concessions have been granted in the past, though there has been a distinct tightening up recently. If the planning system is to become fully efficient, the Department will need to be much firmer about time limits towards the appellant and the local planning authority alike.

11.79 **Standard time scale.** Procedures at all three stages could well be speeded up without endangering the quality of decisions. There is a particularly strong case for the introduction of a standard time scale within which the Secretary of State should normally decide particular types of appeals. This would impose a discipline on all concerned and the Department would be able, in acknowledging receipt of the appeal, to inform each appellant how long the case is expected to take. However, the Secretary of State must retain his discretionary power to extend the time limit for his own decision if necessary.

11.80 If the time limit *is* extended, the Department should either give an alternative timetable within which the case is likely to be determined, or tell him that in the particular circumstances it is not possible to estimate the time needed. Cases of this kind would of course be very rare, but it is important to recognise that there are some in which, exceptionally, for policy reasons, no timetable can be laid down.

11.81 **A firm date for the notice of appeal.** The Department is justly blamed for many of the delays which occur but some fault at least, lies with the parties. In future the date of notice of appeal should be the date on which full grounds of appeal and all the documents required by the Department have been received.

11.82 **Prescribed form of appeal.** It may also be more convenient if the Form of Appeal could be prescribed by the GDO. It would then normally be obtained from the Secretary of State as is now the practice.

11.83 **Role of Administrative Division in reducing delays.** In the immediate past the Administrative Division has responded well to the need to shorten *the waiting period* for an inquiry from 15 months as it was at its worst to approximately 8 months (see para. 5.26 which deals with recent arrangements for reducing the waiting period). There should be a gradual reduction during 1975 to an average at the end of the year of (a) $5\frac{1}{2}$ months from the time when appeal papers are in order to the date of decision in Inspectors' cases and (b) 7 months in Secretary of State cases. For written representations these periods would be (a) $4\frac{1}{2}$ months and (b) 6 months.

11.84 Two changes which are particularly needed. First, there should be clear-cut arrangements for dealing with each appellant individually. I suggest the designation of 'Case Officers'. Second, the Department should temper the understandable tendency to give special consideration to the convenience of local authorities. This was perhaps justified in the difficult days of local government reorganisation, but although local government still suffers from lack of staff there is no longer a special case for favoured treatment.

11.85 Case Officers. The appointment of Case Officers is required to meet the needs of those appellants who find difficulty in locating the officer able to deal with their problems.

11.86 Case Officers' functions. As suggested in the Interim Report I think the Case Officer should be available to discuss with the appellants and local authorities:

(*a*) the choice between written representations and Inquiries;

(*b*) the timing and arrangements for Inquiries; and

(*c*) subsequent progress towards a decision.

11.87 He would also:

(*a*) be expected to inform the appellant, at any time, of the progress of his case, even after it has passed to the decision branch from whom he would then have to obtain the necessary information; and

(*b*) be responsible for ensuring that both the appellants and the local authority comply with the Department's requirements and suggestions and deciding when the appeal papers are complete (see para. 11.81).

11.88 Allocation of Case Officer. The card acknowledging the appeal should always state the name (and telephone number) of the Case Officer to whom all further inquiries on the progress of the appeal may be made.

11.89 Difficulties. I appreciate that this proposal involves difficulties for the Department. Wherever the file happens to be at the moment when the inquiry is made, it certainly will not be with the Case Officer. If the appeal is ultimately to be decided on the advice of one of the regional offices, the file may almost certainly be in the regional office.

11.90 Nevertheless, I think it essential that an appellant should be able to find out as far as possible what progress is being made. Uncertainty is as harmful as delay. It is in everyone's interest that there should be a breakthrough in this respect.

SECTION X: WAYS OF SAVING TIME

11.91 Preparatory stage. Time can be saved by:

(1) keeping the preparatory work for Class A appeals within strict limits; and

(2) arranging that the burden of preparatory work for Class B cases should be shared between authority and appellant. I suggest, for example, that the

form TCP20 3A/74/11 (see Appendix III v) should be completed by the appellant (who would undertake the appropriate research at the local authority offices).

11.92 In all cases, times should not begin to run until the appellant completes all the required appeal documents to the satisfaction of the Case Officer. (See para. 11.87 above.)

11.93 **Fixing dates for Inquiries.** I have already stressed above the importance of adhering to a strict timetable. This is particularly important in relation to Inquiry dates. It would be simplest if the Department fixed the dates for Inquiries without consultation with either party. If an appellant for any reason other than illness or anything equally unavoidable, could not accept the date fixed, his case should be heard after all others pending.

11.94 **Local authorities' objections.** Local planning authorities sometimes plead for delay on the grounds that they lack staff or accommodation but:

(a) whilst it is appreciated that local government reorganisation has caused an upheaval, the time has now come when local authorities, like appellants, will have to accept dates appointed by the Department unless circumstances are wholly exceptional;

(b) lack of accommodation should not be accepted as a reason for altering dates. Accommodation can always be hired if necessary;

(c) if local authorities lack staff they should instruct private practitioners. There is ample precedent for this.

11.95 These rules must be applied strictly for the time being. When delays have been eliminated they may be relaxed.

SECTION XI: COSTS

11.96 **The Secretary of State** should be encouraged to award costs much more readily against a party causing delay in the appeal procedure. He has not done so very often in the past but there seems no reason why he should not make such awards frequently in future both in written representations and public inquiry cases (see para. 11.103).

11.97 **Unforeseen delays** caused by only one of the parties postpone the decision and lead to a serious waste of time for Inspectors and the Inspectorate's staff. In particular, after a last-minute postponement it is not always possible to reassign an Inquiry to the Inspector formerly in charge.

11.98 **Inspectors should have the power to award costs** in cases which have been transferred to them for decision. In Secretary of State cases, the Inspector should make a recommendation and the question of costs should then be dealt with by the Secretary of State as an integral part of his decision letter.

11.99 **A Comprehensive Code for Costs.** There should be a new comprehensive code to deal with costs.

11.100 **Present situation.**   The number of applications to the Secretary of State for an award of costs on grounds of unreasonable behaviour (including those arising from adjourned or abortive inquiries) at present runs at about a hundred a year.   Of these he grants about a quarter and refuses the rest.   Most of these awards are against the appellant – either because he has appealed repeatedly without change of circumstances, or because he has failed to appear at a local inquiry and therefore renders all preparatory work and arrangements abortive.

11.101 **Action against which costs should be awarded.**   I do not propose to produce an exhaustive list of grounds for an order for costs.   Some examples are:

(a) late adjournment of Inquiries;

(b) late amendment of grounds of refusal or of appeal;

(c) frivolous, vexatious or repetitive appeals which prove unsuccessful;

(d) failure to comply with directions on procedure, e.g.

    (i)   the exchange of Proofs of Evidence,

    (ii) the disclosure of technical reports;

(e) insubstantial ('make-weight') grounds of refusal or appeal;

(f) failure to comply with rules of procedure whether laid down by statutory orders or circulars;

(g) introduction of new evidence without reasonable notice (see para. 11.143(5)).

11.102 **No body or person to be exempt from an order for costs.**   I recommend that such sanctions should be applied against both applicant and local planning authorities and also against other statutory bodies; possibly also, at some future date, against other interested parties.   This last suggestion will need careful consideration.   It is, in my view, important that Inspectors should have unfettered discretion to recommend the award of costs which should be to the standard scale (called by lawyers 'party and party') and subject to the normal taxation procedures.

11.103 **Costs in written representation cases.**   An order for costs under Section 250 (5) can only be made where there has been an Inquiry.   An amendment is necessary to enable the Secretary of State to make an order at any time, after an appeal is lodged.   This would also cover orders for costs in respect of appeals in writing.

SECTION XII:

SUGGESTED IMPROVEMENTS IN WRITTEN PROCEDURE

11.104 As I have already indicated, there is a case for encouraging appeals in writing for Class A (11.32).   Therefore a major effort is needed to make this method more attractive for Class B.

11.105 Under the present procedure the appellant's grounds of appeal serve as his written representation.   The local planning authority is then invited to submit a statement of its own.   A copy of the authority's statement is sent to the appellant and he has a chance to comment. This should complete the written procedure. But in the past further comments were allowed or even invited and the procedure dragged on.

11.106 There should be clear limits to the number of representations which each party to the appeal can make. The Department should lay down a code of procedure, widely publish it and also monitor it, so as to ensure that it is strictly observed. This should be followed up by statutory rules, which I assume would be drafted in consultation with the Council of Tribunals, to ensure that the proposed timetable is complied with. The procedures (and rules) should include written representations to:

(a) the appellant's grounds of appeal;

(b) the local authority's observations;

(c) the appellant's reply.

11.107 It has been suggested that the parties should be allowed 'any further representation limited to correcting factual errors'. I am afraid I disagree with this. Both parties will have had an opportunity to state their case twice. The local planning authority in the grounds of refusal and its 'observations' (see (b) above); the appellant in his grounds of appeal and his reply to the local authority's observations. If the Inspector who visits the site requires further information, or if the Department requires it, then a Class A Inquiry should be ordered (see para. 11.117 below).
It is vital that there should be firm application of the rules of procedure for written representations if they are to play a major part in speeding up appeals.

11.108 **Timetable.** The timetable should be as follows:

(1) The appellant's representations are normally inserted on the appeal form and if he wishes to submit further representations, time should not begin to run until these are received by the local authority.

(2) The local authority observations arrive at the Department within the following 6 weeks.

(3) The appellant then has 2 weeks to reply.

(4) An Inspector's site visit is arranged for a date not more than 2 weeks after the date for the appellant's reply.

(5) The Department gives a decision within 5 weeks after the site visit, unless the Secretary of State specifies otherwise. In those exceptional circumstances, the Secretary of State gives notice of the date by which he expects to decide the case, stating the reason for the delay.

(6) The total period for completing this procedure is thus 15 weeks from the date when the local authority receives the appellant's representations as compared with the present average of about a year.

(7) In Inspectors' cases the 5 weeks period mentioned in (5) could reasonably be reduced to 3 weeks.

11.109 This timetable should apply whether the written representations procedure is adopted by agreement or by order of the Secretary of State.

11.110 If neither party complies with the timetable, the Secretaries of State and their Inspectors should be free to reach decisions on the grounds of appeal and refusal only.

11.111 Delays also result if interested parties write in after the representations of the appellant and the local planning authority are complete, and the appeal has moved to the decision stage. This difficulty will be avoided by a procedure which requires interested parties to submit their observations by a specified date to the Department – perhaps the same date as for the local planning authority's reply.

11.112 **Need for firm measures.** These may seem somewhat ruthless measures but they are indispensable if this review is to be at all effective. We have at present a flexible and benevolent written representations system; it works well but far too slowly. My objective is to reduce the period of time required for its operation from about one year at present in Secretary of State cases and 36 weeks in Inspector's cases to 15 and 13 weeks respectively. It should be remembered that written appeals account for 70% of all appeals even now, and could be used more effectively if delays were eliminated. This can only be done if the procedure and the timetable is strictly observed, otherwise there is no point in making any change in the system at all. The choice is reasonable speed, or much the same degree of delay as we have now.

11.113 **Quality will not suffer.** I think it very unlikely that in the type of case which is dealt with by written representations the quality of decisions can be significantly affected even if the decision is made on grounds of refusal and grounds of appeal alone.

11.114 **Site visit crucial.** It is the inspection of the appeal site, and not what the parties say, that matters most in deciding an appeal. If the site visit leaves the Inspector who makes it in doubt, he will be able to recommend that a Class A Inquiry should be held.

11.115 **Power to order Inquiry.** The Secretary of State should use to the full his power (under para. 5(1) of Schedule 9 to the 1971 Act) to order an Inquiry (if the Inspector appointed to view the site recommends this) at any time up to 28 days after the receipt of the appellant's reply. This offers an opportunity to transfer the written case to the Inquiry procedure. It is an important procedural expedient.

11.116 **Visits must not be too casual.** It would be very tempting to suggest that the Inspector should instead have an informal discussion with the parties on an accompanied site visit, but such a procedure would be too casual.

11.117 **Avoiding protracted proceedings.** I have considered and rejected the proposal that the Inspector should have the power to require further information from the parties and that this power should be exercised within 14 days of the site inspection. (A further 14 days would have been allowed for a reply.) In my view it could prove self-defeating to extend the written representation procedure in this way. If a decision cannot be made on the information available under the normal procedure there should be an Inquiry, normally Class A.

11.118 Inspectors should make recommendations. In a transferred case, the Inspector who visits the site merely writes a decision letter. In a Secretary of State case where written representations are used he has to write an unusual kind of report, in that he comments on the site, but offers no conclusions or recommendations. I think that in the latter type of case the Inspector who visits the site should also consider the representations and submit a draft decision letter, at least for a trial period.

SECTION XIII: INQUIRIES AND HEARINGS

11.119 'Hearings' obsolete. There appears to be no appreciable advantage in holding hearings (which the public have no right to attend) instead of inquiries. I do not think that there are any cases nowadays in which there should be a prohibition against the admission of the public or the press and I doubt whether there is any point in keeping this distinction.

11.120 Choice. In some cases (e.g. appeals from a determination of 'alternative use' of land to be compulsorily acquired for a public purpose*) the parties are offered the alternative of a hearing or an inquiry. The small advantage of offering a choice scarcely justifies the extra administrative work it causes.

11.121 I understand that in the past, hearings have often been held when an appeal involved only public authorities. I recommend accordingly that the law should be amended to exclude the option of a hearing.

11.122 Informal inquiries. I suggest, however, that in any future legislation the expression 'informal inquiries' should be used to describe inquiries in Class A appeals. At these no interested parties would normally be involved, though they would have the right to take part should they wish.

SECTION XIV: CONDUCT OF INQUIRY

11.123 Inspector's role. In some Class B cases the Inspector should take a more active role, indicating informally, at a suitable juncture, what issues appear to him most important, and assisting parties, if necessary, to bring out relevant facts (or alternatively dissuading them from wasting time on what is irrelevant).

11.124 Ad hoc Inspectors. The identification of issues and the weighing of evidence are tasks which require long experience and suitable training. It may be that for a time *ad hoc* Inspectors should be appointed in some cases to set a suitable example.

11.125 Use of Assessors. For major Inquiries (or called-in cases) in which the presentation of evidence by the parties is not likely to be sufficiently expert, the Inspector should more frequently have the assistance of an Assessor to elicit information which he needs.

---

*Under S.23 (23) of the Land Compensation Act 1961 or 1973.

138

11.126 **Excessive formality.** As I have already reported (para. 11.4), there is a strong feeling that Inquiries are too formal and legalistic. There is no reason why the atmosphere at an Inquiry should not be one which will help people to feel at ease, although at major Inquiries too much informality would obviously become more of a hindrance than a help.

11.127 **Assisting Inspector.** The opening and closing statements by the parties should have the specific aim of assisting the Inspector in making his findings of fact and conclusions.

11.128 **Cross-examination** plays a vital part in testing the accuracy of evidence, and Inspectors do not always appreciate the value of cross-examination genuinely aimed at eliciting the facts. It is less helpful to cross-examine in detail on matters of opinion. A touch of friendliness is always welcome, especially where interested parties are concerned.

11.129 **Guidance for dealing with the public.** Members of the public make a valuable contribution to Inquiries but some have little idea of what is relevant and Inspectors must be given guidance on how to deal firmly with this aspect of public involvement.

11.130 The following paragraphs deal with the vexed question of enabling 'interested parties' to copy documents used at Inquiries.

The Provisions of the Inquiries Procedure Rules

11.131 Rule 6(4) provides that where the local planning authority intend to refer to, or put in evidence at the Inquiry, documents (including maps and plans), their statement (under Rule 6(2)) must be accompanied by a list of such documents, together with a notice stating the times and place at which the documents may be inspected by the applicant and the Section 29 parties; and the local planning authority must give them a reasonable opportunity to inspect and, where practicable, to take copies of the documents.

11.132 Under Rule 6(5) the local planning authority must give any other person interested a reasonable opportunity to inspect and, where practicable, to take copies of any statements by the Secretary of State under Rule 6(1) or by the authority under Rule 6(2), and of the other documents referred to in Rule 6(4), as well as of any statement served on the authority by the applicant under Rule 6(6).

11.133 Under Rule 10(4) the Inspector has discretion to admit any evidence, and he may direct that documents tendered in evidence may be inspected by any person entitled or permitted to appear at the Inquiry, and that facilities be afforded him to take or obtain copies thereof.

11.134 The Department report that no serious difficulties are known to have occurred in working the procedure under Rules 6(4) and 6(5). The question is whether a person taking a copy of a document (when given the opportunity to do so under the Rules) is in fact breaching the copyright in the work. Sections 6 and 9 of the Copyright Act 1956 set out certain exceptions from the restrictions, but there is no statutory exception for copying under the authority of another enactment. The only exceptions which may be relevant are 'fair dealing' for the purposes of research or private study, and reproduction for the purposes of a 'judicial proceeding'.

11.135 In the opinion of the Department's legal advisers, the copying of a document or plan by a party to an Inquiry (or by a prospective participant) cannot be for the purposes of research or private study. The expression 'judicial proceeding' however is defined in the 1956 Act in such a way as to include a public inquiry held under Section 282 of the Planning Act. Copying for the purpose of such an Inquiry would not therefore seem to constitute an infringement of copyright.

11.136 What is the 'taking a copy of a document for the purposes of an Inquiry'? Clearly, it extends to copying by one of the persons who has a statutory right to appear at the Inquiry (local planning authority, appellant or Section 29 party) when afforded an opportunity under Rule 6(4), and to the copying of a document made available under Rule 10(4). But it seems very doubtful that a 'person interested' who copies Rule 6 statements and other documents made available in pursuance of Rule 6(5), can be said to copy for the purposes of the Inquiry; therefore technically such persons are probably in breach of the Copyright Act.

11.137 The difficulty is that such a person may well be a *bona fide* objector, albeit not a Section 29 party as such. The spirit of my Interim Report recommendation cannot be fulfilled if such persons are liable to infringe the law of copyright, when they seek to inform themselves about the evidence submitted. It should be noted that the Inquiries Procedure Rules also *intend* that any other person should have reasonable access to the evidence. It is the local authority which, as piggy in the middle, finds itself unable to satisfy both the law and the public simultaneously.

The Legal Position

11.138 Section 3 of the Copyright Act, which protects 'artistic works', appears to cover any plan, map or diagram which accompanies an application for planning permission. The general rule is that the architect owns the copyright in the plans which he has prepared. They may not, therefore, be reproduced without his licence. Reproduction includes not merely taking a copy of the plans, but also building in accordance with them.

11.139 Where, therefore, an architect submits plans with an application for planning permission, a question arises: how far has he licensed their reproduction? It would seem clear that he has licensed reproduction for all purposes connected with the consideration of the application for planning permission, e.g. if the local authority needs to make further copies in order to deal with the application. This, I think, includes providing a copy for the parish council. But it would seem unlikely, under the present law, that the local authority could reproduce the plans for other purposes, e.g. to supply to potential objectors or amenity societies. It is not strictly necessary for such persons to be given copies for the planning application to be dealt with.

11.140 If the law were altered so as to provide that any person interested could obtain copies of plans submitted for planning permission, then it seems likely that no change of copyright law would be strictly necessary; for then the architect submitting the plans would know that there is a specific statutory right in others to obtain copies of the plans, and would therefore be held to have implicitly licensed their reproduction for that purpose. Accordingly, I recommend the enactment of a declaratory section stating that the supply of a limited number of copies of plans pursuant to a particular provision shall, for the avoidance of doubt, be deemed not to infringe any copyright in the plans. Such a section could apply equally to the copying of documents deposited for a public Inquiry and to the copyright of application plans (see 10.14).

SECTION XV: PUBLIC INVOLVEMENT

11.141 **The right balance.** The contribution of the public to the appeal process must at the same time be both strongly encouraged and firmly contained. This is more easily said than done. There is sometimes a difficulty in encouraging the general public to participate in even the most important inquiries, except where their private interests are directly affected. It is equally difficult to restrain a sincere but irrelevant objection of a local pressure group.

11.142 **The amenity societies' contribution.** Local and national amenity societies give much assistance. Local societies often start as mere negative pressure groups but continue their work positively in the public interest. It must be remembered that even the most experienced and respected societies depend on local committees where experience and expertise inevitably vary.

11.143 **Changes to help Inspectors.** The Inspectorate have a difficult task to perform. It would help them greatly:

(1) if interested parties were normally expected to give *notice in writing* of their representations;

(2) if in exceptional cases they had power to require the interested parties to provide a summary of their submissions, however informal, along the lines of a Rule 6 statement;

(3) if amenity societies received guidance and help in the presentation of their cases. They would need money and the help of a national or regional amenity society with the necessary experience to give advice;

(4) if there were a general extension of the practice of awarding costs. There is a special case for the appellant or local authority, or both, being responsible for (and ordered to pay) *the costs of an interested party who provides helpful evidence* which would not otherwise have been available. (This would, in turn, encourage societies to adopt a constructive approach at Inquiries.)

(5) There is also a case, in exceptional circumstances, for an award of costs *against interested parties* who, after a warning from the Inspector, pursue an objection which is considered (in transferred cases by him, elsewhere by the Secretary of State) to be frivolous or vexatious.

11.144 **Minority pressures.** Irrelevance and repetition waste time but otherwise do no harm. There is, however, a real danger (as I think has already been seen in some isolated cases) that decisions are influenced by sheer pressure from the few, with 'strong voices' or substantial resources.

11.145 **Balanced, relevant evidence.** Steps must therefore be taken:

(1) to secure full and early publicity for appeals especially those of general and genuine planning importance;

(2) to give positive support and help to amenity and other societies which have established a record of responsible and constructive conduct;

(3) to encourage Inspectors to deal firmly with irrelevant matters which should not be allowed to take up time at Inquiries.

SECTION XVI: CATEGORY B APPEALS

11.146 **Inquiry Procedure Rules.** Experience has shown that it would be better if the now pre-Inquiry procedure were to be sanctioned by a Statutory Instrument. Therefore, the Inquiry Procedure Rules will have to be extended if the proposals of this report are accepted.

11.147 In paragraphs 6.58–6.61 of my Interim Report I made two suggestions connected with the local planning authority's statement under Rule 6 of the Town and Country Planning (Inquiries Procedure) Rules 1969* (which is for all practical purposes mandatory). One was that the time limit within which it must be presented should be related back to a past date rather than forward to the date of the Inquiry. The second was that, following its presentation, a similar statement should be required from the appellant as a rule rather than, as now, very much an exception. I received a considerable volume of support for both these propositions and no criticism of them. The fact that, for one reason or another, it may still be many weeks before the Inquiry opens is no reason whatever why the principal parties should not be required to present their statements to the Department as soon as can reasonably be expected.

11.148 **Rule 6 statements by appellants.** The Committee on Administrative Tribunals and Inquiries had some reservations as to whether appellants should be required to give advance notice of the detail of their case (para. 285). But nowadays in Class B cases complex technical issues frequently arise, and these involve statistical estimates and forecasts. It will help everybody if differences are defined before the Inquiry. In less technical cases it is also helpful to have a clear indication of the appellant's case, especially where the grounds of appeal are not very informative. Anyway, there is already the power to require these statements and it should be used frequently (see Rule 6(6)).

11.149 **Rule 6 Experiments.** In some experiments which the Department carried out, agreement was reached on figures on traffic flows and land availability, and in one case the local planning authority accepted the appellant's offer to contribute to the cost of drainage works, and withdrew its objection on that ground.

11.150 **Timetable for Rule 6 statements.** I therefore adhere to my previous general recommendations. In detail, and as a starting point for further discussion, I suggest that:

---

*Now superseded by Town and Country Planning (Inquiries Procedure) Rules 1974.

(*a*) as soon as the case officer in the Department decides that the appeal papers are complete (para. 11.87), the local planning authority should be instructed to present their Rule 6 statement within 5 weeks (subject to extension at the discretion of the Department) and in any event not less than 8 weeks before the date fixed for the Inquiry;

(*b*) the appellant should normally be required to submit his own **Rule 6** statement within 4 weeks after receiving the local planning authority's;

(*c*) within 14 days of the receipt of the appellant's statement of submissions, the Department should fix the date for the Inquiry and notify the parties in writing.

11.151 A demanding timetable. Experience already shows that this is going to be a taxing timetable. Appellants' expert witnesses are in most cases over-worked and sometimes quite genuinely cannot produce their proofs or plans until the last minute. The question is when should the last minute be.

11.152 Present practice: local planning authorities. Local authorities at present have to produce their plans pursuant to Rule 6(4) 28 days before the Inquiry. Most of them do, because the rules require it. Some also produce their principal proof in the form of a Rule 6 statement at the same time.

11.153 Present practice: appellants. The Rule 6(6) which deals with similar statements by appellants is similarly worded. Requests for such statements are now more frequent but as yet erratic. Local planning authorities generally make them too late to be effective.

11.154 Early exchange of proofs. I also suggested (paragraph 6.62 of the Interim Report) that the parties should be required to agree a statement of facts as far as possible, and to exchange (especially in impact statement cases) all, or at least technical, proofs of evidence. This proposal, too, has evoked strong support. I conclude that it would be particularly useful if the appellant's Rule 6(6) statement was required to contain a statement of facts and matters referred to in the local authority Rule 6(2) statement which are agreed by both parties. An example is Appendix III iv.

11.155 Penalties for failure to meet timetable. Failure by either party to comply with the time limits should result in their having to apply for leave to add to their grounds of refusal or appeal, as the case may be, and this would normally mean an order for costs (see para. 11.96 *et seq.* above). This may not prove a *wholly* effective sanction, especially where an appellant is waiting for the local planning authority's Rule 6 statement in order to prepare his case. But there is at present no effective sanction at all; and, on the whole, local authorities comply with the time limit under Rule 6(2).

11.156 Other suggested changes. If my suggestions in paragraph 11.146 *et seq.* are followed, the Rules must be adjusted accordingly and extended to cover all statistical and technical information. It might also be provided that in some cases the Inspector should have a general power to order an exchange of proofs within a specified period before, or at, the opening of an Inquiry. In some major cases, there would be advantage in the Secretary of State providing a statement (as he does under Rule 6(1) in call-in cases) of the issues which seem to him likely to be relevant to his consideration of the appeal.

11.157 **Public access to documents.** We must not forget other interested parties. Rule 6 statements and all documents and plans exchanged by the parties should continue to be available for inspection by the public. It would also, as already noted, be very helpful if the interested parties were to set out in writing, before the Inquiry begins, the principal points they wish to raise. The rules of procedure could contain requirement to this effect.

11.158 **Flexibility and experiment.** Such a rule must, however, be used flexibly to avoid unfairly penalizing an objector who is not able to express himself clearly in writing. The various borderlines between what is possible in theory and what is practicable should be explored in experiments.

11.159 **Universal agreement not practicable.** It has also been suggested to me that third parties who wish to give evidence at an Inquiry should be placed under the same obligation as the principal parties *to agree statements of fact*. I think this, again, is a counsel of perfection. The stage is soon reached when too many cooks take too long to agree (or even to decide that they cannot agree) not only how the broth should be cooked, but even on what the ingredients should be. This kind of situation will certainly not produce speedier decisions, nor probably would they be better ones.

11.160 **Pre-Inquiry meetings** or similar procedures would be useful in some Class B cases. Ideally these should be held by a Regional Registrar (with at least some legal training or experience) or by the Inspector who has been appointed to hold the Inquiry. They also should be held in public. The Inspector would give appropriate directions, and deal with other interlocutory matters, such as adjournments. A Registrar or Inspector must issue directions:

(1) to agree a statement of facts;

(2) to exchange proofs;

(3) as to whether proofs should be taken as read, if delivered in good time before the Inquiry, and put on deposit for public inspection;

(4) to arrange for a meeting between experts;

(5) to draft a proposed programme with fixed times for the attendance of objectors.

The Direction given for the Inquiry into the Brighton Marina in 1974 is set out as Appendix III iii.

11.161 There is already some evidence that these pre-Inquiry procedures are well worth while.

SECTION XVII: GENERAL

11.162 **Sessions.** My Interim Report recommended that a number of cases with a geographical and policy affinity be dealt with at one Inquiry session. This was done as an experiment in March 1974 at Wokingham. The results were mixed, but they did show that there could be a reduction in time and effort provided the cases had a real homogeneity and were not too many in number. A similar experimental Inquiry session was held in South Glamorgan in June 1974. This proved to be valuable in preventing duplication of evidence, and allowed 7 appeals to be dealt with during a 4-day session. The local planning authority asked subsequently that another such session should be held in their area. The need for sessions remains. But to yield good results they need firmer rules and more guidance from the Department, as well as care in choosing the cases to be taken.

11.163 **Group inquiries.** In addition, the recently established practice for Inspectors to deal with smaller cases in groups works well and should be continued.

11.164 **Wider inquiries.** There are, however, at least two types of cases in which an Inquiry or Public Examination is justified to consider matters of general importance:

(*a*) where there are several alternative sites;

(*b*) where there is a preliminary issue of principle to be considered;

(*c*) where a strategic issue has to be resolved to facilitate development control or as an input for a structure or a local plan (such as the need for out of town shopping in a particular area).

11.165 **The Pilot Inquiry** on matters of planning policy suggested in 8.36–8.41 would determine whether the proposed activity should take place at all. Where its recommendations in principle favours such development, a *Second Stage Inquiry* would determine the merits of a specific site or sites.

SECTION XVIII: JUDICIAL REVIEW

11.166 **Possible later extension.** If the appeal procedure operates more speedily and becomes less formal there may be a case for a very limited extension of judicial power to review the Secretary of State's decisions.

11.167 **Questionable decisions.** In the nature of things, a decision taken by the Secretary of State or one of his Inspectors, may be regarded as a bad decision, by at least one of the parties. Indeed Secretaries of State have occasionally felt so much doubt about their own or their predecessors' decisions that they have arranged a public inquiry to consider whether they should set the revocation procedure in motion.

11.168 **Present limits.** At present a decision by the Secretary of State can be reviewed by the High Court only if he has exceeded his powers or if failure to comply with procedures has caused substantial prejudice. The cases show that the Courts have given a fairly wide interpretation to the phrase 'not within the powers' and that a decision is open to challenge if it can be said that no reasonable person would have made it on the evidence which was before the Secretary of State. However, the Courts have been reluctant to quash a decision on these grounds if they have been able to find any evidence at all to support the decision – unless it can be positively shown that the Secretary of State has failed to take account of the relevant considerations.

145

11.169 **Some scope for extension.** I do not wish to encourage intervention by the Courts in administrative matters. Nevertheless, I consider that there would be advantage in extending the Courts powers to the extent that if a decision is ambiguous, or 'unreasonable in a comprehensive sense', the Court would use their reserve power to remit it for re-consideration by the Secretary of State. As I have said, experience shows that this power is exercised sparingly by the Courts and it may be that the construction of 'unreasonableness' in Lord Green's M.R. judgment in *Associated Provincial Picture Houses Ltd v Wednesbury Corporation* (1948) 1 K.B. 223,229 should now be made somewhat more comprehensive. This would require legislation. If the case were remitted, the Secretary of State would still of course retain the discretion to decide whether another Inquiry should be held in such a case and whether he would alter or adhere to his decision.

11.170 **A help to Inspectors.** The object of this additional jurisdiction would be to encourage the Inspectorate and the Department not to be over-cautious, an attitude which is bred of the knowledge that the Secretary of State's decision is final (though a fresh application can open the door to a fresh decision).

11.171 **Appeal by leave only.** To ensure that this power to apply to the High Court is not abused, I suggest that prospective appellants should need to seek leave from a Judge in Chambers by *ex parte* procedure. The Department would thus not need to be represented when the application was made and this stage of the appeal would impose no additional burden on its staff. In most cases I would expect the judges to grant leave more readily if the appellant had previously obtained the Secretary of State's agreement to the application.

11.172 **No intervention by interested parties.** While I appreciate that this is a matter of opinion, I cannot recommend that interested parties could be permitted to intervene in any Court proceedings.

146

CHAPTER 12

Enforcement

SECTION I: INTRODUCTION

12.1 In my Interim Report, I indicated my intention to consider the problems of enforcement control. My concern has been reinforced both by meetings with planning committees around the country who stressed their anxiety at not being able to fulfil their functions properly in the area of enforcement and by the statistical evidence which supports their complaints.

SECTION II: MAIN PROBLEMS

12.2 **The Main Problems are:**

(a) **The delay caused by appeals.** Enforcement notices do not operate quickly enough, because they can be *suspended* for a long time by the process of appeals. About 1,200 enforcement appeals are decided each year, but at the end of 1973 there were 3,678 outstanding, as compared with 2,889 at the beginning of the year. This is particularly disquieting because authorities feel they do not serve notices in anything like as many cases as they would like, which indicates that planning control in this field is functioning at a wholly inadequate pace. The other disquieting fact is that 65% of all enforcement notices served are taken to appeal.

(b) **The local planning authority's inability to serve a stop notice in respect of changes of uses of land.** As the law stands at the moment, uses commenced in contravention of planning law are not susceptible to any immediate sanction such as a stop notice, and may thus continue for several months while the case goes to appeal, naturally giving rise to considerable local concern. I explained in para. 6.9 the reasons why, under the present system, stop notices only apply to building operations. However, the many cases which have been brought to my attention have led me to question the basis on which stop notices are limited to operational development. For example, businesses, such as car sales, which are carried out on open land, may simply avoid the effect of service of an enforcement notice by moving from one piece of land to another. In this way a business can be conducted for quite a long time in contravention of planning control, though the case of *Attorney General v. Smith* (1958) 2QB 173 indicates that an injunction can eventually be sought to prevent further defiance of the Act.

(c) **Reluctance to serve stop notices because of the risk of liability to pay compensation.** Undoubtedly the main factor which inhibits local authorities from serving stop notices is the fear of cases where substantial claims for

147

compensation might be made against them. As I mentioned in para. 6.3, many local authorities apparently do not realise that it is only in very limited circumstances that the service of a stop notice can render them liable to compensation. Section 177 of the 1971 Act states: 'A person shall be entitled to compensation . . . in respect of a prohibition contained in a stop notice in any of the following circumstances:—

(a) the enforcement notice is quashed on any of the grounds mentioned in section 88(1) (b), (c), (d) or (e) of this Act; [see para. 6.11];

(b) the allegation in the enforcement notice on which the prohibition in the stop notice is dependent is not upheld by reason that the enforcement notice is varied on one of those grounds;

(c) the enforcement notice is withdrawn by the local planning authority otherwise than in consequence of the grant by them of planning permission for the development to which the notice relates or for its retention or continuance without compliance with a condition or limitation subject to which a previous planning permission was granted;

(d) the stop notice is withdrawn.'

(d) **Difficulties of local planning authorities in ascertaining facts.** One of the reasons why so many notices are quashed on appeal is that the facts are not disclosed by the occupier soon enough. There is considerable evidence to suggest that many local planning authorities are in an inherently weak position to deal with apparent breaches of control because the methods of getting information about the development in question are unsatisfactory. Under the present system a local planning authority may attempt to ask the owner, occupier or developer of a site or building for information regarding the history of the building or site, and operations which are being carried out or uses to which the site is presently being put. This sort of information is not always readily available. It may take the owner, occupier or developer time to establish the facts. He may not be willing to give them. Meanwhile the local authority has no power to force the developer to gather the information together nor recourse to any sanctions, should the information be false; they must rely on the developer's goodwill and honesty. If the information is inaccurate (whether the error be deliberate or inadvertent), the local authority's position can be extremely difficult. The person giving the information has not committed himself to anything; but the local authority who serves an enforcement notice on the basis of the information received *has* committed itself.

(e) **The complexity of the law.** It may be that the local authorities' lawyers are not able to give wholly adequate advice. This is quite understandable in this difficult branch of the law.* But Inspectors who are appointed to conduct inquiries into Enforcement Appeals are experienced, and the

---

*Harman, L. J. had this to say about enforcement notices: 'Hard indeed are the paths of local authorities in striving to administer the town and country planning legislation of recent years. It is a sorry comment on the law and those who administer it that between the years 1947 and 1960 they had succeeded in so bedevilling the whole administration of that legislation that Parliament was compelled to come to the rescue and remove a great portion of it from the purview of the Courts. Not for nothing was I offered a book yesterday called Encyclopaedia of Planning. It is a subject which stinks in the noses of the public, and not without reason.'

148

Department's legal advisers are so highly specialised, that they are better equipped to deal with them than any other forum in the country (with the possible exception of the Lands Tribunal). The problem of giving accurate advice has been assisted by a very helpful booklet on enforcement practice recently published by the Department.

12.3 The large number of appeals is not really warranted. Less than 20% of successful appeals succeed on legal grounds; on the other hand over 50% succeed on planning grounds, and in these the same result could be achieved in a less complex way.

(1) **Ground A.** (See para. 6.11 and 6.19.) It worries me that the most successful ground of appeal is ground (a). That simply means that enforcement notices are served in many cases where planning permission should be granted for the contravening development. That represents a wasted use of planning powers.

(2) **Grounds B and D.** The second most successful grounds are (b) and (d). This may indicate one or both of two things:

   (a) that local authorities do not get the full facts before they serve the notice (not necessarily through want of trying, as they may have no means of finding out);

   (b) planning officers do not get sufficient legal briefing before advising that a notice be served.

SECTION III: REFORMS

12.4 **Consideration of Grant of Permission.** The local planning authority should, at the outset, be required to consider whether it would grant permission (and if so, subject to what conditions), and to give reasons if it is not prepared to grant unconditional permission.

(a) An enforcement notice is a drastic remedy, but at present it is the only weapon authorities have to bring an activity under planning control. There are often cases where they would be willing to grant permission provided they could impose conditions. At present they have no power to grant any permission until an application is made. I am attracted by the proposal that in cases where they consider that there has been a breach of planning control they should have power (and indeed be encouraged) to make a formal offer of planning permission (with or without conditions) to the person concerned. I recognize that the number of cases where this would be appropriate are limited; nonetheless, if the authority is prepared to grant planning permission in such cases and the developer is willing to accept it, this would, it seems to me, achieve a reduction in the number of appeals as well as eliminating superfluous argument in the appeals which are made. At the present time, an authority has power to serve an enforcement notice if it considers it 'expedient' to do so on planning grounds; I consider that there should be a positive statutory requirement that before

149

deciding whether to serve an enforcement notice the authority must consider what planning objections there are to the development, and make sure that the developer is informed of them. By having the reasons stated in the notice the developer will know clearly the case against him and the room for possible compromise. This should also help to reduce the number of appeals.

(b) If planning permission is to be granted, the proposal to do so should be given the same publicity as would have been given to an application for the same development made in the ordinary way.

12.5 Expediency. The local planning authority should also state in the notice any reasons in addition to 'reasons for refusal', why it is expedient to serve it. Their reasons for thinking it expedient may be limited to the grounds on which they would have refused an application for permission but there may be other considerations, such as the fact that there have been substantial and seemingly justified public complaints. In such a case the developer should be entitled to know at the outset who has complained and why.

12.6 Model form of Enforcement Notices. The model enforcement notice (issued in Circular 153/74*) (Appendix IV i) should always be used as a basis. (It would have to be amended if these recommendations are implemented.) The many legal pitfalls for local authorities seeking to draft a valid enforcement notice have often resulted in forms of wording which go a long way to conceal from the uninitiated layman the basic message which the notice is intended to convey. A model notice which emphasized, if necessary in red, the really crucial points would be of assistance to authorities and landowners alike. Another advantage of a model form of notice would be that it might prevent the raising of pettifogging legal points (see Templeman, J. in *Eldon Garages v. Kingston-upon-Hull Corporation* [1974] 1 W.L.R. 276). If possible the model form should be given statutory force.

12.7 Power to Require Works or Alterations. There should be the power to include in an enforcement notice a requirement for works to be carried out as an alternative to restoring the land to its previous state. At present the enforcement notice can only require the developer to take steps for the purpose of restoring the land to its condition before the development took place or, in the case of a breach of condition, for the purpose of securing compliance with the condition. There are often cases where some different action would meet any valid planning objection, and it would be useful if the requirements in the notice could specify the action in question as an alternative to restoring the land. (I have in mind, for instance, the case where an extension to a house has been put up without permission. It may be that the only objection is to a window which overlooks a neighbour's garden and this could be met by requiring the window to be bricked up.) In addition, Section 91(1) of the 1971 Act (which empowers the local planning authority (in certain circumstances) to enter the land and itself take the steps required by the notice, if the notice has not been complied with) should be amended so that local planning authorities may carry out works as an alternative to restoring the land to its previous state and be able to recover the cost of doing so from the owner of the land.

---

*Welsh Office Circular 204/74.

12.8 **Stop Notices.** Stop notice procedure should be extended to change of use. The reason generally given for restricting the application of stop notices to operational development is that there is often much greater difficulty in finding out whether a material change of use has taken place. I do not see this as a valid objection in principle, although it may mean that authorities will always be less willing to serve stop notices in respect of uses for fear of attracting a compensation claim. However, I think that these fears should be substantially reduced by the discovery notice procedure which I am recommending (see para. 12.9 below). There is to my mind the overriding need to have an effective means of bringing offensive activities to a halt, without having to wait for months or years while appeal procedures are completed, particularly since the potential profits from the activity may encourage the developer to drag out the appeal process as long as possible.

12.9 Discovery Notices

Section 284 of the 1971 Act should be extended to enable local planning authorities to require the occupier to give factual information as to use of land or other activities carried on ('Discovery Notice'). I see no convincing reason for not extending the powers already conferred by Section 284, to include information as to the nature of activities carried on and other facts which would enable the authority to decide whether enforcement action is appropriate (such as whether there is a planning permission in existence, or when the use commenced). At present Section 284 only enables the authority to require information about interests in land.

12.10 How Discovery Notices Would Work

Where a local planning authority have reason to suspect that there has been a breach of planning control, a discovery notice would be served upon the occupier of the land (or the person who appears to have committed the breach, where there is no occupier as such). The information given in response to such a notice should enable the local authority to determine whether the service of an enforcement notice (with or without a stop notice) is warranted; and thus the use of discovery notices will make it possible for authorities to serve enforcement and stop notices (in respect of either operations or use of land) without fear of becoming liable to pay compensation on the grounds that the service of such notices was inappropriate. In most cases the occupier or developer will need 14 days to complete the discovery notice.

12.11 Cases will clearly arise, however, where the operation or use in question may be of a nature which cannot be accepted even for 14 days – for example a change of use which involves intolerable noise or noxious smell. In these cases a local planning authority ought to be able to serve a discovery notice together with a stop notice, requiring that the development cease forthwith and not be resumed pending completion of the discovery notice and consideration of it by the authority. After completion of the discovery notice a maximum of 14 days might be allowed for its consideration; the local authority would then either serve an enforcement notice and confirm the stop notice, or withdraw the stop notice.

12.12 In these cases the local authority would run some risk of being liable to pay compensation. However, the cases in which use of such a procedure is

151

considered appropriate will probably be very rare. If the local authority do, in the exercise of their discretion, decide that a particular activity is so intolerable that it cannot be allowed to continue for 14 days, they must be prepared to defend such a decision. This does not seem to me to be an unreasonable demand in the circumstances; a developer may, after all, be put into a position of serious financial hardship, or even suffer a ruined business as a result of the local authority's action, and if in the event he proves not to have acted in contravention of planning control, he must have some form of redress.

12.13 Penalties for Refusal to Comply with a Discovery Notice

It has been suggested to me that it is wrong in principle to impose criminal sanctions for delayed or misleading answers 'when questions on what amounts to development can be very difficult and doubtful'. I understand this concern, but I do not see why a suitable standard notice cannot be drafted which makes it clear that the person concerned is only being asked to answer questions of fact so far as they are within his knowledge. 'I do not know' will be an acceptable answer, provided it is true. The main object of such a notice would be to protect authorities from serving stop notices in cases where the activity is in fact lawful and a claim to compensation would result. Accordingly I think it would be appropriate – as an addition or alternative to the criminal sanctions already imposed by Section 284 – for the Lands Tribunal to have a discretion to refuse or reduce compensation where the authority have been misled.

12.14 The legislation would include appropriate safeguards to protect people whose failure to comply with a discovery notice was due to circumstances beyond their control.

12.15 **Inquiry Procedure.** There should be Inquiry Procedure Rules for enforcement appeals (and Rule 6 statements by both the local planning authority and the appellant). I see no reason why enforcement proceedings should generally be transferred to the Courts or made analogous to other Court procedures, as has been suggested to me. I consider it important that all planning inquiries should be governed by similar requirements and that these should be clearly set out in statutory rules. In enforcement cases however, because of the need for historical evidence and documentary material (usually stretching back over several years), it is appropriate that the parties should be informed of each other's cases at an early stage, and in particular that documents should be disclosed by both sides.

12.16 Therefore the Secretary of State should have the power to require the appellant to submit his Rule 6 statement and lists of documents within a prescribed time following lodging of the appeal. The penalty for non-compliance by the appellant in these cases would be striking out. I do not think this is too rigorous a measure to invoke. It is vital that the hearing of cases should be speeded up in every possible way if the system is to remain efficient and, more important, if it is to be improved. Individuals who flagrantly refuse to cooperate by failing to comply with measures demanded by law for the smooth running of the system as a whole must be prepared to suffer the consequences of their actions. It is already accepted in many spheres that time limits should apply; I can see no reasonable arguments against a demand from the Secretary of State to the appellant for a statement of case within a specified period.

12.17 Any system which is to command public respect and confidence must be seen to be fair, and for this reason (and, equally important, because it will also help to reduce the number of cases proceeding to inquiry) it is necessary that the same powers are available to require the local authority to furnish its own statement of case and list of documents within a period prescribed by the Secretary of State.

12.18 **Allowing an Appeal out of time.** A second vital safeguard is that the Secretary of State should have the power to allow an appeal out of time. I anticipate that this power should only be used in extraordinary circumstances, in order not to render nugatory the beneficial effects of the other measures I have proposed.

12.19 **The Four-Year Rule.** Under Section 87(3) of the 1971 Act, an enforcement notice relating to operational development must be served within the period of four years from the date of the breach. It has been suggested that the time limit should be considerably lengthened. I have a great deal of sympathy with this proposal; but the exact period within which the local authority would have to take enforcement action is a matter for further consideration, possibly by local authority associations.

12.20 **Costs.** The power to award costs should be used freely in enforcement appeals. My general recommendations on the greater use of the power to award costs to successful parties apply with particular force to enforcement appeals. The award of costs in favour of authorities should help to discourage frivolous or long drawn out appeals.

12.21 **Challenge in the Courts.** There should be no power to challenge the validity of enforcement notices in Magistrates' Courts on the grounds specified in paragraphs (f) and (g) of Section 88(1) of the 1971 Act (these grounds relate to the steps required by an enforcement notice and the time for compliance). The Secretary of State has the power to vary the above requirements and this power is often used. It is anomalous that a Magistrates' Court on a prosecution for failure to comply with an enforcement notice should be able to decide that the notice is invalid on these grounds, especially as the Court has no power to vary the requirements. These matters, like the other grounds of appeal, should be exclusively within the jurisdiction of the Secretary of State. The effect of *Smith v. King* (1970) 21 P. & C.R. 560, which decided that the validity of an enforcement notice could be challenged in the Magistrates' Court on grounds (f) and (g) of Section 88(1) of the 1971 Act should be referred (for the reasons given in Lord Parker LCJ's dissenting judgement in that case) by an appropriate amendment to Section 243. A further amendment should provide that the Secretary of State is the exclusive tribunal to deal with an allegation that a notice is a nullity (in addition to the grounds of appeal set out in Section 88).

SECTION IV: ADDITIONAL PROBLEMS

12.22 **Breaches of Intermittent and Temporary Nature.** There should be power to serve enforcement notices in respect of intermittent and temporary breaches.

The problem is that the existing procedure cannot operate once a breach has ceased, even though it is likely to be repeated in the near future. What is needed is a power for the authority to serve an enforcement notice in respect of a breach even if it has ceased, provided that the notice is served within a specified time thereafter. If the enforcement notice is upheld, subsequent repetitions of the breach would be dealt with by the Courts as offences under Section 89 as if the notice had been served and taken effect before the earlier breach ceased; the frequency and degree of the contravention would be taken into account. The power to serve stop notices in respect of uses should be made wide enough to ensure that stop notices can be used to prevent repetition of a breach during the period before the enforcement notice takes effect.

12.23 No Advertisement of Enforcement Notices and Appeals. There is no justification for advertising enforcement notices; it would amount to advertising an unproved allegation that a contravention of the planning code had occurred. Only if the planning authority offer a planning permission (see para. 12.4 above) should this be given the appropriate publicity.

12.24 Similarly, no enforcement appeal should be advertised unless ground (a) is pleaded (i.e. that planning permission should be granted). In this case the advertisement should:

(i) specify the land;

(ii) specify the exact purpose of the enforcement notice: e.g. to remove a named use or building (or control it in a specified way);

(iii) say that an appeal has been lodged on the ground that the use or the works (as the case may be) should be permitted;

(iv) invite representations within 21 days (the standard time adopted in this report);

(v) say that any representations received will be taken into account and a copy of them supplied to the main parties to the appeal.

12.25 Intensification. The question of '*intensification of use*' presents some considerable difficulties. They stem not only from the topic itself but also from a line of decisions of the Courts (starting with *Guildford Rural District Council v. Fortescue*; *Same v. Penny* (1959) 2QB 112) which unhappily have not succeeded in giving a unanimous lead to the layman. I am incapable of suggesting a statutory definition of intensification of use, and because of the inherent difficulty I doubt whether even the most skilled parliamentary draftsman would succeed. Nevertheless, it would clear the air somewhat if Section 23(3) of the 1971 Act were amended to declare, for the avoidance of doubt, that intensification of use may constitute development, and that development would occur if as a matter of fact and degree the character of the use has changed materially by reason of the intensification. One of the difficulties is that under Article 3 of the Use Classes Order it is possible to change from one use to another within the same use class. This is a licence which it would be impractical and undesirable to curtail. There are, however, cases where as a result of this kind of change there is an intensification of use which causes injury to the neighbourhood. I consider that the legislation should (if an appropriate provision can be devised) be so framed as to ensure that material changes of use which involve intensification are excluded from the Use Classes Order. This should give the local planning authority some control over many cases of intensification of use, enabling them either to serve an enforcement notice or to grant a conditional permission (e.g. limiting the hours of use) which will render the use less objectionable.

12.26 Third Parties. It has been suggested that third parties should have a statutory right to request the local authority to serve an enforcement notice. I have taken into account the arguments in favour of such a measure:

(a) that the local authority may be unaware of a particular breach which is causing local, if limited, concern;

(b) that neighbours within the immediate area of unauthorised development are those who stand to suffer most through its continuance.

I believe, however, that this would be superfluous. Everyone – neighbours, amenity societies or any interested parties – already has a right, albeit not a statutory one, to ask the local authority to take enforcement action, or indeed to write to the Secretary of State requesting him to take such action. Where the authority decide to take no action, objectors should normally be given the reasons for the decision. But it would be inappropriate for either of these rights to become statutory. To formalise something which exists in practice already would merely cause unnecessary delays and extra difficulties to local authorities, whilst adding nothing to the efficiency and speed of the procedure.

12.27 Enforcement Notices and Discontinuance Orders. It has also been suggested that an enforcement notice which has been quashed (or found by the Secretary of State or the Courts to be invalid) should operate as a discontinuance order at the option of the local authority. The law already provides, however, for a local planning authority to make discontinuance orders (independently of their powers regarding enforcement notices) and I believe it would be unnecessarily complicated to make extra provisions of the kind suggested.

12.28 The Inadequacy of Present Penalties. The penalties in force at present are inadequate. The fines which may be imposed might deter some minor developers from continuing operations or uses in breach of law, but when applied to large-scale developers they are derisory, particularly since Magistrates' Courts rarely impose the full penalty. Sums such as £400 and £50 per day are easily absorbed in building costs, or may be looked upon as a reasonable expense if a profitable contravening use is continued. Greater powers should be available both to local authorities and to the Secretary of State, if penalties against those who do not comply with enforcement and stop notices are to be both a real deterrent and fair to other developers who do stay consistently within the law. Authorities should be more willing to proceed by way of indictment, when the penalties are unlimited. Furthermore, a means should be devised to enable the authority to call evidence as a matter of course relating to the appropriate level of the fine (e.g. the value of the contravening use to the defendant). This is rarely done at present, particularly if the defendant pleads guilty, and the Court has no material upon which to assess the proper penalty.

155

12.29 Furthermore I can see no difficulty in applying to contravening uses the same power to take direct action to secure compliance with the enforcement notice as is given in respect of operations by Section 91 of the Act of 1971. The degree of determination used by those who are intent on ignoring development controls is not limited to those who carry out operations; the need for strong remedies against unauthorised changes of use is apparent.

12.30 **Pop Festivals.** A committee chaired by Mr. Denis Stevenson has recently investigated* the special problems relating to pop festivals and does not recommend any legislative change. Current methods of planning control are not well suited to dealing with transient activities and even an amendment to the provision of the General Development Order (Class IV of Schedule 1) which relates to uses for periods up to a total of 28 days in any calendar year, would not overcome the problems of enforcement. It seems to me that a better procedure is to require a licence** to be obtained under public health or similar legislation rather than to attempt to deal with the matter in a planning Act. I am, however, not making any recommendations on this aspect of enforcement.

---

*Pop Festivals, Report and Code of Practice, HMSO 1973.

**This was the approach of the Night Assemblies Bill, which was withdrawn in spite of initial Government support, partly because of the difficulty of defining the assembly in question in such a way as not to interfere with the ordinary rights of public assembly.

Development by the Crown

1. **Exemption of development by the Crown.** Under Section 266 of the Town and Country Planning Act 1971 development by the Crown of 'Crown Land' is exempt from the development control provisions of the Act, but this exemption does not extend to development of such land by others in so far as they have an interest in such land.

2. **Definition of Crown Land.** 'Crown Land' in this context includes all land which:

(1) belongs to the Sovereign in right of the Crown – the Crown Estate falls into this class – which is administered by the Crown Estate Commissioners, the revenue going to the Exchequer;

(2) belongs to the Sovereign in right of the Duchy of Lancaster, the net revenues of which are transferred to the Privy Purse of the Sovereign herself, or to the Duchy of Cornwall, the revenues of which are at the disposal of the Prince of Wales;

(3) belongs to a Government Department or is held in trust by the Sovereign for the purposes of a Department.

3. **Exemption of governmental bodies.** Governmental agencies and authorities enjoying exemption include:

(1) Departmental Agencies forming part of Government Departments the principal example being the Property Services Agency of the DOE;

(2) authorities appointed by Ministers to act on their behalf or administer estates on their behalf, the principal examples being the Regional Health Authorities, the Forestry Commission and the Industrial Estate Corporations responsible to the Department of Industry.

4. **Bodies which are not exempt.** Bodies which are not exempt include nationalised industries, the Post Office, the Civil Aviation Authority and other 'hived off' public sector bodies such as the Manpower Services Commission and its agencies, and New Town Development Corporations.

5. **2 million acres of Crown Land.** In all, apart from highways there are about 2 million acres (over 800,000 hectares) of Crown land in England and Wales. Over 1 million is held by the Forestry Commission, over half a million by the Ministry of Defence (much of it in agricultural use), about 180,000 by the Crown Estate Commissioners, and over 50,000 by the Department of Health

and Social Security through the Regional Health Authorities. The Defence estate is managed on behalf of the Ministry of Defence by the Property Services Agency of the DOE which also manages a substantial civil estate including offices, stores and workshops.

6. **Crown developers.** The main Crown developers are:

(1) *The Department of the Environment* which:

   (a) through its Road Construction Units and Regional Controllers (Roads and Transportation) is responsible for motorway and other trunk road works in England;

   (b) through its Directorate of Ancient Monuments and Historic Buildings is responsible in England for the buildings of the Royal Palaces, for the Royal Parks, for certain other special buildings including the Palace of Westminster and for ancient monuments;

   (c) through the Property Services Agency which is responsible for most of the functions of the former Ministry of Public Buildings and Works, and provides works services throughout the United Kingdom for Government Departments, the Armed Forces, and certain other public sector clients, notably the Post Office (Post Office works are subject to statutory planning control and the Property Services Agency acts as an agent for the Post Office in the planning process).

(2) *The Department of Health and Social Security* which through the Regional Health Authorities is responsible for hospital works in England.

(3) *The Welsh Office* which has responsibilities in relation to Wales analogous to (1)(a) and (2) above and is responsible for ancient monuments there.

SPECIAL PROCEDURES RELATING TO CROWN DEVELOPMENT

7. **Compulsory purchase.** Although Crown development is exempt from statutory planning control, this does not mean that it is free from all control. Proposals for trunk roads, including motorways, are subject to authorisation procedures under the Highways Act 1959 and the Acquisition of Land (Authorisation Procedure) Act 1946. These are outside my terms of reference.

8. **Non-statutory procedures** are laid down by DOE Circular 80/71* (Welsh Office Circular 164/71). These cover motorway service areas and other facilities ancillary to motorways. I have considered these as they are parallel to the statutory development control procedures. I have also considered the related question of planning clearances for development of land to be disposed of by the Crown.

9. **Consultations and 'reference' to the DOE.** The basic principle of the arrangements set out in DOE Circular 80/71 is that before undertaking any proposal which, but for Crown exemption, would have required planning permission the

---

*DOE Circular 64/74 (Welsh Office Circular 102/74) adapts the arrangements set out in Circular 80/71 to the situation following local government reorganisation.

body concerned will consult the local planning authority and in the event of disagreement refer the issue to the DOE.

10. **Publicity.**   Generally, arrangements for publicity are the same as for private developers, but it is interesting to note that advertisements are not required for 'bad neighbour' development, provided they are within a big establishment.

11. **Substantial departures from development plans.**   Similarly, proposals for substantial departures from development plans are subject to procedures analogous to those applying to statutory planning applications.

12. **Public inquiries.**   When controversial cases are referred to the DOE, public inquiries are arranged before a decision is reached.   The DOE may also decide to hold a public inquiry in any controversial case even if the local planning authority do not oppose the development.   This is equivalent to a call-in.

13. **Time limit for consultations.**   The Circular imposes a time limit of two months for a local authority to express its view on a development proposal of the Crown.   There are, however, '*Special Urgency*' cases for which 14 days only are allowed.   In any case an extension can be agreed.   If no comments are received within the time limit, the Crown is free to proceed with development.   This is an equivalent of a deemed consent.

PLANNING ISSUES ARISING ON DISPOSAL OF CROWN LAND

14. **Normal procedures apply.**   This paragraph deals with private development of land disposed of by the Crown.   In recent years there have been extensive disposals of both surplus Defence lands and surplus hospital lands and in future years one may expect a continuing programme of disposal of Defence lands.   In cases where the issue of development arises only after disposal, there are no special problems, as it is then subject to the normal statutory procedures.

15. **Circular 49/63: Opinion as to development envisaged in the future.**   However, Departments often wish not unnaturally to establish before putting land on offer the use which might subsequently be permitted.   Since it is not possible for the Crown to apply for planning permission, the practice is to seek an opinion from the local planning authority under the procedure laid down by Ministry of Housing and Local Government Circular 49/63.   The local planning authority is asked to say whether the development envisaged would have been permitted if an application had been made.   They are expected in considering this request to treat it in general as they would any application for permission, observing the same time limit and carrying out any consultations which would be appropriate in the case of such an application.   However, any opinion given specifically reserves the position in the event of a future planning application. Disputed cases are referred to the DOE, and the DOE will in any event give an opinion on cases involving substantial departures from a development plan which it is thought necessary to call in.

16. Should Crown Development be subject to formal control? One of the principal questions I have had to consider is whether Crown development should continue to be free from statutory control. This is by no means axiomatic. It has been suggested for many years not only that the immunity of the Crown is outdated, but also that control of Crown development is insufficient. It is pointed out in addition that the Secretary of State for the Environment can authorize development which he carries out himself.

17. The view of PSA. The Property Services Agency's view is that, having regard to the public concern about environment, Ministers and their servants cannot afford to show a bias in favour of the Crown. Further, the Property Services Agency is under increasing pressure to set an example in high architectural standards.

18. No practical reason for change of 'informal' control. I express no view about the Crown's record in this respect, as I have not received sufficient evidence on this topic. I know that the Crown now accepts that it is under an obligation to plan and design its own developments to standards which are an example to others. No convincing practical reason has been advanced why the informal arrangements laid down in Circular 80/71 should not result in an effective control of development by the Crown, *if both the DOE and local authorities treat the Crown's proposals as if they were those of a private developer*. I believe they do this already.

However, I think it would be appropriate in certain circumstances to make more use of the help of outside Inspectors. They could be asked to conduct public inquiries where the DOE is involved both as developer and arbitrator in a major controversial case. While I, of course, do not suggest that the Department's Inspectors are subject to bias in such cases, I think that all concerned would benefit from this way of showing impartiality.

PROPOSALS FOR AMENDING THE PROCEDURE
LAID DOWN BY CIRCULAR 80/71

19. Improving the Circular. I think that the Circular should, however, be amended to take account of my proposals for the handling of planning applications and my recommendations on public participation. Such adjustments are inevitable if the Circular procedure is to continue to be analogous to the formal procedures of statutory control.

20. Examples of changes which may be considered are:

(1) **Class A.** For cases other than those of 'Special Urgency' there should be a distinction between Class A and Class B cases with the appropriate time scales. It should be understood that in Class A cases the Crown has a right to proceed with development failing a definitive expression of view from the local planning authority within 42 days or a transfer of the case to Class B; this would replace the right which exists at present to proceed failing a definitive view within two months or an agreed extension of time.

(2) **Class B.** In Class B cases the three months' limit for decision should replace the two months under Circular 80/71. The present right to proceed with development failing a definitive view should be replaced with a right to refer the case to the DOE.

(3) **Publicity.** The publicity arrangements for Category A and B applications should also generally apply to A and B Crown cases, except that neighbour notification should not be requested where the land to be developed is surrounded by land also owned or controlled by the Crown. Site notices should not be required where the land is so surrounded and where there is no direct access to it from a public highway. The Crown should be prepared to publish notices in the Press if the local planning authority consider this appropriate. Copies of proposals should be made available to parish councils and other local bodies who wish to be notified.

(4) **Preliminary Statements.** In Class B cases which go to public inquiry, the local planning authority and the developing body should both issue preliminary statements on the analogy of 'Rule 6 statements', the local authority making its statement first; there should also be pre-inquiry meetings in appropriate cases and in all cases a firm timetable for handling the various stages.

(5) **Public Participation Meetings.** When a case referred to the DOE arouses some public concern, appearing insufficient to merit a public inquiry under an Inspector, members of the public should be invited to appear and speak at any meeting convened to discuss the issue with the developing body and the local planning authority; the proceedings at any such meeting should be kept informal.

(6) **At the outset.** In Class B cases of major public interest the developing body should arrange for public participation *before* seeking a definitive view from the local planning authority. Arrangements should be made in association with the authority and should provide for an exhibition of plans and related explanations, with an opportunity for members of the public to express views in writing and, in appropriate cases, a question and answer session. Participation of this kind is already arranged by the Road Construction Units of DOE; the exhibition organised by the Property Services Agency of their proposals for developing the Vauxhall Effra site in central London is an example of the approach now needed.

21. **Special Urgency cases.** These procedural suggestions all relate either to Class A or Class B cases. I think it will continue to be necessary, primarily for defence reasons, to have exceptional arrangements for 'Special Urgency cases'. I propose the 14 day period should be retained for the local planning authority's handling of such cases, and I do not think it feasible to do more in such cases by way of publicity than to ask the local planning authority – if security considerations permit – to take what steps it can in the time available to find out what those immediately affected might think about the proposal. The DOE should be notified as soon as possible by the authority (i.e. within the 14 day period) of any proposal which they might find it difficult to agree to.

22. **'Intolerable delays'.** The proposed procedures may seem to impose additional procedural burdens and delays on Crown developers. Like other developers, the Property Services Agency complain of delays; they say that some

161

delays are intolerable. Although under Circular 80/71, they have a right to proceed with development, failing a definitive view from the local planning authority at the end of two months, they do not think it feasible to exercise this right, at least in major cases.

23. **Effective 'right to refer' to DOE.** All delay is contrary to public interest, but especially so in relation to the Crown and may cost the taxpayer substantial sums. It is because of the need to ensure a reasonably speedy handling of such proposals that I am proposing, for Class B Crown cases, abolition of the unreal option to proceed with development failing a statement of view by the local planning authority and substitution of the right to refer the case to the DOE (equivalent to the right of appeal) within 3 months. In Category A cases I propose to retain the option to proceed with development if no view is expressed within the time limit. In this category of case it does not seem to me that such an option is unreal.

PROPOSALS FOR AMENDING MHLG CIRCULAR 49/63

24. **Disposal of surplus Crown lands—Publicity.** It will be necessary to review MHLG Circular 49/63 (see paragraphs 14 and 15). The procedure as it exists at present makes no provision for seeking any views other than those of the local planning authority and the DOE. The Circular should be amended to provide for publicity on the lines proposed above for Circular 80/71 cases.

25. **A and B cases.** The distinction between Class A and Class B cases would also have to be made together with the time limits which, if exceeded, would trigger off a reference to the DOE.

26. **Actual applications in B cases.** In major Category B cases, however, it may well be more satisfactory for the disposing body to encourage a would-be purchaser to submit a planning application to be dealt with in the normal way.

APPENDIX IIA (i)

APPLICATION FOR PLANNING PERMISSION OR APPROVAL OF DETAILS OF DEVELOPMENT

NOTES FOR APPLICANTS

1. These notes are provided to help you with your planning application. It may also be helpful to you to call at the office from which you obtained this form to discuss your proposals before you complete the application.

2. If you are in doubt whether your project requires planning permission because it may not involve development or it may be permitted by the General Development Order, you may apply to the local planning authority to determine the issue under section 53 of the Town and Country Planning Act 1971. This may be done by letter which should give details of the present or last use of the land/building and of the proposed new use including the processes to be carried out and any machinery to be employed. You may at the same time as you seek such a determination apply for planning permission.

3. This form is for the under-mentioned kinds of application and if the information required does not fit the circumstances of your case you should seek further advice from the Council.

(*a*) **Outline planning application.** If you wish to know whether planning permission will be given for the erection of buildings on a site before you have detailed drawings prepared, you should make an application for outline permission. It will help the authority if you give as much information as possible. If you show in reply to question 3 in the application form certain matters as reserved for subsequent approval but send the authority plans showing tentative ideas of how the development might be carried out, those plans will not form part of the application, and any permission granted may require you to obtain approval of these matters. If you show any matters as not reserved for approval you must include in your application plans showing adequate details.

(*b*) **Approval of reserved matters.** Where outline permission has already been granted, you may make application on this form for approval of the reserved matters. Please state in your answer to question 2(*b*) for which reserved matters you are now seeking approval. Approval of details should not be sought if current proposals would not be within the outline permission or would conflict with conditions imposed; in those circumstances you should apply for planning permission. The outline permission will lapse if details of reserved matters have not been submitted to the authority within the period stipulated in the permission or, where no period was stipulated in the permission, as laid down in section 42 of the 1971 Act.

(*c*) **Full planning application.** This is needed if you wish to make a change in the use of land or buildings, or carry out works or operations including the erection of buildings where you do not wish to follow the outline procedure

163

above. It will also apply where development has been carried out without permission and application is being made to regularise the position; in this kind of case you should, in reply to question 2(*b*), make it clear that you wish to retain the existing buildings or continue existing uses.

(*d*) **Renewal of temporary permission or relief from conditional permission.** If you wish to apply for permission to retain works or to continue a use without complying with a condition subject to which the original permission was granted (including any requirement that works should be removed or that the use should cease by a specified date), you should say so in reply to question 2(*b*) and give the date of the original permission and identify the particular condition, in reply to question 3(iv).

4. **Renewal of time-limited permission** (Section 41 or 42 of the 1971 Act). Where the application is made before the appropriate time limit expires, provision is made for a simplified application. It is not necessary for this form to be completed; the application may be by letter, giving sufficient detail of the previous planning permission to enable the authority to identify it: such application must be accompanied by the appropriate certificate under section 27 of the Act.

5. **Industrial Development.** If you are seeking planning permission (outline or detailed), other than in a Development Area, for the erection of more than 15,000 square feet (1,393·5 square metres) of industrial floor space, including ancillary space such as staff rooms, storage, etc., your application cannot be considered unless you attach a copy of an Industrial Development Certificate issued by the Department of Trade and Industry. A certificate is also needed where an application relates to a change of use affecting a corresponding floor area. Industrial floor space is measured internally.

6. **Minerals.** The form does not include questions dealing with the special matters on which information is needed in the case of a mineral application. On request the council will say what information they need in such a case.

DRAWINGS AND PLANS

7. **Site Plans.** Each application (except for approval of reserved matters) and each copy thereof should be accompanied by a plan or sketch of not less than 1/2500 scale, showing the site to which it refers and its boundary. The application site should be edged or shaded in red and any other adjoining land owned or controlled by the applicant edged or shaded blue.

8. **Other drawings.** Except in the case of outline applications where additional drawings are not normally needed, these should normally be to a scale of not less than 1/100 if in metric or ⅛in. to a foot if imperial measure is used. They should show the existing features of the site including any trees, and be in sufficient detail to give a clear picture of any new building. They must indicate clearly the location of the proposed development within the site and the amount of floor space to be used for different purposes. Where existing and new works are shown on the same drawing, new work should be distinctively coloured. The materials to be used in the external finish of walls and roofs and their

164

colour should be indicated on the drawings. The means of access to the site, and the type of wall, fence or other means of enclosing the site and any landscaping details, etc., should be shown. Applications for change of use of part of a premises must be accompanied by floor plans showing the extent of the existing and proposed uses unless the areas are readily identifiable by description.

9. Plans and drawings are open to inspection by the public. Applicants are not, however, required to disclose any proposed security arrangements.

CERTIFICATES

10. **Certificates under section 27 of the Town and Country Planning Act 1971.** Section 27 of the Act provides that the local planning authority shall not entertain an application for planning permission unless it is accompanied by one of 4 certificates, A, B, C or D. One copy of the relevant certificate should be attached to this application. If you are the freehold owner or have a tenancy of all the land, Certificate A is appropriate. If you are not, you will have to give notice to the other owners and complete Certificate B. Certificates A and B and two copies of the notice for service on other owners (Notice No. 1) are printed at the end of the application form. Further copies of Notice No. 1 can be obtained from the office where you obtained this form if more than two owners are involved. Certificates C and D are appropriate only if you have made efforts to trace the other owners and have failed. Owner for the purposes of certificates B, C and D includes a person having a tenancy with 10 or more years to run as well as the freehold owner. If any of the land to which the application relates constitutes or forms part of an agricultural holding, you will also have to give notice to any agricultural tenant, and certify accordingly. The forms of these notices and certificates are prescribed in the General Development Order 1973. The forms are set out in schedule 3 to the Order: (Copies can be obtained from the office where you obtained this form).

11. **Certificates under section 26 of the 1971 Act.** Section 26 of the Act provides that applications for special kinds of development cannot be entertained unless accompanied by a certificate that the applicant has published an advertisement in the local paper and displayed a notice on the site. The kinds of development to which the section applies are designated in Article 8 of the Town and Country Planning General Development Order 1973 (S.I. 1973) No. 31, namely:

(*a*) construction of buildings for use as public conveniences;

(*b*) construction of buildings or other operations, or use of land, for the disposal of refuse or waste materials or as a scrap yard or coal yard or for the winning or working of minerals;

(*c*) construction of buildings or other operations (other than the laying of sewers, the construction of pumphouses in a line of sewers, the construction of septic tanks and cesspools serving single dwelling-houses or single buildings in which not more than ten people will normally reside, work or congregate, and works ancillary thereto) or use of land, for the purpose of the retention, treatment or disposal of sewage, trade waste or sludge;

(*d*) construction of buildings to a height exceeding 20 metres;

(e) construction of buildings or use of land for the purposes of a slaughter-house or knacker's yard; or for killing or plucking poultry;

(f) construction of buildings and use of buildings for any of the following purposes, namely, as a casino, a funfair or a bingo hall, a theatre, a cinema, a music hall, a dance hall, a skating rink, a swimming bath or gymnasium (not forming part of a school, college or university), or a Turkish or other vapour or foam bath;

(g) construction of buildings and use of buildings or land as a zoo or for the business of boarding or breeding cats or dogs;

(h) construction of buildings and use of land for motor car or motor-cycle racing;

(i) use of land as a cemetery.

The forms of notices and certificates are prescribed in the General Development Order. You will find the forms set out in schedule 3 to the Order (Copies can be obtained from the office where you obtained this form).

OTHER MATTERS

12. Hazardous Materials. The use or storage of any of the following materials in the quantities stated will require special consideration as to siting and any proposals to use or store these materials should be clearly indicated in the application form.

Acrylonitrile	50 tons
Ammonia	250 tons
Bromine	100 tons
Chlorine	25 tons
Ethylene Oxide	20 tons
Hydrogen Cyanide	50 tons
Liquid Oxygen	135 tons
Liquified Petroleum Gas	100 tons
Phosgene	5 tons
Sulphur Dioxide	50 tons
Flour	200 tons
Refined white sugar	200 tons

Petrochemical and Plastic Polymer Manufacture Industry – All Materials.

13. Building Regulations. This application relates only to planning procedures. You may also need to apply for approval under the Building Regulations on forms available from the office where you obtained this form.

14. Statutory Undertakers. Where the development will involve the provision of gas, electricity, water or telephone service, the developer should give notice of his proposal at the earliest practicable date to the undertakings responsible for the services needed.

15. Development Control Policy Notes. The Department of the Environment and the Welsh Office have published guidance for all concerned with the development, on a variety of topics in a series entitled 'Development Control Policy Notes'. A list of the current notes can be obtained from the Council.

16. **Buildings of Special Architectural or Historic Interest.** The Secretary of State for the Environment has compiled Lists of Buildings of Special Architectural or Historic Interest under section 54 of the 1971 Act. Proposals for alterations, extensions or demolition of a building on the Secretary of State's Lists require Listed Building Consent. Planning permission also is often required for such works, except in the case of demolition proposals, and it is advisable to apply for planning permission and Listed Building Consent simultaneously. The forms for making an application for Listed Building Consent can be obtained from the office where you obtained this form.

Town and Country Planning Act 1971
Application for Planning permission or
Approval of Details of Development

Application No / /
(for official use only)

The top three completed copies of this form
and the top copy of the appropriate certificate,
together with three plans (see notes) must be
submitted to

PART 1 — to be completed by or on behalf of all applicants as far as applicable to the particular development.

1. **Applicant** (in block capitals)	**Agent** (if any) to whom correspondence should be sent (in block capitals)
Name	Name ....
Address	Address ....
....	....
Tel No.	Tel. No. ....

2. Particulars of proposal for which permission or approval is sought

(a) Full address or location of the land to which this application relates and the area (if known)

(a)

(b) Brief particulars of proposed development including the purpose(s) for which the land and/or buildings are to be used

(b)

(c) State whether applicant owns or controls any adjoining land and if so, give its location

(c)

(d) State whether the proposal involves:—

State Yes or No

(i) New building(s)

(i) [ ]

If residential development, state number of dwelling units proposed and type if known, e.g. houses, bungalows, flats.

(ii) Alteration or extension

(ii) [ ]

(iii) Change of use

(iii) [ ]

(iv) Construction of a new access to a highway — vehicular / pedestrian

(iv) [ ]

(v) Alteration of an existing access to a highway — vehicular / pedestrian

(v) [ ]

3. Particulars of Application (see note 3)

State whether this application is for:—

State Yes or No

(i) Outline planning permission

(i) [ ]

If yes, tick any of the following which are reserved for subsequent approval
1 siting ☐
2 design ☐
3 external appearance ☐
4 means of access ☐
5 landscaping ☐

(ii) Full planning permission

(ii) [ ]

(iii) Approval of reserved matters following the grant of outline permission

(iii) [ ]

If yes, state the date and number of outline permission
Date
Number

(iv) Renewal of a temporary permission or permission for retention of building or continuance of use without complying with a condition subject to which planning permission has been granted

(iv) [ ]

If yes, state the date and number of previous permission and identify the particular condition (see note 3d).
Date
Number
The condition

168

4. Particulars of Present and Previous Use of
   Buildings or Land
   State
      (i) Present use of buildings/land   (i)

      (ii) If vacant, the last previous use   (ii)

---

5. Additional Information

   (a) Is the application for Industrial, office,
          warehousing, storage or shopping purposes?
          (see note 5)

   State
   Yes or No

   (a) [＿＿＿＿＿]   If yes, complete Part 2 of this form

   (b) Does the proposed development
          involve the felling of any trees?

   State
   Yes or No

   (b) [＿＿＿＿＿]   If yes, indicate positions on plan

   (c)   (i) How will surface water be disposed of?   (c) (i)

          (ii) How will foul sewage be dealt with?   (ii)

---

6. Plans (See Notes 7, 8 and 9)

   List of drawings and plans submitted with the
   application

I/We hereby apply for

   *(a)   planning permission to carry out the development described in this application and the accompanying plans, and in accordance therewith.

OR *(b)   planning permission to retain buildings or works already constructed or carried out, or a use of land already instituted as described on this application and the accompanying plans.

OR *(c)   approval of details of such matters as were reserved in the outline permission specified herein and are described in this application and the accompanying plans.

*Delete whichever is not applicable.

Signed ....

On behalf of ....
               (insert applicants name if signed by an agent)

Date...

Note—*An appropriate certificate must accompany this application unless you are seeking approval to reserved matters—see Note* **10.**

PLANNING APPLICATION FORM. PART 2

Application No.
(For Official Use Only)

Additional Information required in respect of Applications for Industrial, Office, Warehousing, Storage or Shops

(Those questions relevant to the proposed development to be answered)

1. In the case of industrial development, give a description of the processes to be carried on and of the end products, and the type of plant or machinery to be installed.	
2. If the proposal forms a stage of a larger scheme for which planning permission is not at present sought, please give what information you can about the ultimate development.	
3. Is the proposal related to an existing use on or near the site? If so, please explain the relationship	State Yes or No
4. Is this a proposal to replace existing premises in this area or elsewhere which have become obsolete, inadequate or otherwise unsatisfactory? If so, please give details including gross floor area of such premises and state your intentions in respect of those premises.	State Yes or No

5.		Existing (if any)	Proposed new floor space
(a)	What is the total floor space of all buildings to which the application relates?	(a) m^2/sq. ft.	m^2/sq. ft.
(b)	What is the amount of industrial floor space included in the above figure?	(b) m^2/sq. ft.	m^2/sq. ft.
(c)	What is the amount of office floor space?	(c) m^2/sq. ft.	m^2/sq. ft.
(d)	What is the amount of floor space for retail trading?	(d) m^2/sq. ft.	m^2/sq. ft.
(e)	What is the amount of floor space for storage?	(e) m^2/sq. ft.	m^2/sq. ft.
(f)	What is the amount of floor space for warehousing?	(f) m^2/sq. ft.	m^2/sq. ft.

6.		(a) Office	(b) Industrial	(c) Other staff
(i)	How many (a) office (b) industrial and (c) other staff will be employed on the site as a result of the development proposed?			
(ii)	If you have existing premises on the site, how many of the employees will be new staff?	(i) (ii)		
(iii)	If you propose to transfer staff from other premises, please give details of the numbers involved and of the premises affected.			

170

7. In the case of industrial development is the
   application accompanied by an industrial
   development certificate?

   If "No" state why a certificate is not required.

   State
   Yes or No
   [   ]

8. What provisions have been made for the parking,
   loading and unloading of vehicles within the
   curtilage of the site?
   (Please show the location of such provision
   on the plans and distinguish between parking
   for operational needs and other purposes)

9. What is the estimated vehicular traffic flow to
   the site during a normal working day? (Please
   include all vehicles except those used by
   individual employees driving to work).

10. What is the nature volume and proposed means
    of disposal of any trade effluents or trade
    refuse?

11. Will the proposed use involve the use or
    storage of any of the materials of type
    and quantity mentioned in note 12?

    If "Yes" state materials and approximate
    quantities.

    State
    Yes or No
    [   ]

171

CERTIFICATE UNDER SECTION 27 OF THE TOWN AND COUNTRY PLANNING ACT 1971

Certificate A*

I hereby certify that:-

1. *I am   *the estate owner in respect of the fee simple

    The applicant is   entitled to a tenancy   of every part of the land to which the

    accompanying application relates.

*2.   None of the land to which the application relates constitutes or forms part of an agricultural holding:

      or:-

*2.   *I have   *myself

      The applicant has   given the requisite notice to every person other than   himself

    who, 20 days before the date of the application, was a tenant of any agricultural holding any part of which was
    comprised in the land to which the application relates, viz:-

Name of Tenant	Address	Date of service of notice

Signed ....   *On behalf of ....

Date ....

Certificate B*

I hereby certify that:-

1. *I have

    The applicant has   given the requisite notice to all the persons who, 20 days before the date of the

    accompanying application, were owners of any of the land to which the application relates, viz:-

Name of Owner	Address	Date of service of notice

*2.   None of the land to which the application relates constitutes or forms part of an agricultural holding ;

      or:-

*2.   *I have   *myself

      The applicant has   given the requisite notice to every person other than   himself   who, 20 days before

    the date of the application, was a tenant of any agricultural holding any part of which was comprised in the land
    to which the application relates, viz:-

Name of Tenant	Address	Date of service of notice

Signed ....   *On behalf of ....

Date ....

* Delete where appropriate

172

TOWN AND COUNTRY PLANNING ACT, 1971

Notice under Section 27 of application for planning permission

TO : .... (owner of the undermentioned land)

....

TO : .... (agricultural tenant)

....

(a) Insert address or location of proposed development.

Proposed development at (a)...

....

TAKE NOTICE that application is being made to the

(b) Insert name of Council.

(b) .... Council by

(c) Insert name of applicant.

(c) ....

....

(d) Insert description and address or location of proposed development.

for planning permission to (d) ....

....

....

If you should wish to make representations about the application you should do so by writing within

20 days of the date of service of this notice to the $\dfrac{\text{*Town Clerk}}{\text{Clerk of the Council}}$

(e) Insert address of Council.

at (e) ....

....

Signed ....

*On behalf of ....

Date ....

*Delete where inappropriate.

PROCEDURAL STAGES OF AN APPLICATION

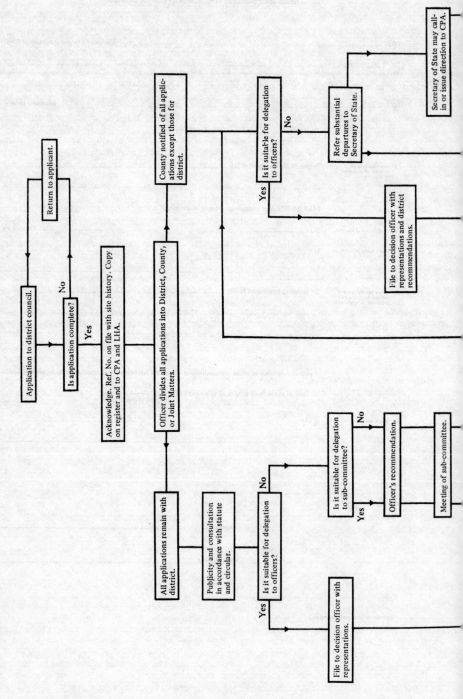

Application to district council.	
Is application complete?	No → Return to applicant.
Yes	
Acknowledge. Ref. No. on file with site history. Copy on register and to CPA and LHA.	
Officer divides all applications into District, County, or Joint Matters.	

All applications remain with district.

Publicity and consultation in accordance with statute and circular.

Is it suitable for delegation to officers?

Yes → File to decision officer with representations.

No → Is it suitable for delegation to sub-committee?

Yes → Officer's recommendation.

No → Meeting of sub-committee.

County notified of all applications except those for district.

Is it suitable for delegation to officers?

Yes → File to decision officer with representations and district recommendations.

No → Refer substantial departures to Secretary of State.

Secretary of State may call-in or issue direction to CPA.

DEVELOPMENT CONTROL SCHEME
ADOPTED BY THE C. ...

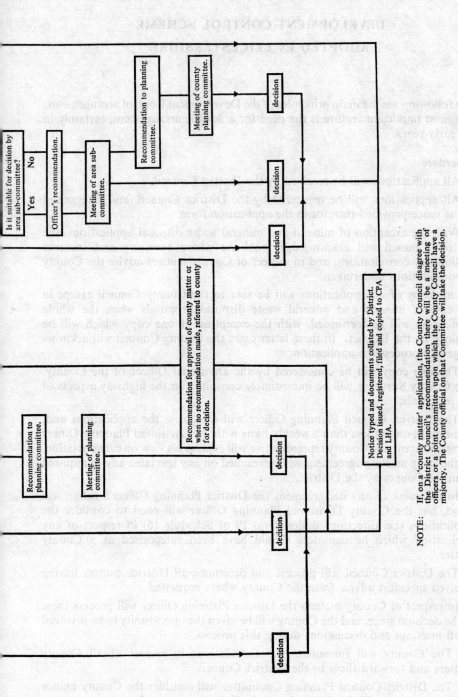

DEVELOPMENT CONTROL SCHEME
ADOPTED IN LEICESTERSHIRE

The following are the main principles of the Development Control arrangements. The most important feature is the need for a flexible arrangement, certainly in the early years.

Procedure

1. All applications will be received by the District Council.

2. All applications will be registered by the District Council, and categorised in the space provided therefor in the application form.

3. With the exception of mineral and mineral waste disposal applications, the District Council will acknowledge, publicise where necessary and institute preliminary consultations, and in respect of County matters advise the County of consultations undertaken.

4. One copy of all applications will be sent to the County Council except in the case of mineral and mineral waste disposal proposals when the whole application will be forwarded, with the exception of one copy which will be retained by the District. In these latter cases the County Council will acknowledge and process the application.

5. The one copy will be considered by the Divisional Officer of the County. The County Surveyor will be immediately consulted on the highway aspects of the proposals.

6. The District Council Planning Officer will categorise the applications and, at meetings on not less than a weekly basis with the Divisional Planning Officer or his Assistant, the County representative will express his view on categorisation. At the same meeting agreement will be reached on any specialist advice required from the County by the District.

7. In the event of any disagreement the District Planning Officer's ruling will stand, but the County Divisional Planning Officer will need to consider the implications (i.e. directions under Para. 19 of Schedule 16) in respect of any application which he considers should have been categorised as a County matter.

8. The District Council will process and determine all District matters having received specialist advice from the County where requested.

9. In respect of County matters the District Planning Officer will process these to the decision stage, and the County will be given the opportunity to be involved in all meetings and discussions during this process.

10. The County will formulate recommendations in respect of all County matters and forward them to the District Council.

11. The District Council Planning Committee will consider the County matter applications and will determine those which they wish to refuse, incorporating the County's reasons for refusal, and return to the County Council those

applications which they would wish to permit together with any recommendation relating to them.

12. The County Planning Committee will determine those County matter applications referred to them as described in the preceding paragraph.

13. In the matter of appeals the District Council will deal with all appeals arising from the determination of District matters, but may ask for a County witness if they require one. In respect of County matters which are determined by the District Council, i.e. refusals, either the District Council or the County Council will deal with these, but will have available a County witness. The County Council will deal with any County matter where the refusal contains matters with which the District Council are not in full agreement. In respect of County matters determined by the County Planning Committee, the County Council will assume full responsibility for appeals, but may ask for a District witness if appropriate.

14. Copies of all decisions taken by the District Council will be sent to the County Council and copies of County decisions will be sent to the District Council. At this stage the decision will be fed into the County data bank.

M

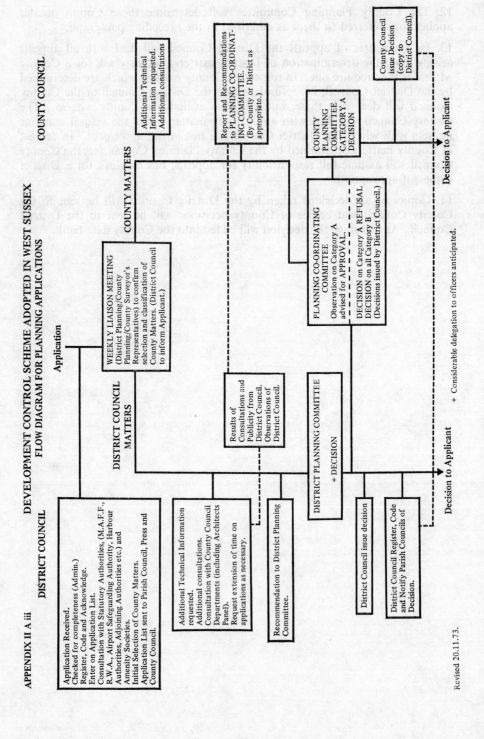

APPENDIX II A iii   DEVELOPMENT CONTROL SCHEME ADOPTED IN WEST SUSSEX
FLOW DIAGRAM FOR PLANNING APPLICATIONS

DISTRICT COUNCIL

COUNTY COUNCIL

COUNTY MATTERS

DISTRICT COUNCIL MATTERS

Application

Application Received.
Checked for completeness (Admin.)
Register, Code and Acknowledge.
Enter on Application List.
Consultation with Statutory Authorities, (M.A.F.F.,
R.W.A., Airport Safeguarding Authority, Harbour
Authorities, Adjoining Authorities etc.) and
Amenity Societies.
Initial Selection of County Matters.
Application List sent to Parish Council, Press and
County Council.

WEEKLY LIAISON MEETING
(District Planning/County
Planning/County Surveyor's
Representatives) to confirm
selection and classification of
County Matters. (District Council
to inform Applicant.)

Additional Technical
Information requested.
Additional consultations.

Report and Recommendations
to PLANNING CO-ORDINAT-
ING COMMITTEE.
(By County or District as
appropriate.)

COUNTY
PLANNING
COMMITTEE
CATEGORY A
DECISION

County Council
issue Decision
(copy to
District Council).

Additional Technical Information
requested.
Additional consultations.
Consultation with County Council
Departments (including Architects
Panel).
Request extension of time on
applications as necessary.

Results of
Consultations and
Publicity from
District Council.
Observations of
District Council.

PLANNING CO-ORDINATING
COMMITTEE
Observation on Category A
advised for APPROVAL.

DECISION on Category A REFUSAL
DECISION on all Category B
(Decisions issued by District Council.)

Recommendation to District Planning
Committee.

DISTRICT PLANNING COMMITTEE
+ DECISION

District Council issue decision

District Council Register, Code
and Notify Parish Councils of
Decision.

Decision to Applicant

Decision to Applicant

+ Considerable delegation to officers anticipated.

Revised 20.11.73.

178

WEST SUSSEX COUNTY COUNCIL AND

DISTRICTS COMMITTEE RESPONSIBILITY

Type of Development	District Planning Committee	Planning Co-ord. Committee	County Planning Committee

Private Development
  Non County Matter
  County Category B
  County Category A (Refusal)
  County Category A (Approval)
	*
	o
	o
	o
		
		*
		*
		o
			
			*

†Circular 80 (Government Departments)	As for Private Development		

County Council Development
  (Deemed Permission)
District Council Development
  (Deemed Permission)			

†Electricity Lines (and associated Sub-Stations) Processed under Circular 63/51	*		*
†Electricity Sub-Stations (Permitted Development)	*		

Section 17 Determinations
Land Compensation Act 1961
  District Council Acquiring
  County Council Acquiring
  All other cases
	*
	
		o
		o
			
			*

	As for Private Development		
Section 53 Determinations (Except District Council cannot say 'No' to a County Matter)	*		
Established Use Certificates—Section 94 (Except District Council cannot say 'Yes' to a County Matter)	*		
Listed Building Consent	*		
Advertisement Consent	*		

Notes:

* Committee making decision.

o Committee giving observations.

‡ Where adverse comment received from the District/County, observation obtained of Joint Co-ordinating Committee.

† Probable delegation of decisions and formal observations to officers, Committee to be advised of action taken.

'Departures from Development Plan' to be processed through same Committee as determines application.

Applications

1. The County and District Councils will endeavour to secure uniformity in the forms used throughout the County.

2. The County Council will prepare and submit for the consideration of the District Councils, a portfolio of draft forms and will review the same when required.

3. In accordance with the provisions of the Town and Country Planning General Development Order 1973, all planning applications are to be made to the District Council in whose area the land is situated.

(Four copies of the application form and plans accompanying them are required in each case.)

4. The boundaries of the District Councils are shown on the plan which follows.

5. In many cases a separate form will also be required for a consent under the Building Regulations. Where any works affect a building listed as being of special architectural or historic interest, a special application form may be required in certain circumstances. There are specific types of development (e.g. the erection of an industrial building) where additional information is required by the Planning Authority. WHENEVER IN DOUBT, AN APPLI-CANT SHOULD SEEK ADVICE FROM THE DISTRICT COUNCIL.

6. Application and associated forms, together with any advice on their completion can be obtained from the District Councils.

Administration on Receipt of Application

7. The District Council will:

8. Ensure that an application is fully completed.

9. Acknowledge its receipt. (Unless subsequently informed to the contrary, the applicant can assume it will be determined by the District Council.)

10. Enter details of the application on the statutory register.

11. Code the application.

12. Complete a standard pro forma for the file.

13. Carry out consultations with statutory authorities and amenity societies.

14. Carry out all advertising and display of notices on site.

15. Make the initial selection of County Matters.

16. Where required, notify the Parish Council of the application.

17. Notify the County Council at agreed intervals of all applications received with the following information:

> Application Number
>
> Development proposed
>
> Address or location of site

(Where under paragraph 16 a list of applications is supplied to a Parish Council, such a list will satisfy the provisions of this paragraph.)

The Planning Applications System — Coding

18. Information about planning applications and the implementation of those applications is an essential element of the Information System for the County. It is part of the basic data of the Residential Land Availability Survey which

is subsequently used for population forecasting, in the monitoring of commercial development, in the production of lists of expirations, and in returns required by Central Government and other bodies.

19. The information is collected in the normal course of the Development Control and Building Inspection processes. The District and County Councils have agreed that the District Councils will forward the information in a suitable form to the County Council who will process, collate and store the information on their computer and make available to the District Councils such information or the product of such information as is required.

COUNTY MATTERS – DEFINITION AND CLASSIFICATION – WEEKLY LIAISON MEETING

20. **Introduction.** The responsibility for control of development is divided between County and District Authorities. While the majority of planning decisions are to be taken at District Authority level, there are certain categories of application which will be a County responsibility known as 'County Matters'.

21. These are defined in general terms only in paragraph 32 of the 16th Schedule of the 1972 Local Government Act, and there needs to be a more explicit definition if doubt, uncertainty and confusion are to be avoided.

22. In accepting an explicit definition of County Matters the County Council have assumed that the District Authorities, when exercising their Development Control functions will as a matter of general principle adhere to already established planning policies. Any modification of these policies, and any new policies will be a matter for District and County Authorities through their co-ordinating machinery.

23. The County Council are given powers of direction (Paragraph 19, 16th Schedule 1972 Act) in respect of proposals that concern county policy, but the use of these powers would be in direct conflict with the co-operative approach now adopted. Consequently, it is not intended they should be used save in the event of a serious breakdown in joint working arrangements.

24. **Basic Principles.** In seeking to establish a more explicit definition the following principles have been adopted:

 (i) Notwithstanding the divisions of responsibility for exercising planning functions, the overall objective shall be the provision of a fully co-ordinated planning service in West Sussex.
 (ii) Local planning matters are the concern of the District Authorities, and as long as these do not affect policy issues, the County Authority has no part in the decision making.
 (iii) A stage can be reached when an accumulation of decisions on essentially local matters begins to have an impact upon county policies.
 (iv) When that stage is reached, the County Authority will become concerned with decisions which hitherto have not been their responsibility.
 (v) From the outset, major proposals which do not accord with approved policies and certain categories of development (e.g. minerals) will be County Matters.
 (vi) The Planning Co-ordinating Committee will consider and determine those proposals defined as *potential* County Matters, notwithstanding

181

the provision of Section 15(2) of the 16th Schedule of the 1972 Local Government Act.

25. The aim has been, therefore, to decide what applications are County Matters at the time they are submitted. For this purpose development has been divided into various categories. Each application which falls into a category of County Matters will be examined to decide its relative importance and which Committee should have the responsibility for determining it.

26. In categorising County Matters, regard has been given in the first place to an overall definition without, at that stage, taking into account the forum at which a decision would be made. Subsequently the categories have been sub-divided between those for which the Planning Co-ordinating Committee will have an executive responsibility and those for which it will advise the County Planning Committee *that it wished to approve.*

27. The categories of County Matters are set out at Annex 1.

28. The procedure by which County Matters will be agreed between County and a District Council, will be by means of informal, yet regular, meetings between the officers of the two authorities.

29. Weekly Liaison Meetings

(i) Regular weekly meetings between representatives of the District Planning Officer, County Planning Officer and County Surveyor, together with such other officers as might from time to time be concerned, will be held at the District Council offices.

(ii) The County Surveyor's representative will advise, or where appropriate make recommendations, on the highway aspects of applications brought forward by District Council representatives.

(iii) The officers will confirm the selection and classification (A or B) of County Matters and will undertake an initial appraisal of each.

(iv) Subsequently a copy of County Matter applications, fully documented will be handed to the County Planning Officer's representative, in order that policy advice may subsequently be provided by the County Council.

(v) The District Council will notify those applicants whose applications have been transferred to the County Council for determination (classification A).

30. The Committee which determines an application will also have the power to determine, in the appropriate cases, whether or not such application should be permitted as a departure from the Development Plan. Departure procedures will be undertaken by the authority responsible for issuing the decision.

Planning Co-ordinating Committees

31. As part of their policy for achieving a fully co-ordinated planning service in West Sussex, the County and District Councils have agreed to establish, as joint sub-committees of their principal planning committees, planning co-ordinating committees for each of the Districts in the following manner:

32. *Constitution.* Four members of the County Planning Committee and four members of the District Planning Committee.

33. *Chairman.* A County or District member alternating year by year unless the Committee determine otherwise.

34. *Terms of Reference.*

(*a*) To consider and advise the Constituent Authorities on those Structure Plan and Local Plan matters which affect the overall responsibilities of the County and District.

(*b*) (i) To consider and decide Category B County Matters and Category A matters which it wishes to refuse.

(ii) To advise the County Planning Authority on those Category A County Matters which it wishes to approve.

35. Each District Council will be responsible for the administration of the Planning Co-ordinating Committee for its District.

36. The County Secretary and County Planning Officer will be entitled to receive copies of all agendas, reports, minutes, memoranda and notes and any other like material relating to any Planning Co-ordinating Committees.

37. The officers of the County and District Councils shall have the right to attend any Planning Co-ordinating Committee and to advise the Committee on any matters under discussion.

Administration of Non-County Matters

38. The District Council is entirely responsible for processing applications for non-County Matters.

39. Where appropriate District Council may consult the County Services.

40. All consultations with the County Council Departments (other than the County Surveyor's) will be made through the County Planning Officer.

41. The District Council will issue all decision notices except where the County Planning Committee determine the application (see paragraph 49 (ii)).

Administration of County Matters

42. The County Council will be responsible for processing applications from the time of the Weekly Liaison Meeting to the stage of sending recommendations on to the District Council for consideration by the Planning Co-ordinating Committee (see paragraph 46 below).

43. When necessary, the District Council will request an extension of time for an application after discussion at the Weekly Liaison Meeting.

44. The District Planning Officer will supply to the County Planning Officer, one copy of the application and accompanying plans, together with any supporting correspondence and will transmit to him the results of all consultations and any observations received as a result of advertising the receipt of the application, or other publicity, together with any observations of the District Council.

45. The County Planning Officer will carry out all consultations with County Departments (including the Highway Department) and any special consultations required and will notify the District Planning Officer of the results of the same.

46. Category A and B applications will be referred to the Planning Co-ordinating Committee with the written recommendations of the District and County Planning Officers, given either jointly or separately as they shall agree.

47. Category B applications determined by the Planning Co-ordinating Committee and thereafter:

(i) One copy of application will be returned by the County Planning Officer to the District Council.

(ii) District Council will issue decision.

(iii) District Council will register decision.

(iv) District Council will complete coding of application.

(v) District Council will notify the Parish Council or persons having made representation.

48. Category A applications where decision is to refuse.
(As for paragraph 47 above.)

49. Category A applications where approval advised by the Planning Co-ordinating Committee:

(i) Considered and determined by the County Planning Committee.

(ii) County Council will issue decision notice, with copy of application to applicant.

(iii) The County Council will supply a copy of the decision notice to District Council.

(iv) District Council will register decision.

(v) District Council will complete coding of application.

(vi) District Council will notify Parish Council and persons having made representation.

Central Services

50. There are a number of features common to the planning services of both the County and District Planning Authorities, notably in information requirements and specialist services. To provide these economically to all planning authorities and at the same time to conserve the scarce specialist skills necessary for them, it has been agreed that they shall be provided centrally by the County Council to be available without charge to all the District Councils of West Sussex. In providing such services the County Council will not seek to dictate programme or staff investment of the District Councils. On the other hand the District Councils making use of the services will be able to join in forming programmes of work and specifications so that an overall County service is provided.

51. A County-wide information system, providing basic data for all local and central government services as well as for the more specialist planning services, is a foremost requirement. Much of the input to the system will be supplied by the District Councils under the foregoing provisions. The central services to be provided by the County Council are:

(a) Processing of Census data.

(b) Information arising from the Planning Application System.

(c) Residential Land Availability.

(d) Population forecasting.

(e) Monitoring of Industry, Offices and Shops.

52. The Central Design Section of the County Planning Department will be available to the District Planning Officers for advice on the control of design standards, the development of conservation programmes and work on the

preservation and restoration of buildings of architectural or historic interest, including all applications affecting Listed Buildings.

53. An integral part of the service is its inter-relationship with the Panel of Architects. The Central Design Section will be available for discussions with a District Planning Officer on any matters of design and site lay-out, whether as a preliminary to submission to the Panel of Architects or otherwise, and as support to a District Planning Officer in negotiations with applicants about such matters.

54. In addition to the above, the following specialist services will be made available by the County Council:

(a) Landscape Architecture.

(b) Archaeological advice.

(c) Arboreal advice.

(d) Agricultural advice on development for agricultural purposes or of agricultural land unless referred to the Ministry of Agriculture, Fisheries and Food.

55. The County and District Planning Authorities will from time to time review the operation of the central services and will by agreement amend, add to or delete any of the services, systems or programmes in accordance with the needs of the County for the time being.

The Architects' Panel

56. The maintenance of the highest standards of design is related to the standard of professional advice available to the planning authorities. The Government recommend that one way of utilising professional resources is by using Architects' Panels to provide advice which is both expert and independent of the planning authorities on architectural, townscape and urban conservation matters. Such a Panel operated effectively for the old West Sussex County Council as a supplement to the Central Design Section and the County and District Planning Authorities have agreed that it should be reconstituted in the following manner:

57. The Panel will be known as "The West Sussex Planning Authorities' Architects' Panel".

58. The members of the Panel will be practising architects comprising not less than twelve architects in private practice nominated by the Chairman of the R.I.B.A. South Eastern Region, together with architects employed by the District Councils and in the Central Design Section of the Planning Department and nominated by such Councils or the County Planning Officer respectively.

59. The administration of the Panel will be undertaken by the County Council, who will bear the costs of such administration, together with the claimable expenses of the private architects.

60. A Panel meeting will consist of five members; three architects in private practice serving on a rota basis and one each from the District Councils and the Central Design Section.

61. The Chairman of a Panel meeting will be a member in private practice.

62. A Panel meeting will be convened weekly or at such other intervals as is found expedient for the discharge of the Panel's business.

63. The County Council will notify all District Councils of the venue and other arrangements for Panel meetings.

64. In order to maintain an even workload at meetings, District Planning Officers will, unless there are exceptional circumstances, send the files of all applications for consideration by the Panel to the County Council at least three days before a meeting. The District Planning Officer or his representative will have the right to attend any Panel meeting whilst an application submitted by him is being considered.

65. The Panel functions solely as an advisory service to the planning authority using it.

The Highway Input in Development Control

66. The respective responsibilities of the County and District Councils in the highway aspects of development control and the principles which could govern the arrangements between authorities are examined in the paper approved by a Working Party of officers, entitled the 'County Surveyor's Role in Development Control'. This part of the Scheme is a resumé of the procedures outlined in that paper.

67. The Local Government Act 1972 not only divides development control between the County, with its County Matters, and the District Council, but also responsibility for the highway content of development control, and the divisions in the planning and the highway aspects are not always the same. Therefore any application with a highway content can fall into one of the following four groups:

(1) **Non-County Matters**

   (a) Where the highway content can be determined by the District Council without reference to the County Council.

   (b) Where the highway content must by definition be referred to the County Council.

(2) **County Matters**

   (a) Where the highway content can be determined by the District Council without reference to the County Council.

   (b) Where the highway content must by definition be referred to the County Council.

68. The classes of application which must be referred to the County Council for highway advice are:

(a) Any application for development within a curtilage which is affected by a road improvement scheme or a new road scheme. To achieve this, County must notify Districts of 'Bands of Interest'.

(b) Development for housing comprising 50 units or more.

(c) Development other than residential where the application of County car parking standards requires provision of 50 or more car-parking spaces.

(d) Car parks for 50 or more cars.

(e) Applications affecting Principal (paragraph 69) or Trunk Roads (paragraph 69) except cases listed in paragraph 70.

(*f*) Applications on principal traffic roads (paragraph 69) included in a Development Plan except cases listed in paragraph 70.

(*g*) Public transport inter-changes.

(*h*) Any development proposal which would not of itself necessitate reference to the County Council but which adjoins land which is being developed or is to be developed, or may be reasonably expected to be developed within a period of five years, where the combined effect of these proposals would bring the original proposal into one of the classes defined above.

(*j*) (i) Development of any site on unallocated land where three or more heavy commercial vehicles will be parked.

    (ii) Development of any site on allocated land where twenty-five or more heavy commercial vehicles will be parked.

(*k*) Except where Agency agreements have been made with District Councils in respect of Private Street Works, Advance Payments Code and Section 40 Agreements or where the agreed Code of Practice is applied in relation to that application, any application involving the layout of a new street or system of new streets.

69. Definitions

Trunk Road

(Section 14 Highways Act, 1959) A highway for which the Highway Authority is the Central Government. Maintenance is frequently undertaken by Agent Authorities. Planning applications affecting such highways have to be referred to the Department of the Environment and the Secretary of State is empowered to make Directions in respect of refusals or conditions to be imposed on any permission. These are binding on the Planning Authority.

Principal Road

(M.O.T. Circular 9/66) Primarily concerned with grant arrangements to Highway Authorities. They comprise in general the more important traffic routes and in West Sussex include all Class I roads with one or two minor exceptions as well as one or two of lower categories.

Principal Traffic Roads

A term used in planning schemes prepared under former Town and Country Planning legislation. The majority of Class I and Class II roads are shown as such in the present County Development Plan.

Classified Roads

Section 27 paragraph 3 of the Local Government Act 1966 refers to principal roads and any road which before the commencement of that part of that Act was classified in Class I, II or III.

70. With regard to the classes of development which are referred to as being matters which the highway authority must determine, the following need not be referred to the County Surveyor and may be determined by the District Council:

(*a*) The erection, construction, maintenance, improvement, or alteration of small ancillary buildings, or alterations of existing buildings, and the erection or construction of fences, walls and other means of enclosure abutting on a highway provided:

(i) that no new means of access or material alteration to an existing means of access is involved;

(ii) that the development will not result in an increase in the use of an existing access which in the opinion of the District Council would interfere with or cause danger to traffic on the highway concerned;

(iii) that any building is behind the existing building line;

(iv) that the District Council is satisfied that the development will not obstruct the view of persons using any road used by vehicular traffic at or near any bend, corner or junction so as to be likely to cause danger to such persons.

(b) Changes of use which in the opinion of the District Council will not result in an increase in the use of an existing access which would interfere with or cause danger to traffic on a highway maintainable at the public expense.

The above exemptions do not extend to development affecting Trunk Roads or to development within 'Bands of Interest' notified to the District Council concerned.

71. The County and District Councils have agreed common Standards and Code of Practice relating to the highway aspects of Development Control — the Code of Practice referred to in sub-paragraph (k) of 68 above.

Procedures

72. The highway aspects in applications falling within Classes 1(a) and 2(a) will be dealt with by the District Council. Advice from the County Surveyor in respect of such applications will be available if required.

73. Those falling within Classes 1(b) and 2(b) will be discussed at the Weekly Liaison Meetings (see paragraph 29) and the classification confirmed in cases of doubt.

74. In respect of Class 1(b) applications, requiring further consideration by the County Surveyor, the District Planning Officer will pass to him one copy of the application together with the District Council's observations in writing. The County Surveyor will return the copy of the application to the District Planning Officer together with his recommendation.

75. In respect of Class 2(b) applications, requiring further consideration by the County Surveyor, the consultation will be through the County Planning Officer (see paragraph 45).

Procedure in the event of a dispute

76. *Class* 1(b)

If the District Planning Committee wish to determine an application in this class contrary to the recommendation of the County Surveyor, they will refer the application to the Planning Co-ordinating Committee who will determine the application.

77. *Class* 2(b)

If the Planning Co-ordinating Committee wish to determine an application

188

in this class contrary to the recommendation of the County Surveyor, they will:

(i) where they are agreed on the principle of development on land use grounds but disagree solely on the highway aspect, consult with the Roads and Transportation Committee of the County Council to ascertain whether they require a Direction to be issued, or

(ii) where there is no agreement on either the planning or highway issues, refer the application to the Joint Planning/Roads and Transportation Sub-Committee of the County Council.

Appeal Procedure

78. In any appeals against decisions, the District Council will provide the witnesses in classes 1(a) and 2(a) and the County Council in classes 1(b) and 2(b), but in any event the respective authorities will provide assistance when it is needed or in appropriate cases.

COUNTY AND DISTRICT COUNCIL DEVELOPMENT ETC.

79. **County Council Development.** Before granting itself Deemed Permission for any development, the County Council shall consult the District Planning Officer in writing, and where adverse observations are given, the observations of the Planning Co-ordinating Committee shall also be obtained and taken into consideration.

80. **District Council Development.** Before granting itself Deemed Permission for any development, the District Council shall consult the County Planning Officer in writing, and where adverse observations are given, the observations of the Planning Co-ordinating Committee shall also be obtained and taken into consideration.

81. **Circular 80 Consultation.** Consultations by Government Departments under Circular 80/71 as amended by Circular 64/74 will be treated similarly to private applications depending on whether they are Non-County Matters or County Matters.

82. **Section 17 Determinations (Land Compensation Act, 1961).** Applications for certificates of appropriate alternative development will be taken to the Planning Co-ordinating Committee to give advice either to the District or the County Planning Committee.

83. **Section 94.** Applications for established use certificates will be processed and determined by the District Planning Committee, with the proviso that if the District Committee wish to grant the certificate on a County Matter, then the application will be referred to the County Planning Committee for decision.

84. **Section 53.** Applications submitted to determine whether or not a planning application is necessary shall be processed and determined by the District Planning Committee, with the proviso that if the District Committee decide that an application is *not* necessary when a County Matter is involved, then the application will be referred to the County Planning Committee for decision.

85. **Applications for Electricity Lines.** The existing procedures under Circular 63/51 are continued and will be reviewed in the event of any changes of policy by the Departments of the Environment or Energy.

Appeal Procedures

86. The District Council will be responsible for the administration of all appeals relating to non-County matters or arising from the decisions of the Planning Co-ordinating Committee for the area, including the advocacy and provision of technical witnesses at any local inquiry held in respect of such an appeal.

87. The County Council will be responsible for the administration of all appeals, including the advocacy and provision of technical witnesses at any local inquiry held in respect of such an appeal, arising from a decision of the County Planning Committee or a decision of a Planning Co-ordinating Committee in respect of Category 'A' County matters.

88. The procedures defined in paragraphs 86 and 87 hereof are subject always to the provisions of paragraph 78 and to the following paragraphs.

89. In any appeal, where the authorities agree it is necessary, the County Council will provide the evidence on matters of strategic importance and arising out of specialist services and the District Council will provide the evidence on matters of local issue.

90. In any appeal arising from a decision of the Planning Co-ordinating Committee, where the authorities agree that it is of special significance, then the following arrangements, or any part of them or combination of them or their parts may also be undertaken as is appropriate to the circumstances:

(a) The authorities may contribute in such proportions as shall be agreed between them to fees incurred in the employment of counsel and any consultant required for specialist evidence.

(b) The County Council may, if so required, undertake the administration of the appeal and be responsible for the advocacy at the local inquiry.

Concurrent Powers

91. The County Council and District Council will exercise those planning functions for which they have concurrent powers in accordance with the general principles, namely, the District Council will be responsible for local issues and the County Council for matters of strategic importance or more than local significance.

92. The authorities will consult with one another upon any action proposed by them and will endeavour to agree which authority should consider the proposal.

93. Nothing in this part of this Scheme shall over-ride any requirement of a statute or subordinate legislation or limit the power of either authority to take such action as they think proper.

Review Procedure

94. This Development Control Scheme will be amended from time to time to accord with the requirements of any statute or subordinate legislation or Circulars and in any event its provisions will be reviewed by the participating authorities at the end of two years from its adoption by them and thereafter at such regular intervals as the authorities agree. By such reviews the authorities will ensure that the Scheme will continue to be updated and improved.

INTERPRETATION

95. In this Scheme, any reference to a statute shall be construed as referring also to any statutory extension, modification or re-enactment thereof.

96. Any reference in this Scheme to a County or District Council shall be deemed to include the appropriate Committee, member or officer of that Council to whom responsibility for the exercise of the part of the Scheme in question has been delegated, and any reference to a designated officer shall be deemed to include any officer authorised by him to act on his behalf in the course of his duties.

ANNEX 1

PART 1

DEFINITION OF 'COUNTY MATTERS' under Paragraph 32 (except sub-paragraph (d)) of Schedule 16 of the Local Government Act, 1972

In the foregoing provisions of this Schedule 'county matter' means in relation to any application, order or notice—

(a) The winning and working of minerals in, on or under land (whether by surface or underground working) or the erection of any building, plant or machinery —

    (i) which it is proposed to use in connection with the winning and working of minerals or with their treatment or disposal in or on land adjoining the site of the working; or

    (ii) which a person engaged in mining operations proposes to use in connection with the grading, washing, grinding or crushing of minerals;

(b) The carrying out of searches and tests of mineral deposits or the erection of any building, plant or machinery which it is proposed to use in connection therewith;

(c) The disposal of mineral waste;

(e) The carrying out of operations in, on, over or under land, or any use of land, which is situated partly in and partly outside a National Park;

(f) The carrying out of any operation which is, as respects the area in question, a prescribed operation or an operation of a prescribed class or any use which is, as respects that area, a prescribed use or use of a prescribed class.

PART 2

DEFINITION OF "COUNTY MATTERS"

In accordance with Paragraph 32(d) of Schedule 16 of the Local Government Act, 1972

1	2	3
Overall definition of County Matters	*To be decided by a Planning Co-Ordinating Committee* (*Category B*)	*To be decided by the County Planning Committee where the P.C.C. wish to approve* (*Category A*)

Rural Areas (areas away from towns and villages, i.e. outside defined areas)

1. Residential

Any proposal for more than 2 units where these are detached from any town or village.	3 – 10 units.	Exceeding 10 units.

2. Offices, Industry, Shopping and Warehousing

(a) Proposals for the establishment of new uses.	Not exceeding 10,000 sq. ft.	Exceeding 10,000 sq. ft.
(b) Extensions of existing uses where the scale is substantially altered.		

3. Glasshouses

(a) Proposals establishing new glasshousing.	Not exceeding 50,000 sq. ft.	Exceeding 50,000 sq. ft.
(b) Major extensions outside areas of approved policy exceeding 10,000 sq. ft. or 40 ft. in height.		

4. Caravans

(a) Residential—		
(i) New sites for more than two caravans.	(i) 3 – 10 caravans.	(i) Exceeding 10 caravans.
(ii) Extensions of an existing site by more than 10% of its area provided the proposed increase is more than ½ acre.	(ii) Not exceeding 20%.	(ii) Exceeding 20%.

1	2	3
Overall definition of County Matters	*To be decided by a Planning Co-Ordinating Committee* (*Category B*)	*To be decided by the County Planning Committee where the P.C.C. wish to approve* (*Category A*)

(*b*) Holiday (including Touring sites and tented camping sites)—		
(i) New sites.	(i) 3 – 10 caravans.	(i) Exceeding 10 caravans.
(ii) Extensions of an existing site by more than 10% of its area provided the proposed increase is more than ½ acre.	(ii) Not exceeding 20%.	(ii) Exceeding 20%.

5. Recreational Uses

The provision of new facilities on an area exceeding 10 acres, and all uses provided as a commercial enterprise.	All proposals falling within column 1 but not column 3.	All proposals in a Rural Conservation Area* or where a proposal is of regional significance.

6. Airfields

(*a*) New airfields and helicopter pads.	None.	All proposals.
(*b*) Proposals for hard runways and their extensions.		
(*c*) Proposals which would extend the potential of the airfield.		

7. Car Parks

Proposals for more than 50 car parking spaces in a Rural Conservation Area*.	50 – 200 car parking spaces.	Above 200 car parking spaces.

8. Overhead Electricity Lines

Proposals for the routing of 33Kv lines and above, and their attendant switching stations, sub-stations, etc.	All proposals falling within column 1, but not column 3.	All proposals for the routing of 132 Kv lines and above and their attendant switching stations, sub-stations etc.

1	2	3
		To be decided by the County Planning
	To be decided by a Planning Co-Ordina-	*Committee where the P.C.C. wish to*
Overall definition of County Matters	*ting Committee*	*approve*
	(Category B)	*(Category A)*

9. **Hotels, Schools and Institutional Establishments**

   (*a*) New buildings providing for more than 10 bed spaces (excluding staff).

   (*b*) Change of use of existing building providing for more than 20 bed spaces (excluding staff).

All proposals falling within column 1, but not column 3.

All proposals providing for more than 50 bed spaces (excluding staff).

Defined Areas

10. **Residential**

    Schemes over 50 acres on land not allocated in a plan.

   (*a*) **New Plan after 1st April 1974**

       Proposals in excess of 1 acre on land not allocated in the plan where the number of units already existing, allocated or permitted exceeds the Local Plan provision by more than 10%.

   (*b*) **Existing Plan at 1st April 1974**

       Proposals in excess of 1 acre on land not allocated in the plan where the number of units already existing, allocated or permitted exceeds the Local Plan provision, plus permitted departures as at 1st April 1974, by more than 10%.

   (*c*) **No Plan**

       Proposals in excess of 1 acre where the number of units already existing and permitted exceeds those existing at 1st April 1974 by more than 10%.

Where the 10% tolerance has been exceeded, all proposals exceeding 1 acre but not exceeding 10 acres.

All schemes over 50 acres on land not allocated in a plan or, where the 10% tolerance has been exceeded, all proposals in excess of 10 acres.

195

1	2	3
Overall definition of County Matters	*To be decided by a Planning Co-Ordinating Committee* *(Category B)*	*To be decided by the County Planning Committee where the P.C.C. wish to approve* *(Category A)*
11. Offices, Industry and Warehousing Schemes over 5,000 sq. ft. on land not allocated in the plan.	Not exceeding 20,000 sq. ft.	Exceeding 20,000 sq. ft.
12. Shopping (Area not allocated) (*a*) Proposals which have a new shopping centre where the proposals is for more than 10 shopping units or where the gross area exceeds 10,000 sq. ft. (*b*) Proposals which substantially affect the economic character of an existing shopping area or alter the extent of its catchment area.	(*a*) Not exceeding 20,000 sq. ft.	(*a*) Exceeding 20,000 sq. ft. (*b*) Where the impact of the proposal affects more than one district.
13. Recreational The provision of new facilities on un-allocated land on an area exceeding 10 acres and all uses provided as a commercial enterprise.	All proposals falling within column 1 but not column 3.	All proposals in a Rural Conservation Area* or where a proposal is of regional significance.
14. Glasshouses (*a*) Proposals establishing new glasshousing. (*b*) Major extensions outside areas of approved policy exceeding 10,000 sq. ft. or 40 ft. in height.	Not exceeding 50,000 sq. ft.	Exceeding 50,000 sq. ft.

15. Caravans
(*a*) Residential –
  (i) New sites for more than two caravans.
  (ii) Extensions of an existing site by more than 10% of its area providing the proposed increase is more than ½ acre.
	(i) 3 – 10 caravans.
	
	(ii) Not exceeding 20%.
		(i) Exceeding 10 caravans.
		
		(ii) Exceeding 20%.

1	2	3
Overall definition of County Matters	To be decided by a Planning Co-Ordinating Committee	To be decided by the County Planning Committee where the P.C.C. wish to approve
	(Category B)	*(Category A)*
(b) **Holiday (including Touring sites and tented camping sites) –**		
(i) New sites.	(i) 3 – 10 caravans.	(i) Exceeding 10 caravans.
(ii) Extensions of an existing site by more than 10% of its area providing the proposed increase is more than ½ acre.	(ii) Not exceeding 20%.	(ii) Exceeding 20%.

16. **Airfields**

   (a) New airfields and helicopter pads.

   (b) Proposals for hard runways and their extensions.

   (c) Proposals which would extend the potential of the airfield.

(a) New airfields and helicopter pads.	None.	All proposals.

17. **Car Parks**

Proposals for more than 50 cars on land not allocated.	All proposals.	None.

18. **Overhead Electricity Lines**

Proposals for the routing of 33 Kv lines and above and their attendant switching stations, sub-stations etc.	All proposals falling within column 1 but not column 3.	All proposals for the routing of 132 Kv lines and above and their attendant switching stations, sub-stations etc.

* The Rural Conservation Areas are:

   Areas of Outstanding Natural Beauty

   Areas of Scientific Interest

   Areas of High Landscape Value

   Country Parks

   Areas where the County's Coastal Gap policy applies

   Nature Reserves

APPENDIX 11A (iv)

DEFINITION OF CLASS A DEVELOPMENT

1. **All simple cases.**
2. **Development which conforms with specific land use provisions in either:—**
(1) a statutory local plan adopted following approval of a structure plan;
(2) the whole or part of a statutory development plan still in operation under the 1947 Act development plan system;
(3) a non statutory local plan adopted by a local authority following a programme of public participation.

But at least for an experimental period some specified limit on size would be desirable:—

(a) housing — maximum of five houses;
(b) industrial and commercial development — maximum of 5,000 sq. ft.;
(c) applications for the approval of reserved matters relating to cases classed as 'A' when outline permission was sought.

3. **Development which falls just outside the GDO.** Para 7.9 (iii) refers to developments that just exceed those permitted by the General Development Order. Particular uses which should come within Class A irrespective of whether they are shown within the specified land use or not are:—

4. Class 1 (Development within the curtilage of a dwelling house):
(i) all development within the curtilage of a dwelling house;
(ii) any development which would have been within Class 1 but for the fact that the house was not used as a single dwelling house (e.g. because part of the house was used as an office or because the house was used as two or more flats or was in multi-occupation).

5. Class VI (Agricultural buildings, works and uses):
(i) buildings which would have come within Class VI but for the fact that their use, although for accommodating livestock, would not be requisite for the use of the land for agriculture (e.g. stables for riding horses; intensive breeding units for pigs not dependent on the land, because they were fed wholly or almost wholly on imported food);
(ii) buildings within 25 metres of a trunk or classified road but otherwise within the GDO limitations.

6. Class VIII (Development for Industrial Purposes):
(i) operations which would be within the GDO permission but for the fact that the external appearance of the premises of the undertaking would be materially affected or that an industrial development certificate was needed;
(ii) where the tolerance for extensions permitted under the GDO has already been exhausted, any extension which in itself does not create more than 500 square metres floor area or does not amount to more than 5% of the existing floor space of the industrial undertaking, whichever is the greater.

7. **Reserved matters** relating to cases classed as 'A' when outline permission was sought.

198

APPENDIX II A (v)

PRACTICE OF SELECTED LOCAL AUTHORITIES IN DEFINING MINOR AND MAJOR APPLICATIONS

Authority	Definition of Major/Minor Applications	Differences in Procedure in Processing Major/Minor Applications	Numbers Major/Minor Applications	Percentage of Major/Minor Applications
Southants	Minor: extensions to existing building, carports, garages, renewals etc. Major: all cases where a policy implication is involved.			1973 Jan. – Sept. 80% minor 20% major 1974 Jan. – Sept. 72% minor 28% major
Brentwood DC		Minor: decision delegated to officer. Major: committee decision.		Minor: 33% Major: 67%
Liverpool	Minor: house extensions etc.	Minor: 2 copies of plans and applications. Major: 4 copies of plans and applications.		Minor: 30% (some turn out to be GDOs). Major: 70%
Lancaster	Minor: under 3 dwellings. Major: over 3 houses, flats, large buildings, major extensions, industrial applications, all over 5,000 sq. ft.	Minor: sometimes delegation. Major: committee decision.	Minor 423 Major 83	Minor 84% – 85% Major 15% – 16%
South Lakeland DC	Part 2: simple applications; decision is clear cut. Part 3: more complex; decision needs more thought.	Part 2: no discussion. Part 3: sub-committees debate application.	Minor applications: 604 Major applications: 710	Minor: approx. 46% Major: approx. 54%

199

Authority	Definition of Major/Minor Applications	Differences in Procedure in Processing Major/Minor Applications	Numbers Major/Minor Applications	Percentage of Major/Minor Applications
East Cambridgeshire		Major applications: detailed reports prepared on application for planning committees/sub-committees.	Since April 1974 570 cases. 81 major cases.	Minor: approx. 86% Major: approx. 14%
City of Plymouth	Major application: (a) substantial development which involves a lot of time in processing; (b) development which is not large in itself but is complicated and contentious involving much public participation.		Major applications: (a) 143 (b) 106 Total major applications: 249	Major applications: (a) 10.72% (b) 9.74% Total % major applications: 20.46% of total number of applications.
Stevenage		All applications go to committee, but consultation more extensive on major applications.		Minor: 90% – 95% Major: 5% – 10%
Mid Suffolk	Minor: development under 12 – 15 houses which is *not* contentious; Major: development over 15 houses in village; Others: large broiler house; open Sunday market.		*Since April:* Minor: 909 Major: 41	Minor: approx. 95% Major: approx. 5%
Newcastle		250 – 300 applications dealt with at each committee meeting. Officer selects important ones at initial stage.		Minor: approx. 70% Major: approx. 30%

200

APPENDIX IIA (vi)

STAFF DEPLOYED ON PLAN-MAKING
AND DEVELOPMENT CONTROL

Stockton-on-Tees BC	Development control staff	1 qualified planner.
		2 graduates.
		1 enforcement officer.
		1 administrative assistant.
		5 clerical staff.
		2 senior posts (vacant)
	Plan-making	5 qualified planners.
		1 planning graduate.
		1 administrative assistant.
Leeds	Planning staff	230 divided into 4 sections – 1 of which includes development control staff.
Bucks	For 5 districts	Total professional planning establishment 42.
Birmingham	Development control staff	55 (19 professionals).
Berkshire/Nottingham RDC	Planning staff (inc. d.c.)	County Council 11 District Councils 37
Breckland DC	Development Control	9 professionals (38 in planning department).
Luton DC	Development Control	6 full-time professionals. 2 part-time professionals (2 on enforcement).
Bedfordshire CC	Development control	5/4 professionals.
Elmbridge DC	Development Control	c. 27 (professional and non-professional).
City of Oxford	Development Control	5 professional. 3 admin/clerical support. 3 professionals on conservation, also 20 work on listed building applications and tpos.
Leicester City	Development Control	9 professionals. 3 admin/clerical support.
Leicester CC	Development Control	8 professionals.
Devon/Plymouth	Planning Dept.	77
	Plan-making	9
	Urban Design	16
	Development Control	9
Woking City/District	Development Control	7 full time. 2 professionals part-time. 3 clerks part-time.
Hertsmere DC	Development Control	13

Hertfordshire CC	Development Control	30
Southampton	Planning Dept.	65
	Development Control	17 (half professionals)
Mole Valley DC	Planning Dept.	35
	Development Control	71 – technical staff.
South Cambridgeshire	Development Control	42% of planning staff.
Blackburn	Planning Dept.	32 professional/technical.
	Development Control	12/13

202

APPENDIX IIB (i)

EXTRACTS FROM THE GENERAL DEVELOPMENT
(AMENDMENT) ORDER 1974
ARTICLES 5, 6, 7, and 16

"Applications for planning permission

5.—(1) Subject to the following paragraphs of this article, an application to a local planning authority for planning permission shall be made on a form issued by the local planning authority and obtainable from that authority or from the council with whom the application is to be lodged and shall include the particulars required by such form to be supplied and be accompanied by a plan sufficient to identify the land to which it relates and such other plans and drawings as are necessary to describe the development which is the subject of the application, together with such additional number of copies, not exceeding three, of the form and plans and drawings as may be required by the local planning authority: and a local planning authority may by a direction in writing addressed to the applicant require such further information as may be specified in the direction to be given to them in respect of an application for permission made to them under this paragraph, to enable them to determine that application.

(2) Where an applicant so desires, an application may be made for outline planning permission for the erection of a building and, where such permission is granted, the subsequent approval of the local planning authority shall be required to such matters (being reserved matters as defined) as may be reserved by condition. The application shall be made on a form, as required by the preceding paragraph, shall describe the development to which it relates, shall be accompanied by a plan sufficient to identify the land to which it relates (together with such additional copies, not exceeding three, of the form and plan as may be required by the local planning authority) and may contain such further information (if any) as to the proposal as the applicant desires:

Provided that where, in Greater London, the local planning authority, and elsewhere, either the authority to whom the application is made or the authority by whom the function of determining the application is exercisable are of the opinion that in the circumstances of the case the application ought not to be considered separately from the siting or the design or external appearance of the building, or the means of access thereto or the landscaping of the site, they shall within the period of one month from receipt of the application notify the applicant that they are unable to entertain it unless further details are submitted, specifying the matters as to which they require further information for the purpose of arriving at a decision in respect of the proposed development; and the applicant may either furnish the information so required or appeal to the Secretary of State within six months of receiving such notice, or such longer period as the Secretary of State may at any time allow, as if his application had been refused by the authority.

(3) Where a planning permission has previously been granted for development and that development has not yet been commenced, and where a time limit imposed by or under section 41 or section 42 of the Act (that is to say, a time

limit on the commencement of the development or, in the case of an outline planning permission, on the submission of an application for the approval of reserved matters) has not yet expired, an application may be made for planning permission for the same development without complying with paragraphs (1) and (2) of this article; but such application shall be in writing and shall give sufficient information to enable the authority to identify the previous grant of planning permission. Where the local planning authority are of the opinion that further information is necessary to enable them to deal with the application, they may by a direction in writing addressed to the applicant require the submission of information, plans or drawings on such matters as may be specified in the direction.

(4) A local planning authority may by a direction in writing addressed to the applicant require to be produced to an officer of the authority such evidence in respect of an application for permission made to them as they may reasonably call for to verify any particulars of information given to them.

(5) This article shall be the regulations to be made for the purposes of section 25 of the Act.".

(c) For article 6 there shall be substituted the following article:—

"Other forms of application

6.—(1) An application to a local planning authority for approval of reserved matters shall be in writing, shall give particulars sufficient to identify the outline planning permission in respect of which it is made and shall include such particulars and be accompanied by such plans and drawings as are necessary to deal with the matters reserved in the outline planning permission together with such additional number of copies of the application and plans and drawings as were required in relation to the application for outline planning permission.

(2) An application to a local planning authority for a determination under section 53 of the Act shall be in writing and shall contain a description of the operations or change of use proposed and be accompanied by a plan sufficient to identify the land to which the application relates. Where the proposal relates to the carrying out of operations, the application shall in addition be accompanied by such plans or drawings as are necessary to show the nature of the operations which are covered by the proposal. Where the proposal relates to a change of use, full descriptions shall be given of the proposed use and of the use of the land at the date when the application is made (or, where the land is not in active use at that date, the purpose for which it was last used). The local planning authority may by a direction in writing require the applicant to furnish such further information as may be specified in the direction, to enable the application to be dealt with.".

(d) For article 7 there shall be substituted the following article:—

"General provisions relating to applications

7.—(1) Any application made under article 5 or 6, where the land in respect of which the application is made (a) is in Greater London shall be lodged with the council of the London borough in which the land is situate or with the Common Council, as the case may be, and the authority with whom the application is lodged shall, if necessary, transmit it to the local planning authority, (b) is elsewhere than in Greater London shall be made to the district planning authority.

(2) On receipt of any such application the local planning authority in Greater London, and elsewhere the district planning authority, shall send to the applicant an acknowledgement thereof in the terms (or substantially in the terms) set out in Part I of Schedule 2 hereto. In the case of an application which falls to be determined by the county planning authority the district planning authority shall as soon as may be notify the applicant that the application will be so determined and shall transmit to the county planning authority all relevant plans, drawings, particulars and documents submitted with or in support of the application and notify the county planning authority of all action taken by the district planning authority in relation to the application.

(3) The period within which the local planning authority shall give notice to an applicant of their decision or determination or of the reference of an application to the Secretary of State shall be two months or (except where the applicant has already given notice of appeal to the Secretary of State) such extended period as may be agreed upon in writing between the applicant and (*a*) in Greater London, the local planning authority, (*b*) elsewhere, the district planning authority or, in the case of an application which falls to be determined by the county planning authority, either the district planning authority or the county planning authority.

(4) Every such notice shall be in writing and—

(*a*) in the case of an application for planning permission or for approval of reserved matters, where the local planning authority decide to grant permission or approval subject to conditions or to refuse it, the notice shall:—

   (i) state the reasons for the decision; and

   (ii) where the Secretary of State has given a direction restricting the grant of permission for the development referred to in the application or where he or a government department has expressed the view that the permission should not be granted (either wholly or in part) or should be granted subject to conditions, give details of the direction or of the view expressed; and

   (iii) where a local highway authority has given a direction restricting the grant of planning permission for the development referred to in the application or a county planning authority have given a direction as to how the application is to be determined, give details of the direction, and shall be accompanied by a notification in the terms (or substantially in the terms) set out in Part II of Schedule 2 hereto;

(*b*) in the case of an application for a determination under section 53 of the Act (whether forming part of an application for planning permission or not), the local planning authority shall (except where they determine that the carrying out of operations or the making of a change in the use of land would not constitute or involve development of the land) state in such notice the grounds for their determination and include a statement to the effect that if the applicant is aggrieved by their decision he may appeal to the Secretary of State under section 36 of the Act (as applied by section 53 of the Act) within six months of receipt thereof or such longer period as the Secretary of State may at any time allow.

(5) A local planning authority shall furnish to such persons as may be prescribed by directions given by the Secretary of State under this order such information as may be so prescribed with respect to applications made to them under article 5 or 6 of this order including information as to the manner in which any such application has been dealt with.".

"Appeals

16.—(1) An applicant who desires to appeal—

(*a*) against a decision of a local planning authority refusing permission to develop land, refusing to grant any approval required under this order, or granting permission or approval subject to conditions; or

(*b*) against a determination of a local planning authority under section 53 of the Act; or

(*c*) on the failure of a local planning authority to give notice of their decision or determination or of the reference of the application to the Secretary of State,

shall give notice of appeal to the Secretary of State within six months of notice of the decision or determination or of the expiry of the appropriate period allowed under article 7(3) of this order, as the case may be, or such longer period as the Secretary of State may at any time allow. In the case of an appeal in respect of an application for a determination under section 53 of the Act (whether the appeal is made under sub-paragraph (*b*) or sub-paragraph (*c*) above) the notice shall be given in writing; and in every other case it shall be given on a form obtained from the Secretary of State.

(2) Such person shall also furnish to the Secretary of State a copy of each of the following documents:—

    (i) the application;

    (ii) all relevant plans, drawings, particulars and documents submitted with the application (including, in the case of an application for planning permission, a copy of any notice provided in accordance with section 26 of the Act and of the relevant certificate under that section and a copy of the certificate given in accordance with section 27 of the Act);

    (iii) the notice of the decision or determination, if any;

    (iv) all other relevant correspondence with any local planning authority.".

APPENDIX II C i   DIAGRAM SHOWING PROPERTIES FOR INCLUSION IN NOTIFICATION ARRANGEMENTS

[1] Single storey extensions

[2] Two storey extensions (or larger)

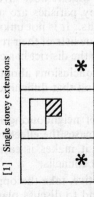

[3] Redevelopment (residential)

Notify — immediately adjacent properties to front, side and rear plus one or two next but one, as appropriate
    those opposite the site
    those opposite any access

[4] Other forms of development or redevelopment (e.g. offices, industry, etc)

Notify — surrounding area within reasonable radius distance from site

✳ NOTIFY

▨ DEVELOPMENT

LOCAL COUNCILS (PARISH AND COMMUNITY COUNCIL)

1.   Formal links have existed since April 1974 between planning authorities and the public, as represented on parish and community councils.

2.   Local councils are called 'parish councils' in England and 'community councils' in Wales. A parish (or community) is a unit of administration, with a parish meeting and, where the electorate exceeds 200, it has an elected council. Over 10 million people live in such parishes, and there are about 7,200 parish councils. With the re-organisation of local government, municipal boroughs and urban districts with populations less than 20,000 and less than one fifth of the new district, were provided with successor councils, with the same functions as parish councils. All councils at this level of local government have a common voice and representation in the National Association of Local Councils and its County Associations.

3.   Local councils vary considerably in size, from less than 200 to 20,000 inhabitants. The number of such councils in a district also varies considerably: many urban and metropolitan districts have none or only a few, usually rural districts have 50 to 100 parish councils, but some have nearly 200. The larger of these local councils have full-time staff and their elected members often include a number with experience of planning. Smaller councils often have only part-time staff or rely entirely on voluntary efforts.

4.   District planning officers reported in a survey, to which nearly 90 per cent sent in their observations, that in nine out of every ten districts parish councils are in fact being kept informed about planning applications within their area. Over 40 per cent always provide plans, a further 10 per cent do so on request, and another 20 per cent if additional copies of plans are provided by applicants, or for larger applications, or on loan.

5.   By a 5:3 majority, they expressed their view that parish council notification is effective. Reasons given range from the stimulation of local interest by such notification, to the local knowledge drawn to the attention of planning officers.

6.   But in a substantial minority the existing consultative processes are not working well. Consultation as required under Statute does involve the districts in a significant amount of extra work. Many parishes are asking for more information, sometimes with mischievous results. It is not unknown, where the parish council is a town council, for them to issue lists of their recommendations to the local press as 'planning decisions' before the district has considered them.

7.   It may be too early to come to any firm conclusions about the working of this formal public involvement, but I understand that difficulties in some areas are being overcome in the following ways:—

(a)   In several districts, informal groupings of neighbouring smaller parishes co-operate in planning matters. This increases the effectiveness of council members with planning experience, and it makes it easier for planning staff to make regular contacts with parish councils.

(b)   Planning staff, usually on their own initiative, take the opportunity of site visits to meet parish council members and to discuss planning proposals on the spot.

(c) Members of parish and community councils must be provided with:

   (i) explanatory literature designed for their special needs;

   (ii) conferences and training sessions to increase their appreciation of planning.

(d) Parish councils can involve the public with planning, by regular posting on parish notice boards of planning news, holding parish meetings to discuss major developments and encouraging the formation of local amenity societies.

o

AN ACCOUNT OF EXISTING PLANNING
INFORMATION CENTRES

1. My review included visits to several Planning Advice Centres already in operation and an appraisal of the way in which they were operating. The Centre run by Winchester District Council was visited several times, as were similar Centres in Camden, Lambeth, Chelsea, Leeds and Leicester. In addition, Bristol has had a Planning Exhibition for a number of years where planning advice is available, and Brighton is about to set up a similar Centre.

2. Winchester is the natural Centre for most of its district except those parts that were joined to it in April 1974 – which are nearer to Portsmouth. The Planning Advice Centre is situated centrally in the City and staffed by non-technical information officers, hence only able to give class 1 advice* without reference to staff of the planning department. The location of that department in the building makes communication rather difficult, enquirers needing more specialised advice either have to be referred to an enquiry desk and consulting room at some distance, or they have to wait for the information officers to obtain the information from there. Though small, the Planning Advice Centre is comfortable and convenient. In a mainly non-urban district, the pressure for planning advice is not very great.

3. The Planning Advice Centre of the London Borough of Camden is in Holborn Town Hall, at the extreme southern end of the Borough which stretches as far as Hampstead. The Centre is staffed by a non-technical assistant as well as a planning officer, the records office is a few feet away, so that advice of classes 1, 2 and 3* can be given. The officers on duty deal with about 30 – 50 enquiries per day. Between technical enquiries, the planning officers are able to carry on with their own work. They man the Centre on a rota basis, and the Borough has a relatively large number of junior staff sharing this rota for each to be on duty about once a month for a day.

4. The Lambeth Centre has a somewhat different rôle: most of the advice is sought by members of the general public concerned with the effects of development. It is very spacious and well furnished, with plenty of room for exhibits of a planning nature; it is easily accessible on the ground floor, with a completely informal atmosphere – it looks more like a showroom than a council office, an important consideration in view of the kind of person most likely to need its advice. Planning records, maps, etc., are kept in the Centre, the staff of which is non-technical but experienced, so that class 1 and class 2 advice* is readily available. The planning department is not far away to deal with more technical enquiries.

5. The Planning Advice Centre at Leeds is situated on the ground floor of a high-rise office block, which contains the planning department. It is in premises originally designed to be a shop, it is well laid out and furnished, contains exhibits of a planning nature, e.g. larger developments being discussed, and being in a pedestrian shopping precinct it is easily accessible to the public. The Centre is the permanent office of two records officers who deal with all kinds of property enquiries, land charge searches, etc., from the records kept there. The

planning enquiries desk is manned by qualified planning officers, who are attached to the office for two weeks: in the mornings by a member of the Policy Formulation Section, in the afternoons by a member of the Implementation Section. Leeds District is now much larger than the City on its own was before the reorganisation of local government: its area is doubled and the population half as much again. When the Planning Advice Centre was being discussed, the difficulty of vertical access was solved by having the Centre on the ground floor, and that of distance from the City by opening area offices to planning advice. This is done by one of the planning assistants attending a 'planning surgery' periodically in every area office. Planning problems can be discussed with members of the public in their own neighbourhoods, and direct contact with local groups and parish councils is established.

---

*The type of advice given falls most easily into four classes:

1. General non-technical advice. Distribution of explanatory literature and planning forms, general advice on completing standard forms, administrative information about the progress of current applications, dates and agenda of planning committee meetings, applications received, council decisions, etc.

2. Specific non-technical information. Consultation of records, maps, planning history of specific properties.

3. General technical information, of the kind that only qualified staff can give. Interpretation of local plans, specialised advice on making applications, discussion of legal aspects (e.g. whether planning permission is required for some proposed minor work). Discussion on general planning principles, as they affect either applicants or the general public.

4. Specific technical enquiries, referring to particular properties or applications which can only be dealt with by the technical officer in charge of the file.

APPENDIX II C (iv)

NEWSPAPER COVERAGE OF PLANNING

SURVEY BY BUILDING RESEARCH ESTABLISHMENT

The summary in Table 1 shows that nearly half of the local newspapers surveyed gave either full or selected lists of planning applications. These two categories are broken down further in Table 2 to indicate the nature of applications contained in these lists.

TABLE 1: BREAKDOWN OF CUTTINGS

Full list of applications	31
Selection from full list	68
Appeals	10
Inquiries	4
News of new/proposed development	33
Letters of objection to plans	10
Letters of support for plans	1
Reports on planning Committee/Council	42
Parish Council reports/objections	7
Editorials on planning	1
	207

TABLE 2: BREAKDOWN OF INDIVIDUAL APPLICATIONS MENTIONED IN PUBLISHED LISTS

Category of application	House-hold extensions	New buildings		Outline Appli-cations	Altera-tions and improve-ments	Change of use	All other appli-cations
		Dwellings	Others				
Full list published	159	105	81	65	61	41	72
Selections from full list	182	128	102	29	56	50	88

The Rôle of the local press as seen by planning officers

In a survey, District Council planning officers were asked about the rôle of the local press in relation to development control. Table 3 gives the questions and summarises the replies of this section of the questionnaire. Some areas are covered by several newspapers and the variety of replies often indicated the way different newspapers treated planning, and their relative local importance. The Table shows the amount of publicity local newspapers give to the lists of planning applications which councils make available to them.

212

TABLE 3: ANSWERS GIVEN BY PLANNING OFFICERS TO THE QUESTION: WHAT ARRANGEMENTS HAVE YOU WITH THE LOCAL PRESS TO GIVE PUBLICITY TO PLANNING APPLICATIONS?

(i) DOES THE COUNCIL PUBLISH LISTS IN THE FORM OF ADVER-TISEMENTS?

   Yes: 20%   No: 76%   Other answers: 4%

(ii) DO SOME (OR ALL) LOCAL PAPERS PRINT LISTS OF ALL APPLICATIONS?

   Yes: 36%   No: 60%   Other answers: 4%

(iii) DO THEY PRINT SELECTIONS FROM SUCH LISTS?

   Yes: 43%   No: 41%   Other answers: 16%

Yes to (ii) or (iii): 67%

No to both (ii) and (iii), i.e. no lists published within district: 33%

DO YOU CONSIDER THAT THE LOCAL PRESS GIVE SUFFICIENT PUBLICITY TO APPLICATIONS, DECISIONS AND APPEALS?

   Yes: 71%   No: 25%   Other answers: 4%

213

APPENDIX III i

PROCEDURAL STAGES OF AN APPEAL

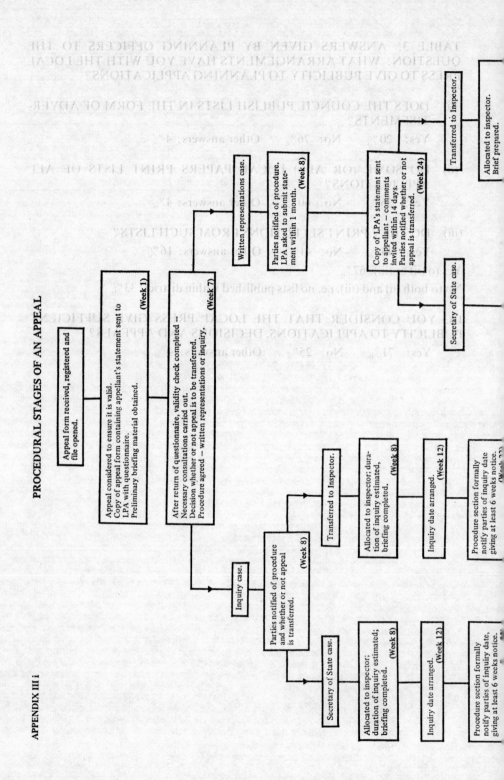

214

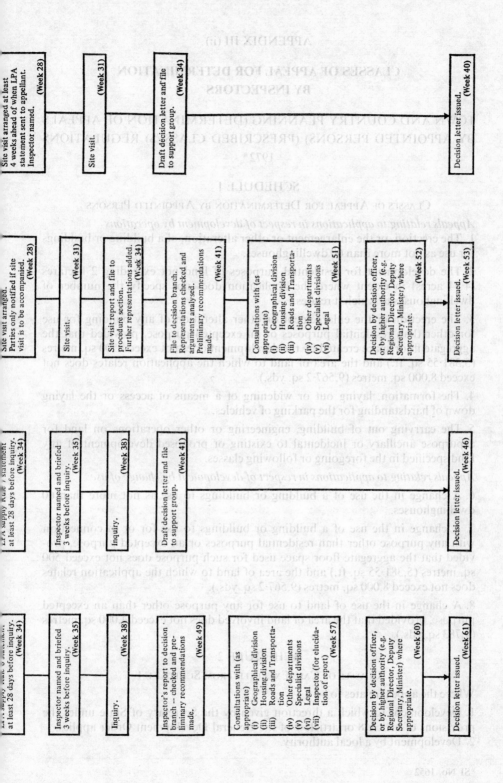

215

APPENDIX III (ii)

CLASSES OF APPEAL FOR DETERMINATION BY INSPECTORS

TOWN AND COUNTRY PLANNING (DETERMINATION OF APPEALS BY APPOINTED PERSONS) (PRESCRIBED CLASSES) REGULATIONS 1972*

SCHEDULE 1

CLASSES OF APPEAL FOR DETERMINATION BY APPOINTED PERSONS

Appeals relating to applications in respect of development by operations

1. The erection, or the enlargement or other alteration, of a building or buildings for use as not more than 60 dwellinghouses.

2. The development for residential purposes of land not exceeding 2 hectares (4·94 acres) in extent where the application does not specify the number of dwellinghouses to which it relates.

3. The erection or the enlargement or other alteration of any building for use for other than residential purposes or an excepted purpose, provided that the aggregate floor space created by the development does not exceed 500 sq. metres (5,381·55 sq. ft.) and the area of land to which the application relates does not exceed 8,000 sq. metres (9,567·2 sq. yds.).

4. The formation, laying out or widening of a means of access or the laying down of hardstanding for the parking of vehicles.

5. The carrying out of building, engineering or other operations on land for a purpose ancillary or incidental to existing or proposed development of any kind specified in the foregoing or following classes.

Appeals relating to applications in respect of development by change of use

6. A change in the use of a building or buildings to use as not more than 60 dwellinghouses.

7. A change in the use of a building or buildings to use for or in connection with any purpose other than residential purposes or an excepted purpose, provided that the aggregate floor space used for such purpose does not exceed 500 sq. metres (5,381·55 sq. ft.) and the area of land to which the application relates does not exceed 8,000 sq. metres (9,567·2 sq. yds.).

8. A change in the use of land to use for any purpose other than an excepted purpose, provided that the area of land involved does not exceed 4,000 sq. metres (4,783 sq. yds.).

SCHEDULE 2

CLASSES OF CASE EXCEPTED FROM SCHEDULE 1

Where the appeal relates to :—

1. Development to which a direction given by the Secretary of State under the provisions of article 8 or article 9 of the General Development Order applies.
2. Development by a local authority.

---

*SI No. 1652

3. Development by statutory undertakers on operational land or on land in the case of which the circumstances mentioned in section 225(2)(*b*) of the Act apply.

4. Development by the National Coal Board on land of a class specified in regulations made pursuant to section 273 of the Act.

5. Development for which planning permission has been refused by a local planning authority, or granted by them subject to conditions, where the local planning authority have included in their reasons for their decision the statement that it has been made following an expression of views, by a government department or new town development corporation, that the application should not be granted wholly or in part, or should be granted only subject to conditions.

6. Development where the same development or the same land is concurrently the subject or part of the subject of another appeal to the Secretary of State, not being an appeal within any of the classes specified in Schedule 1 to these regulations, or of an application referred to him, under any provisions of the Act, or of an order made under section 45 or 51 of the Act.

BRIGHTON MARINA INQUIRY, 1974
PRE-INQUIRY MEETING
INSPECTOR'S PRELIMINARY NOTE

(A) Before the Pre-Inquiry Meeting

(1) All parties are asked to send the Inspector a list of the witnesses proposed to be called, together with a statement of the subject matter to be covered by each witness.

(2) All parties are asked to send the Inspector a note of any suggestions for steps to be taken before the Inquiry in addition to those listed below which they wish to have considered at the meeting.

(3) The County Council are asked to send the Inspector a list of conditions required to be imposed on any planning permission in order to implement the County Council's views, like the list at the end of the Brighton Corporation's Rule 6 Statement.

Copies of documents supplied to the Inspector will be circulated at the meeting.

(B) At the Meeting

(1) The purpose of the meeting is (a) to discuss, on a provisional basis, the procedural arrangements for the public Inquiry and (b) to agree steps to be taken by the parties before the Inquiry in order to facilitate the Inquiry generally and if possible to shorten it.

(2) The procedural arrangements to be discussed will include e.g. the programme, the order of appearances, the need for a programme officer for the third parties, lists of attendances, sitting days and hours, etc.

(3) The parties will be asked to agree that proofs of evidence should be circulated at least 24 hours before a witness gives evidence, and that sufficient copies should be available for supply to the public attending the Inquiry.

(4) All parties are asked to ensure that their evidence is directed towards, and covers, the six points listed by the Secretary of State in his letter of 17th June 1974 as likely to be particularly relevant to his consideration of the application. Within the framework of those points, the following steps are proposed.

(C) Action by the parties

(1) The Applicants to confirm that the list of plans accompanying the application is still valid, or to supply particulars and copies of any variations or substitutes which will be produced.

(2) The Applicants to specify with precision which matters raised in the application should in their view be dealt with in any permission granted, and which matters should be reserved for subsequent approval.

(3) The Applicants to specify the programme for construction of the Marina if permission is granted, and to state their views as to phasing.

(4) The Applicants to indicate which of Brighton Corporation's proposed conditions, and which of the County Council's proposed conditions (see note (3) 'Before the Meeting', above), are acceptable and which are not acceptable. Any issues thus disclosed to be considered further for possible resolution by meetings and discussion.

(5) The Applicants and the two local authorities to agree a fully detailed statement on the traffic position (item (f) in the Secretary of State's letter). The statement to include Ove Arup's estimates of traffic generation by the Marina, and the County Council's analysis of the distribution and effect of the traffic on the existing and proposed road system. Objectors to indicate precisely which aspects of these figures (if any) they propose to challenge, and to supply any alternative traffic figures to which they will refer.

(6) The Applicants, if they intend to refer to the general housing need in Brighton and area, to agree any facts and statistics with the two local authorities, and to produce an agreed statement.

(7) The County Council to supply full particulars of its calculations on shops referred to on page 3 of the Rule 6 Statement.

(8) The County Council to supply its 'further submissions on the educational and social service aspects of the proposal', referred to on page 4 of the Rule 6 Statement.

(9) The County Council to supply a Rule 6 list of documents.

(10) The objectors, if it is intended to raise the question of sewage disposal or other health matters, to specify precisely the points to be raised, and to agree the factual basis of the submission with the relevant public bodies.

(11) All parties who have supplied a Rule 6 Statement to supply the Inspector and Assessor with copies of all listed documents which have not already been sent to the Department.

(12) Such further action as may be agreed at the pre-Inquiry meeting.

All documents resulting from the implementation of agreed pre-Inquiry action are to be treated as part of Rule 6 Statements and circulated accordingly.

APPENDIX III (iv)

AGREED STATEMENT OF FACTS

This is based upon, but does not comprise, a full statement of facts agreed in a recent appeal. Details that are not essential in an illustrative statement have been deleted. Names and locations have also been changed where this is necessary to preserve anonymity.

A. Introduction

1. The appeal is made by United Confederates Ltd. against the refusal of the local planning authority to grant planning permission for the erection of buildings containing not more than 250,000 sq. ft. of office floor space and construction of roads and carparks in connection therewith at Hornby, Surrey. The original application was supported by an office development permit.

2. The reason given for refusal was that the development would conflict with the local planning authority's intention to discourage the introduction of major new sources of employment into an area of high labour demand within which established local industrial and commercial concerns need to be given priority.

3. The Notice of Appeal gave the following grounds:

1. The Appellants are the British subsidiary of a large international company whose Head Office is at present in Central London. Expansion in Central London is neither practicable nor in accordance with national planning policy.

2. The only suitable site for the location of the Head Office outside London is the appeal site.

3. Under the Strategic Plan for the South-East, Hornby is in a growth area. The issue of an office development permit for 250,000 sq. ft. of office floor space shows that the location of the Head Office in the Hornby area would be in accordance with national policy for the distribution of employment. The only ground given by the local planning authority for refusal is directly contrary to national policy for the distribution of employment.

4. The development would not lead to a requirement for industrial workers. On the contrary, it would provide opportunities with career prospects to the present and future population of Hornby and surrounding areas.

B. The Site and Surroundings

4. The appeal site ('the site') is about 2 miles north of Hornby town centre, on the west side of the London/Brighton trunk road A.23 (London Road) and directly adjacent to the Exchange Way roundabout.

5. The site is $16\frac{1}{2}$ acres in area and roughly rectangular in shape. Two and a half acres of the site are owned by United Confederates Ltd. and the remainder (14 acres) is owned by the Hornby Borough Council. The site includes a vacant residential property with a large garden, a public open space, some disused property and unused land. An unadopted public highway known as Corker Lane crosses the site diagonally. No other public rights of way affect the site.

6. The land to the north and west of the site is mainly farm land with a few houses. The eastern boundary (northern half) adjoins the A.23 and the roundabout; the eastern boundary (southern half) abuts the backs of older properties fronting the A.23 beyond which is the Homefrith Industrial Trading Estate. The southern boundary abuts the council maintenance depot and a sewage pumping station.

C. Administrative Boundaries and Planning History

7. Until 1st April 1974 the site was within the former County of Surrey and the Urban District of Hornby; since 1st April 1974 it has been within the new County of Surrey and the Borough of Hornby.

8. The following planning boundaries are relevant:

(a) Planning Area 6, Hornby/Bredon Hill as defined in the Strategic Plan for the South-East 1970.

(b) The Hornby/Darkwell Sub-Region as defined in the Sub-Regional Study Final Report to the Joint Planning Advisory Committee (West Sussex, East Sussex, Surrey) October 1972.

(c) The Districts as have existed since 1st April 1974.

9. The aggregate residential population of the following Employment Exchange Areas:— Marston; Redbury and Newick; Newbury Heath and Bredon Hill; East Milborough; Hornby and Wolverton is larger than that of the Hornby/ Darkwell Sub-Region, but it is agreed that the geographical differences are not significant.

10. In 1961 the former Surrey County Council submitted to the Minister a Town Map for Hornby making provision for a population of 70,000 persons. As a result of representations by Hornby Urban District Council, the Minister formally deferred a decision in order to consider whether provision should be made for a larger population and subsequently the County Council formally withdrew the Town Map while resolving that it continued to be used as a basis for development control decisions.

11. The non-statutory Wednesbury Review Town Map 1973 was completed by Surrey County Council too late to be submitted for the approval of the Secretary of State under the 1962 Town and Country Planning Act, but is similarly used as a basis for development control.

12. In 1965 the former Surrey County Council commissioned the Hornby Expansion Study which was completed in 1969.

13. On 20th January 1971 conditional planning permission was granted for the erection of a 250 twin-bedroomed hotel at Northwood Omnibus Depot and 233 Landsdowne Road, which forms part of the appeal site.

14. The Strategic Plan for the South-East was published in 1970 and in October 1971 the Secretary of State for the Environment issued a statement that the Government had decided that the Strategic Plan represented a reasonable framework for the future planning of the region.

15. After submission of the Final Report of the Hornby/Darkwell Sub-Regional Study, the Joint Planning Advisory Committee recommended to its constituent councils (West Sussex, East Sussex and Surrey) that in preparing their structure plans they should plan for some expansion in the vicinity of Newbury Heath and Bredon Hill, at Hornby and at Wolverton.

D. The Appellant Company

16. United Confederates Ltd. is the British subsidiary of a large international company, United Mining and Manufacturing Company of Longlake, Arizona USA. In 1973 its sales were just over £50 million including almost £7·3 million in exports.

17. United Confederates has 5 factory locations in the UK of which four are in development areas. The company has throughout the country 6 warehouses, 11 regional offices and demonstration rooms and a research laboratory.

18. The Head Office has the overall responsibility for the administration and operation of United Confederates' sales, marketing, manufacturing and distribution functions. It is currently located at United House, 24 Barton Street, London, W1, which is a leased building of 131,000 sq. ft. (gross). The Head Office establishment (920 persons) now exceeds the capacity of United House and it has been necessary to obtain overflow offices at Streatham and Guildford Road. These offices are now full.

19. United Confederates Ltd. require a site for their new Head Office large enough to prevent their having to move again if future expansion is required. Any extensions that are needed would be built in phased units and would have to be the subject of further planning consent. Certain forecasts of employees at the Head Office were given in the Explanatory Memorandum submitted with the planning application. These were based on the growth of the Company, and a large number of other circumstances, remaining constant. Subject to the above United Confederates would anticipate requiring a maximum of 3,000 employees by the year 2000 although it is impossible to forecast this far ahead with any accuracy.

E. The Search for Office Accommodation

20. In 1968 United Confederates foresaw the need for additional office space for Head Office and in 1969 they commenced to search for a site outside London that would meet the following criteria:

  A. Site area to be minimum 15 acres freehold.

  B. Distance from Central London not to exceed 40 miles.

  C. Location to ensure minimum disturbance of present employees.

  D. Resident population of 100,000 within adjacent towns and 200,000 within easy daily travel.

  E. Within one hour's travel of a major international airport, Heathrow or Gatwick.

  F. Good site environment and attractive living areas.

21. The site meets the criteria set out in paragraph 20 above and is the only site that United Confederates had been able to find up to March 1972 which does so. Of the other 168 sites which were investigated the one which, subject to an office development permit and planning permission, comes closest to meeting the criteria was a site south of Basingstoke. For a number of reasons, however, this site was considered less suitable than the appeal site.

22. The County Council are unable to suggest any site within Surrey which would meet the United Confederates' criteria, and to which there would be no planning objection.

F. Outline Concept of Development Presently Intended

23. The development concept is put forward by United Confederates and accepted by the County Council as illustrative only and does not form part of the application the subject of this appeal.

24. The site would thus be divided into a northern section and a southern section by an access road running westwards from the Exclusive Way roundabout. The office building, with an overall area of 250,000 sq. ft., would be in the northern section and would be of the order of 325 feet long by 180 feet wide, 5 storeys in height.

25. Car parking will be provided on the standard local planning authority scale of one space for every 350 sq. ft. of office space with an additional 10% allowance for visitors, a total of 780 spaces. The main car park will be on the southern section with the entrance and exit at the western end of the new road. A small car park for management and visitors will be provided in the northern section.

26. It should be practicable to retain most of the major trees on the site and a high standard of landscaping would be created.

27. The new road would provide a vehicular and pedestrian way from the A.23 to that part of Corker Lane that would remain (to the west of the site). United Confederates would apply for the closure of that part of the land which crosses the site and the extinguishment or diversion of the bridle way.

G. Traffic Consideration

28. The Department of the Environment has no objections in principle to the proposed office development on traffic grounds provided that all access is obtained from the new dual carriageway road connecting to the roundabout. It would also have to be a condition that this road was constructed prior to any work commencing on the site, in order to ensure minimum interference with trunk road traffic by construction traffic.

29. A classified traffic count taken by Surrey County Council on the A.23 adjacent to the appeal site showed that in July 1971, the 16 hour 2-way flow was 25,736 vehicles or 28,867 urban pcu's; the peak hour (5.00 pm to 6.00 pm) 2-way flow was 2,328 vehicles or 2,481 urban pcu's (1,364 pcu's northbound and 1,117 pcu's southbound). The length of the M.29 between Corby and Blackwell (with links to the A.23 at Darkwell, $2\frac{1}{2}$ miles north of the appeal site and to Hornby, $\frac{3}{4}$ mile south of the appeal site) is expected to reduce the traffic flow on the A.23 adjacent to the appeal site by at least 55% and will provide easy access for the appeal site to the national road network.

30. The Surrey Bus Company provides two fairly frequent services along the A.23 passing the site and the Exchange Way roundabout. London Transport's Green Line Road Service Route No 843 (Hornby to Watford via Central London) also passes the site. The service has an hourly frequency.

31. Train Service: Darkwell Station is two miles from the site and Four Elms Station is $2\frac{1}{4}$ miles from the site. There are good services to London and the south coast.

H. Consultations and Provision of Services

32. The former Hornby Urban District Council considered, and the present Borough Council consider, that permission should be granted for the develop-

ment. That Council are prepared to sell to United Confederates the part of the site which they own and to grant any necessary easements of drainage over adjoining land owned by them and to provide equivalent open space elsewhere to replace the loss of public open space on the appeal site.

33. Public Utilities

(i) The Southern Water Authority, the South Eastern Gas Board and the South Eastern Electricity Board have been told of United Confederates' requirements should this development be permitted. They state that adequate supplies of water, gas and electricity can be provided.

(ii) Telephones: the Post Office state that United Confederates' requirements can be provided.

(iii) Foul Sewage: the Hornby Borough Council state that the site is adequately served by the existing drainage system.

(iv) Surface Water Drainage: surface water drainage will be taken from the west of the site to the Byfleet stream and the Thames Conservancy state that this is acceptable.

NOTE:
In paragraphs 3, 19 and 20 the facts therein recorded are agreed as facts but it should be noted that the merit or suitability of opinions or judgements involved are not agreed.

FORM TCP 20 3A/74/11 QUESTIONNAIRE

Our Ref: APP..

TOWN AND COUNTRY PLANNING ACT 1971—SECTION 36 APPEAL

Please complete this questionnaire and return it to the Department within 14 days. A copy may be retained.

1. Are the council agreeable to the appeal being dealt with by the written representation procedure? (Please see paragraph 3 of Circular 23/72.) — Yes/No

2. Is the appeal site within 67 metres of a trunk road? — Yes/No

3. If yes, have the council consulted the Regional Controller (Roads and Transportation)? If Yes, please attach a copy of any comments made by him; if no, please consult him and let the Department have his comments. — Yes/No Not Applicable

4. Has the Secretary of State issued any direction relevant to this appeal? Details should be forwarded to the Department. — Yes/No

5. Is the proposed development likely to affect an Ancient Monument? — Yes/No

6. If yes, was the Secretary of State consulted? If yes, please provide details. — Yes/No Not Applicable

7. Has any other Government Department or New Town Development Corporation or statutory undertaking expressed any view regarding the application? (If so copies of any relevant correspondence should be forwarded.) — Yes/No

8. Does the development involve alteration, extension or demolition of a listed building or the demolition of a building in a conservation area. — Yes/No

9. Is the development such that, if planning permission were given, it would be necessary for an order stopping up or diverting a footpath, bridleway or other highway to be made in order to enable the development to be carried out? If so please give the number, if any, of the footpath, bridleway or other highway. — Yes/No

(This information is needed so that the Secretary of State may consider, if appropriate, the making of a draft order under section 216 of the Act.)

10. Is the site in a Conservation Area? (If it is and the application falls within the terms of section 28 of the Act please enclose a copy of the notice published in accordance with that section.) — Yes/No

225

P

11. i.   Does the appeal relate to an application for planning permission as distinct from an application for approval of details reserved by an outline planning permission?   Yes/No

ii.   Was a section 27 certificate submitted with the application?   Yes/No

iii.   Were any representations received as a result of any notice given under section 27 of the Act?   Yes/No Not Applicable

12.   Where the appeal comes or appears to come within the provisions of section 26 of the Act and Article 8 of the General Development Orders 1973 to 1974 was the development advertised and the appropriate certificate submitted?   Yes/No Not Applicable

Note:—

Any persons who made representations in response to such a notice should now be informed by the council that an appeal has been made to the Secretary of State and that they will be given an opportunity of making representations at a local inquiry if one is held. If no inquiry is held they will be invited to express their views in writing on the understanding that copies will be sent to the parties to the appeal. A copy of the council's letter to the objectors, if any, should be forwarded to the Department.

13.   If the appeal is in respect of the council's failure to give notice within the appropriate period of their decision on an application for planning permission, have the council any observations to make on the application?   Yes/No Not Applicable

(If yes, please attach a copy of such observations and send a copy to the appellant.)

14.   Does the appeal concern the use of land as a caravan site?   Yes/No
If yes:—

i.   Could the local licensing authority express their opinion whether they consider the proposed site is suitable (or could be made suitable by the imposition of conditions on the site licence) for caravan use?

ii.   For the purposes of section 3 of the Caravan Sites and Control of Development Act 1960, may we please have any comments which the local licensing authority wish to make?

iii.   In the event of the appeal being allowed what matters would the licensing authority particularly wish to be regulated by licensing control, bearing in mind the overlap between that and planning control (e.g. Section 5(1)(d) of the 1960 Act)?

15.   Would consultation under Article 13 of the General Development Orders 1973 to 1974 or under departmental circulars have been necessary if the council had proposed to grant planning permission? If so, the council are asked to carry out now any such consultation if they have not already done so   Yes/No

and to send any comments received to the Department and the appellant.

16. Is there any other information relevant to the appeal   Yes/No
which the council consider the Secretary of State should be
aware of?

Council's Reference .... Signature ....

Status ....

Date ....

TCP 203A/74/11

EXTRACT FROM RULES GOVERNING PROCEDURES AT INQUIRIES THE TOWN AND COUNTRY PLANNING (INQUIRIES PROCEDURE) RULES 1974*

Statements to be served before inquiry

6.—(1) In the case of a referred application, the Secretary of State shall (where this has not already been done), not later than 28 days before the date of the inquiry (or such later date as he may specify under proviso (i) to paragraph (1) of rule (5)), serve or cause to be served on the applicant, on the local planning authority and on the section 29 parties a written statement of the reasons for his direction that the application be referred to him and of any points which seem to him to be likely to be relevant to his consideration of the application; and where a government department has expressed in writing to the Secretary of State the view that the application should not be granted either wholly or in part, or should be granted only subject to conditions, or, in the case of an application for consent under a tree preservation order, should be granted together with a direction requiring the replanting of trees, the Secretary of State shall include this expression of view in his statement and shall supply a copy of the statement to the government department concerned.

(2) Not later than 28 days before the date of the inquiry (or such later date as the Secretary of State may specify under proviso (i) to paragraph (1) of rule (5)), the local planning authority shall—

(a) serve on the applicant and on the section 29 parties a written statement of any submission which the local planning authority propose to put forward at the inquiry, and

(b) supply a copy of the statement to the Secretary of State.

(3) Where the Secretary of State or a local authority has given a direction restricting the grant of permission for the development for which application was made or a direction as to how the application was to be determined, the local planning authority shall mention this in their statement and shall include in the statement a copy of the direction and the reasons given for it and shall, within the period specified in paragraph (2) above, supply a copy of the statement to the Secretary of State or local authority concerned; and where a government department or a local authority has expressed in writing to the local planning authority the view that the application should not be granted either wholly or in part, or should be granted only subject to conditions, or, in the case of an application for consent under a tree preservation order, should be granted together with a direction requiring the replanting of trees, and the local planning authority propose to rely on such expression of view in their submissions at the inquiry, they shall include it in their statement and shall, within the period specified in paragraph (2) above, supply a copy of the statement to the government department or local authority concerned.

---

*SI No. 419

(4) Where the local planning authority intend to refer to, or put in evidence, at the inquiry documents (including maps and plans), the authority's statement shall be accompanied by a list of such documents, together with a notice stating the times and place at which the documents may be inspected by the applicant and the section 29 parties; and the local planning authority shall afford them a reasonable opportunity to inspect and, where practicable, to take copies of the documents.

(5) The local planning authority shall afford any other person interested a reasonable opportunity to inspect and, where practicable, to take copies of any statement served by the Secretary of State under paragraph (1) or by the authority under paragraph (2) and of the other documents referred to in paragraph (4) as well as of any statement served on the authority by the applicant under paragraph (6) of this rule.

(6) The applicant shall, if so required by the Secretary of State, serve on the local planning authority, on the section 29 parties and on the Secretary of State, within such time before the inquiry as the Secretary of State may specify, a written statement of the submissions which he proposes to put forward at the inquiry; and such statement shall be accompanied by a list of any documents (including maps and plans) which the applicant intends to refer to or put in evidence at the inquiry, and he shall, if so required by the Secretary of State, afford the local planning authority and the section 29 parties a reasonable opportunity to inspect and, where practicable, to take copies of such documents.

Model Enforcement Notice

IMPORTANT—THIS COMMUNICATION AFFECTS YOUR PROPERTY

(a)

TOWN AND COUNTRY PLANNING ACT 1971

ENFORCEMENT NOTICE

To .... (b)

of ....

....

The (a)   Council (hereinafter called "the Council") being the local planning authority for the purposes of Section 87 of the Town and Country Planning Act 1971 in this matter HEREBY GIVE YOU NOTICE as a person [owning] [occupying] [having an interest in] the land described in Schedule 1 hereto [and shown   on the attached plan] (hereinafter referred to as "the said land") that:—

(c)

1.   It appears to the Council that there has been a breach of planning control [after the end of 1963] [within the period of 4 years before the date of service of this notice] (d) in that the said land has been developed in the manner described in Schedule 2 hereto without the grant of planning permission required in that behalf.

1.   (i) On   19   planning permission was granted under Part III of the Town and Country Planning Act [1947] [1962] [1971] for (e) subject to the following condition(s) [among others]:—

(f)

(ii) It appears to the Council that [after the end of 1963] [within a period of 4 years before the date of service of this notice] (d) there has been a breach of planning control in that the condition(s) recited above has/have not been complied with in the respect(s) set out in Schedule 2 hereto.

2.   The Council in pursuance of the powers contained in the said section 87 and considering it expedient to do so, having regard to the provisions of the development plan and to all other material considerations, HEREBY REQUIRE you within   days/months of the date when this notice takes effect to take the following steps to remedy the said breach of planning control, namely:—(g)

    (i)

    (ii)

    (iii)

    etc.

3.   THIS NOTICE SHALL TAKE EFFECT, subject to the provisions of section 88(3) of the Town and Country Planning Act 1971, at the end of the period of   days beginning with (h)   19 .

SCHEDULE 1

(j)

SCHEDULE 2

(k)
The making of a material change in the use of [the land] [the building(s) on the land [marked . . . on the attached plan]] [part of the building on the land [marked . . . on the attached plan], namely . . .] to use for the purpose of

The carrying out on the land of building, engineering, mining or other operations, namely

Failure to comply with the condition(s) in that

Dated   19 .

Signed

(Council's address)

YOUR ATTENTION IS DIRECTED TO THE ATTACHED NOTES WHICH EXPLAIN YOUR RIGHT OF APPEAL AGAINST THIS NOTICE. YOU SHOULD READ THEM CAREFULLY.

List of those who have submitted evidence

GOVERNMENT DEPARTMENTS

Council on Tribunals
Countryside Commission
Crown Estate Commission
Department of the Environment
Department of Industry (Department of Trade and Industry)
Forestry Commission
Home Office
Ministry of Agriculture Fisheries and Food
Ministry of Defence
The Parliamentary Commissioner for Administration
Property Services Agency
Welsh Office

LOCAL AUTHORITY ASSOCIATIONS

Association of County Councils
Association of District Councils (Rural District Councils Association, Urban District Councils Association)
Association of Metropolitan Authorities (Association of Municipal Corporations)
London Boroughs Association
National Association of Local Councils
New Towns Association

LOCAL AUTHORITIES

Borough of Ashford
Bracknell District Council
Braintree District Council
Bray Parish Council
Broxtowe District Council
London Borough of Brent
London Borough of Camden
Chelmsford District Council
Chesterfield Town Council
Borough of Cleethorpes
Borough of Darlington
Dacorum District Council
Devon County Council
Dover Rural District Council

Durham County Council
East Sussex County Council
Elmbridge Borough Council
Essex County Council
Fareham District Council
Gateshead Metropolitan Borough Council
Greater London Council
Greater Manchester County Council
Hampshire County Council
Hertfordshire County Council
Borough of Heywood
London Borough of Hillingdon
Borough of Ipswich
London Borough of Islington
Kent County Council
Lake District National Park
Lancashire County Council
Leeds City Council
City of London
Maidstone Borough Council
Mole Valley District Council
City of Newcastle-upon-Tyne
City of Norwich
City of Oxford
Peak Park Planning Board
City of Plymouth
City of Portsmouth
Salop County Council
South Cambridgeshire District Council
South Yorkshire County Council
City of Southampton
Stockton-on-Tees Borough Council
Suffolk County Council
Surrey County Council
London Borough of Sutton
Taunton Deane District Council
Tyne and Wear County Council
Uckfield Rural District Council
London Borough of Wandsworth
County Borough of Warrington
Borough of Watford
Waverley District Council
West Sussex County Council
Westminster City Council
City of Winchester
Windlesham Parish Council
Woking Borough Council
Wokingham District Council
Wootton-under-Edge Town Council and Burial Board
Wrekin District Council
Zetland County Council

PUBLIC BODIES, NATIONALISED INDUSTRIES AND RESEARCH ESTABLISHMENTS

Association of River Authorities
British Broadcasting Corporation
British Gas Corporation
British Railways Board
British Waterworks Association
Central Electricity Generating Board
Committee on Minerals Planning Control
Council for Small Industries in Rural Areas
Economic Planning Council, South-East Region
Independent Broadcasting Authority
Institute of Advanced Urban Studies
London Transport
National Bus Company
National Coal Board
National Economic Development Office
National Freight Corporation
Nature Conservancy Council
Post Office
Sports Council
Trent River Authority

PROFESSIONAL INSTITUTIONS AND TRADE ORGANISATIONS

Association of British Chambers of Commerce
British Property Federation (National Association of Property Owners)
Central Committee for the Architectural Advisory Panels
Confederation of British Industry
Construction Surveyors' Institute
Country Landowners Association
City of Westminster Chamber of Commerce
Essex Planning Officers' Association
Faculty of Architects and Surveyors
Federation of Civil Engineering Contractors
Federation of Master Builders
General Council of the Bar of England and Wales
House-Builders Federation
Incorporated Association of Architects and Surveyors
Incorporated Society of Valuers and Auctioneers
Institute of Registered Architects
Institution of Civil Engineers
Institution of Municipal Engineers
Justice
The Land Institute Ltd.
The Law Society
London Chamber of Commerce and Industry
Multiple Shops Federation
The National Farmers' Union
National Chamber of Trade
National House-Building Council

234

National House-Builders' Registration Council
National Housing and Town Planning Council
National and Local Government Officers Association
Royal Fine Art Commission
Royal Institute of British Architects
  [RIBA Eastern Region
  RIBA North-West Region
  RIBA South-East Region Practice Committee
  RIBA Southern Region
  RIBA Teesside Branch
  RIBA Yorkshire Region]
Royal Institution of Chartered Surveyors
Royal Town Planning Institute
  [RTPI South-East Branch]
Sand and Gravel Association Ltd.
Trades Union Congress
Water Companies Association

AMENITY SOCIETIES AND OTHER REPRESENTATIVE 'THIRD PARTY' ORGANISATIONS

Civic Trust
Committee for Environmental Conservation
Commons Open Spaces and Footpaths Preservation Society
Conservation Society
Council for British Archaeology
Council for the Protection of Rural England
Council for the Protection of Rural Wales
Friends of the Earth Ltd.
The Georgian Group
National Council of Women of Great Britain
National Federation of Womens Institutes
Ramblers' Association
Shelter Community Action Team
Society for the Protection of Ancient Buildings
Town and Country Planning Association
Transport Reform Group
Victorian Society
William Morris Society
Youth Hostels Association

The Amwell Society
Barnes Riverside Residents' Association
Barry Constituency Committee of Plaid Cymru
Bournemouth and District Civic Society
Branksome Park and District Residents' Association
Bratton Fleming Area Conservation Society
Brighton Society
Bristol Civic Society
Bristol Visual and Environmental Group
London Borough of Bromley Residents' Federation

235

The Chelsea Society
Chesterfield Heritage Society
Chislehurst Residents' Association
Codsall and District Civic Society
CPRE Keston and District Branch
CPRE Lincolnshire Branch
CPRE Oxfordshire Branch
CPRE Somerset Branch
Dickens Country Protection Society
Dorset Lake Association
'Down Town' Tenants Association
East Chiswick Residents Association
East End Docklands Action Group
Faversham Society
Frithcare
The Greater London Group
Hammersmith Society
Hazelwood Grove Residents' Association
Horsley Countryside Preservation Society
Joint Committee for Planning and Preservation (Sussex)
Joint Docklands Action Group
Kent Rights of Way Council
Leeds Civic Trust
The Lincoln Society
London Association for Saving Homes
Lyme Regis Society
Margate Civic Society
Meadfoot-Wellswood and Area Residents' Association
New Milton, Barton and District Ratepayers' and Residents' Association
The Newnham Society
North Barnes Residents' Association
North Southwark Community Development Group
Northenden Civic Society
Northumberland and Newcastle Society
Pershore Civic Society
Ramblers' Association—Wessex area
Save Piccadilly Campaign
Sheffield Amenities Council
Southampton Civic Trust
Staines Town Society
Surrey Docks Action Group
Talbot Woods Residents' Association
Todmorden Conservation Group
Tolmers Village Association
The Trust for Devizes
Trustees of St Margaret's Residential Grounds
Victorian Society—Manchester Group
The Ware Society
Wirral Green Belt Council
Woolton Society
Wootton Basset and District Civic Trust

236

PROFESSIONAL FIRMS AND COMPANIES

Algrey Developments
Archer Parker and Townsend
J Sydney Barker & Co
E H Bradley & Sons Ltd
Bryant Homes Ltd
Raymond J Cecil and Partners
J M Clark and Partners
William Cowburn, Bers and Bray
Dacre, Son & Hartley
Denton Hall and Burgin
Design Group Partnership
Dexter & Staniland
Gouldens
R Green Properties Ltd
Brian Lingard and Partners
Lovell White and King
Arthur Mull Associates
Murgatroyds
Pearsons
Gordon Pearson and Partners
Porter Cobb with Hamilton
Redfern, Gilpin and Riley
Robertson and Company
Savills
Shaw and Fuller
Kingsley Smith and Company
Smiths Gore
Strutt and Parker
S B Tietz and Partners
Wates Ltd
Welfare Properties Ltd
Wild, Hewitson and Shaw
Mark Wilks and Company

INDIVIDUALS

R Adley Esq MP
Mr and Mrs J B Allt
C Erik Andren Esq
R C Arnold Esq
J B Arthur Esq
M Barnard Esq
D Beecham Esq
J H Benson Esq
R G Bevan Esq
A T Bicheno Esq
D M Booth Esq
A R Boucher Esq
H Braun Esq
R C H Briggs Esq
I Campbell Esq
Mrs S Carmichael
J H Carr Esq
Mrs B Carvalho
L F Cave Esq
A F Clarke Esq
A Cooper Esq
J A Cunnington Esq
E F Dearman Esq
P G Dixon Esq
T E Easterfield Esq
W E Edleston Esq
B E A Evans Esq
J H Evans Esq
E V Eves Esq
D Field Esq
R France Esq
A Fraser Esq
A S Freeman Esq
Mrs K A Geary
H Gee Esq
J Gillam Esq
D Gilmore Esq
R P Harris Esq
K Harrison Esq
R F Harrison Esq
Group Capt E A Harrop
P M Hart Esq
L Hatt Esq
J R Hickmott Esq
S Hodgson Esq
J C Holliday Esq
N G Hotchkiss Esq
J Hutchinson Esq
D W Insall Esq
W James Esq

K H Jessop Esq
Evelyn King Esq MP
L Lane Esq
R L Langley Esq
R B Leaver Esq
G Lee Esq
D Magne Esq
C J Marchant Esq
H E Markson Esq
J P W B McAuslan Esq
J D McConaghy Esq
J McGarva Esq
H I Meyer Esq
R Moate Esq MP
J W Olsen Esq
H J Palmer Esq
F Payne Esq
J L Phillips Esq
S Proctor Esq
E J Razzell Esq
M Read Esq
N Roberts Esq
Dr A Robinson Thomas
Mrs F Roaner
A J Rowe Esq
H Sales Esq
D Serjeant Esq
G Shankland Esq
Miss E M Smith
L G R Stevens Esq
C Streatfield Esq
M J Thompson Esq
A Todd Esq
Mrs M M Turner
W Tyas Esq
R Tym Esq
R Vane Esq
J Wakes Esq
Sir Derek Walker-Smith QC MP
J S G Warren Esq
Mrs J Webb
B West Esq
B Whalley Esq
R O L Wickam Esq
B Wiehaham Esq
N E Wigg Esq
Mrs A Wilks
W Young Esq
R Zetter Esq

Printed in England for Her Majesty's Stationery Office by Daniel Greenaway & Sons Ltd.   Dd 289032 KOO 1/75